The Last Great Sea

The Last Great Sea

A Voyage through the Human and Natural History of the North Pacific Ocean

TERRY GLAVIN

David Suzuki Foundation

GREYSTONE BOOKS

Douglas & McIntyre Publishing Group
Vancouver/Toronto

Greystone Books
A division of Douglas & McIntyre Ltd.
2323 Quebec Street, Suite 201
Vancouver, British Columbia V5T 4S7

The David Suzuki Foundation
219-2211 West 4th Avenue
Vancouver, British Columbia V6K 4S2

CANADIAN CATALOGUING IN PUBLICATION DATA

Glavin, Terry, 1955–
    The last great sea

    Copublished by: David Suzuki Foundation.
    Includes bibliographical references.
    ISBN 1-55054-809-3

    1. Natural history — North Pacific Ocean. 2. North Pacific Ocean — Discovery and exploration. I. David Suzuki Foundation. II. Title.
QH95.1.G52 2000   508.3164'4   C00-910969-2

Editing by Nancy Flight
Jacket design by Chris Dahl
Text design and typesetting by Julie Cochrane
Maps by Stuart Daniel
Printed and bound in Canada by Friesens
Printed on acid-free paper

The publisher gratefully acknowledges the support of the Canada Council and of the British Columbia Ministry of Tourism, Small Business and Culture. The publisher also wishes to acknowledge the financial support of the Government of Canada through the Book Publishing Industry Development Program (BPIDP) for its publishing activities.

Contents

Foreword

I WAS BORN IN Vancouver in 1936. My earliest childhood memories are of fishing in British Columbia before World War II. I remember Dad rowing around Siwash Rock in Stanley Park trolling for sea-run cut-throats; we'd jig for halibut off Spanish Banks; and it was easy to catch sturgeon in the Fraser River.

But the war cut off my childhood idyll, and in 1945 we were expelled from the west coast. I didn't return until 1963, when I accepted a job at the University of British Columbia. By then, the abundant fish I knew as a child were gone; still, I remember quickly filling a bucket with her-ring jigged off the dock at Squamish, joining thousands of others in the annual *Vancouver Sun* Salmon Derby, lifting a gillnet shimmering with hundreds of smelt on Kitsilano beach, and scuba diving for lingcod near Horseshoe Bay. Today, my grandchildren have no chance of fishing as I did even in the '60s. Like everyone else, I just took it for granted that there were plenty of fish and unwittingly contributed to the loss of those "resources." Reflecting over my life, I am struck by the speed of the demise of the kinds and abundance of fish around Vancouver.

One problem is that when we view the ocean, we tend to see a cor-nucopia of separate "resources," "commodities," or "opportunities" instead of a complex, mysteriously interconnected world of biological, physical, and chemical entities. As a result, we set policies to "harvest" herring, abalone, salmon, dogfish, kelp, shrimp, and so on as if they are unrelated and manageable separately. We also persist in the illusion that we can scientifically manage resources and that we are using them in a sustainable way when, in fact, we lack sufficient knowledge of the components of marine ecosystems and their interconnections. To top it all off, the global economy is predicated on maximizing profit at a level and within a time frame far beyond nature's capacity to sustainably fulfill. Trees and fish can only grow so fast, and all attempts to accelerate productivity with plantations, hatcheries, and fish farms are merely temporary illusions of control. Nature cannot be shoehorned into human jurisdictions or priorities; we must adapt and try to emulate nature if we mean it when we say we care about the fate of future generations.

Terry Glavin's magnificent book provides a picture of an ecological jewel on the planet, the North Pacific Ocean. Taken over tens of millennia, this picture includes the place of the First Nations people and their worldview. For more than 10,000 years, First Nations people lived lives so rich in food and materials that they were able to achieve high population densities and create rich cultures. Now, as resources are dwindling while habitat is being trashed, the First Nations perspective and values hold out the promise of a sustainable future.

Viewed over millennia, the massive changes in the ocean and its surrounding forests occur within a geological blink. Within a century, hundreds of distinct races of salmon vanish, dozens of watersheds fall, while the numbers of other fish, birds, and mammals plummet. But there is hope. Because these changes have taken place so quickly, such destructive practices may not yet be encrusted in tradition. It is still possible to rediscover the principles and practices of true sustainability.

The Last Great Sea is an eye-opener, a visceral plea to recognize our need to find other ways and practices, a powerful antidote to the religion of modernity, the belief that the latest is inevitable and best and that we have little to learn from the past or traditional peoples. Best of all, Glavin imparts a sense of wonder and love for this incredible part of the world and the life it sustains.

David Suzuki, Chair, David Suzuki Foundation

Acknowledgments

IT'S CONVENTIONAL THAT friends and family members are mentioned affectionately somewhere near the end of a book's acknowledgment pages. Not this time. Of everyone who contributed in one way or another to the writing of this book, my gratitude goes first and foremost to my family — Yvette, Zoe, Eamonn, and Conall. Each of them made their own contributions, not infrequently in the form of just putting up with me and granting me a degree of slack I did not deserve. I am also especially grateful to Barry Manuck, Rick Bailey, and Craig Orr, whose perseverance in fisheries conservation inspires me and whose friendship I cherish, even though it must not have seemed so during the year or so I spent writing this book. I am thankful to Robert Harlow, who listened to me carry on about my difficulties with this project and always offered wise advice. I also thank my colleagues on the Pacific Fisheries Resource Conservation Council, whose patience, all the while, was also sorely tried. They are the Honourable John Fraser, Mark Angelo, Mary-Sue Atkinson, Paul LeBlond, Murray Chatwin, Rick Routledge, Don Ryan, and Carl Walters.

Of the many scientists whose patience I tested during my research, the one that stands out more than any other is Dick Beamish. His guidance and advice, over several years of my attempts to write about these subjects, has been immeasurable. By noting this, I must also stress that he bears no burden of blame arising from anything that appears in these pages and cannot be held accountable for anything I have written that does not accord with the world as scientists understand it. I am indebted to many scientists and academics, including several of Dick's colleagues at the Pacific Biological Station, and the list is too long to name them all. There are certain chapters in this book in which I rely far more heavily on certain scholars than the endnotes come close to indicating. Among them are the Russian historian Svetlana Fedorova, whose brilliant work on the history of the Russian Pacific has never been properly acknowledged on the North American side of the ocean, and the Canadian historian Daniel Francis, whose research on the history of industrial whaling significantly informs several pages of this book. I also relied heavily on the work of Canadian writer and historian Peter Murray for my understanding of the history of the fur seal industry and the events leading up to the North Pacific fur seal treaty of 1911. I am also heavily indebted to the work of certain Canadian archeologists, such as Knut Fladmark and Roy Carlson, among others, and I borrowed liberally from the findings of dozens of academics from throughout the Pacific Rim who participated in the 1989 Circum-Pacific Prehistory Conference in Seattle.

Portions of this book have appeared in different form over the years in articles I have written for the *Vancouver Sun,* the *Globe and Mail, Canadian Geographic,* and the *Georgia Straight.* More than any other newspaper editor, Martin Dunphy is owed my thanks and praise, not just for sharpening my prose, but for sharpening many of the ideas that appear in this book. I owe particular thanks for the efficient and cheerful assistance of Stephen Watkinson of the University of British Columbia Fisheries Centre, who met all my many requests for obscure papers in long-forgotten academic journals, on time, and under budget. I owe thanks as well to Dick Beamish, Knut Fladmark, and Jim Lichatowich for kindly reviewing the manuscript. Similarly, without the help of the David Suzuki Foundation, much of the research that went into this book could not have been done. Ian Gill of Ecotrust Canada deserves the same sort of thanks, as does Greystone editor Nancy Flight, and last, but certainly not least, Jennifer Barclay, of Westwood Creative Artists.

The fear of you and the dread of you shall be
upon every beast of the earth and upon every
fowl of the air, upon all that moveth upon the
earth, and upon all the fishes of the sea.

— Genesis 9:2

The Whole Haunted Sea:
An Introduction

THE LONGNOSE LANCETFISH IS what you might imagine a deep-sea dinosaur would look like. It is known to taxonomists as *Alepisaurus ferox*, meaning scaleless serpent, which is a good description. Big, nasty teeth jut from a gaping mouth. A dorsal fin rises like a sail from a long and skinny body that can reach more than 2 meters (7 feet) in length. It is allegedly edible. It doesn't look it. Some sharks are apparently quite fond of lancetfish, which are routinely found in the stomachs of whitetip sharks. But whitetip sharks will eat almost anything, including other sharks, seabirds, limpets, periwinkles, garbage, and several of the crew of the steamship *Nova Scotia*, which was torpedoed by a German submarine off the South African coast during World War II. Similarly, a lancetfish will eat just about anything it can fit between its jaws. In the stomach of one lancetfish that found its way into a trawl net were the remains of two juveniles of the genus *Architeuthis*, the legendary giant squid.

A fish that eats baby krakens, looks like a skinny, legless stegosaurus, and is known to inhabit depths of 1800 meters (6000 feet) is not the type of thing Peter Binner expected to see in a crevice on the sandstone shoreline of Browning Harbour, a shallow bay on the north side of Pender Island, one of the Gulf Islands between British Columbia's mainland coast and Vancouver Island. But a dead lancetfish is just what Peter saw, on an early evening in March 1999. He was walking down the dock in front of his house to check on his 8.5-meter (28-foot) gaff-rigged cutter, the *Friday*. The sun was low in the sky, and at first, Peter thought the fish was just an odd piece of driftwood. When he looked closer he saw that it was a fish of some kind, but it wasn't like any fish he'd ever seen before. It was more than a meter (almost 4 feet) long. It was obviously dead.

Peter's story unfolds with the involvement of a local naturalist, a friend's freezer, and a phone call or two to the Pacific Biological Station in Nanaimo. It concludes with the contribution of the fish to a thankful Kelly Sendall, manager of the invertebrates, fish, and herpetology section of the Royal British Columbia Museum in Victoria. Sendall added the specimen to the growing list of oddities that were turning up in the museum's collections catalog.

But Peter Binner's discovery in a Browning Harbour tidepool is not just a story about another little astonishment in a brief spate of curiosities that were washing up on the shores of British Columbia's south coast. During the final years of the 20th century, something was clearly happening throughout the North Pacific. It wasn't just overfishing or pollution. It wasn't just El Niño, the recurring climate event that serves as the popular culprit whenever a California beach house washes into the sea, a Philippine ferry capsizes in a storm, or an Alaskan glacier starts calving icebergs the size of mountains into the shipping lanes. It was more than that.

In June 1997, mariners traversing the Bering Sea were reporting that the ocean had turned a strange aquamarine color. Hardy little seabirds known as shearwaters were found floating around in the water, dead. What ships' crews were seeing was an enormous phytoplankton bloom, a bizarre explosion in the population of free-floating, microscopic marine plants. Nothing like it had been seen before. By September of that year, scientists with the U.S. National Oceanographic and Aeronautics

Administration reported that they were tracking the bloom by satellite scanner. It was visible from space.

Off the California coast, in the early 1970s, the sea was a soup of macroplankton, those microscopic animals that are such a crucial food source for everything from herring to baleen whales. By the late 1970s, the macroplankton in the ocean off California had all but disappeared. As the 20th century limped to a close, common murres, Oregon's most numerous seabird, were abandoning their colonies all along the Oregon coast. Even the largest of coastal animals — gray whales — were delaying their winter migrations and swimming farther out into the Pacific on their southward journeys. At about the same time, lighthouses up and down the B.C. coast were reporting sea-surface temperatures that were higher than any they had measured in sixty-five years of record keeping. Ocean sunfish and albacore were swimming up the west coast's inlets, and for families in small towns from Gray's Harbor, Washington, to Port Edward, on British Columbia's north coast, the old ways of understanding the world had simply stopped working. Sockeye runs that once swarmed British Columbia's central coast just stopped coming home. Mackerel were biting hooks set for chinook. It was like waking up in the morning to find that we all lived on the shore of some distant, foreign sea.

The Pacific coast's fishing communities had already developed artful repertoires of who or what to blame when things went wrong. It was the seals, it was urban development, it was logging, or the pollution of rivers, and always, it was the politicians and the bureaucrats and the Indians. Washington State fishermen liked to blame Canadian fishermen. Washington's sports fishermen often blamed Washington's commercial fishermen. Canadians always blamed Americans, and when Canadians looked out on the Pacific at the end of the 20th century, they had cause enough to be less than articulate about what they saw. On Canada's east coast, the 1992 cod moratorium would have been disastrous enough if all it meant was that 30,000 workers in Canada's poorest province were suddenly pitched onto the dole. It was not just that one of the world's major fisheries crashed. It was not just that Newfoundland's inshore fishermen, in the years before the 1992 cod moratorium, begged and pleaded and rioted about the Canadian trawlers that were fishing out on the banks and nothing was done. It was that the North Atlantic cod fishery was the world's oldest high-seas fishery. It was the largest fishery collapse in human history. It was one of last great assemblages of wild protein on the planet, and it was over and gone. Canadians did it. It happened on our watch, in the late 20th century. In Alaska, meanwhile, when the bread-and-butter Bristol Bay sockeye runs failed to show as expected in 1998, Alaskan scientists tried to explain that something pretty serious was going on, and that complex ecosystem changes were somehow involved. Many fishermen would hear none of it. They blamed the Japanese and the Russians.

It was against this backdrop of incoherence, uncertainty, and despair that this book was written. It was written at the close of a century that began when the world's oceans were giving up about 5 million tonnes of fish every year and ended with about twenty times that amount being taken. Most of the world's great oceanic fishing grounds either had become barren or were being fished beyond sustainable limits. The North Pacific had become the planet's last greatest producer of fish, giving up about 25 million tonnes annually, which is an amount of fish roughly equal to the weight of the combined human population of Canada and the United States.

It was also a time when the North Pacific had suddenly become a region of key geopolitical importance in human events. The Soviet Union had collapsed, leaving in its North Pacific wake a degree of confusion not unlike the mayhem that followed the American purchase of Alaska from the Russian American Company in 1867. The Pacific Ocean itself, by the 1980s, had finally surpassed the Atlantic Ocean as the most important of the planet's oceans in matters of commerce, just as the Atlantic had surpassed the Mediterranean five centuries before. In the 1970s, Europe was North America's main trading partner. By the 1980s, Asian nations outranked Europe in the purchase and sale of goods and services to and from North America. In 1977, the world's busiest port was Rotterdam. In 1987, the world's busiest port was Hong Kong. British Columbia, Washington, and Oregon had come to comprise the fastest-growing region of North America, and much of that

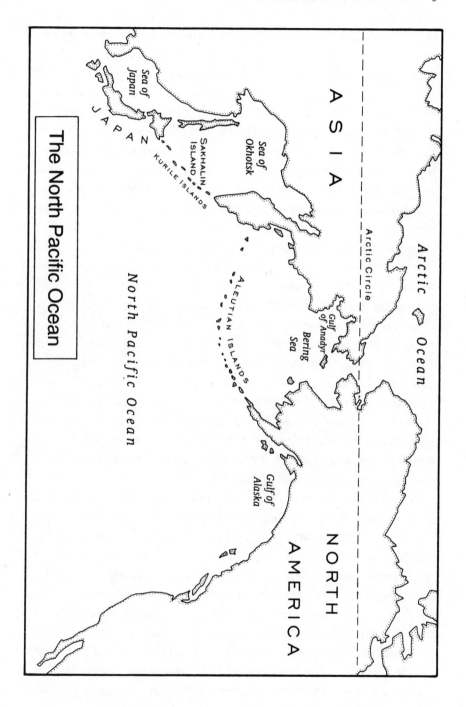

The North Pacific Ocean

growth was due to Asian immigration. During the last twenty-five years of the 20th century, Vancouver International Airport had more than tripled its air traffic, and much of that growth was on trans-Pacific flights. As the 20th century came to a close, many Canadians watched with growing nervousness as one rusty ship after another, each carrying scores of illegal Chinese immigrants, arrived uninvited on British Columbia's coast. Around the same time, many Americans were becoming similarly skittish after they learned that Japan held the mortgages on fully one-third of the U.S. national debt. While all this was going on, oceanographers and climatologists studying the ecological changes under way in the North Pacific were writing technical papers that sounded like passages from the Apocalypse of Saint John.

But this book is not about the end of the world. This is a book about the North Pacific, and because salmon have played such an important part in the story of the North Pacific, the ocean this book describes is the ocean encompassed by the range of North Pacific salmon. That ocean occupies almost one-seventh of the planet's surface, an area larger than the space taken up by the continent of North America, from Ellesmere Island to the Yucatán Peninsula. It is the ocean that lies between the streams where remnant steelhead salmon spawn in the hills above Los Angeles and the last few chum salmon creeks on the east coast of South Korea. It is also the Bering Sea and the Sea of Okhotsk, the Gulf of Alaska, the Gulf of Anadyr, the Strait of Georgia, and other bodies of water, real and imagined.

This book is also about the imaginary ocean, because it is only the human imagination that comprehends the implications of those disturbing things under way out there, beyond the sight of land. In the Western imagination, the North Pacific began and remains a place of great wonder, madness, illusion, and hope. Centuries after fairly precise cartography had established the shape and form of the Atlantic Ocean, the North Pacific was still a place where Jonathan Swift could locate his Brobdingnag and all its fantastic creatures. It was where Spanish kings could imagine the opening of a magical portal to Marco Polo's Orient known as the Strait of Lorenzo Ferrer Maldonado, where Dutch mariners expected to encounter a lost continent, and where one might find the

Pacific terminus of the Northwest Passage that so tormented the sleep of merchant emperors in London and Montreal. It was here, somewhere, that Russian naval officers expected to find a lost colony of refugees from Ivan the Terrible's 16th-century siege of Novgorod.

North America's Pacific coast was the last place on earth to find its way onto the marine charts of European naval officers, Yankee traders, and Upper Canadian cartographers. Although the coast from the Columbia River to the top of the Alexander Archipelago is little more than 2000 sea miles long, it is so ragged, so deeply pierced by inlets and sounds, and so strewn with islands that it takes in about 25,000 nautical miles of linear shoreline. Even the most sober and earnest attempts at chart making in the early days of exploration were overshadowed by accounts of great spectacles and the occasional sea monster. The enormous contribution of Georg Steller himself, the great naturalist who sailed the North Pacific with Vitus Bering for the Russian tsar in the 1740s, took on comical aspects after his alleged encounter with some kind of sea monkey — a beast described as having a head like a dog, large eyes, and a beard. The creature was said to "stand erect like a man" above the waves and play "a thousand apish tricks" alongside ships.

Sea monkeys were rarely sighted at the close of the 20th century, but the ocean of the imagination was undergoing upheavals and tumults every bit as dramatic as the Bering Sea's phytoplankton blooms. Orthodoxies, doctrines, and ways of thinking were collapsing under the weight of their own absurdity. Long-cherished ideas about the equilibrium of the North Pacific's ecosystems, about the antiquity of the North Pacific human cultures, about the relationship between terrestrial and aquatic species, even about the way "nature" works, were being abandoned as surely as murres were abandoning their colonies on the Oregon coast.

Sorting out the history of the North Pacific involves the business of considering questions not only about the observed but also about the observer and the observer's own culture and ideology. Considering such questions is difficult without resorting to unhelpful terms such as "ethnocentrism." There is nothing inherently wrong with being "ethnocentric," but there is no question that the cultural baggage white settlers brought with them to the North Pacific included a number of presumptions and perspectives that were not always helpful in making sense of what they were seeing. These things persist in North American culture, and they include an enduring faith in science that sometimes borders on a sort of religion that disregards however crude, tentative, or jerry rigged the science may be. There is also that blind faith in technology to which North Americans have tended to resort, imagining that technology is always a reliable means to fix the messes humans make. And there are all those lingering convictions about "progress," besides.

To discern the real from the imagined, the Western tradition has conventionally relied upon reason and science. This book, too, is significantly informed by the history of scientific inquiry in the North Pacific and upon the work of several brilliant scientists who have allowed us to see the North Pacific in new and different ways. But as the physicist and historian Thomas Kuhn pointed out, science is not really about the advance of human intelligence through rational processes of inquiry and experiment. It is really about maintaining the hegemony of certain assumptions, proving cherished hypotheses, and often just ignoring data that won't conform with expectations. It is about upholding the tenets of certain paradigms, which, every now and again, collapse in the face of overwhelming contradiction, exception, and anomaly. Such collapses trigger what Kuhn called "intellectually violent revolutions" among scientists, and an exploration of the North Pacific at the advent of the 21st century occurs at a moment in history in which such upheavals were shaking a variety of disciplines, in the ecological sciences, biology, archeology, and anthropology.

It was a bit like loosing the mooring lines and setting out in a small boat, and leaving the old charts back at the dock along with the compass, the depth sounder, and the radio. When such familiar shores are left behind, a different ocean spans the horizon.

The first thing you notice is that there are people out there, and they have been out there for a long, long time. There are mariners from the most unlikely ports. There are cultures of great antiquity around the top of the Pacific, and nothing about them fits very well with conventional theories about social "evolution" and the history of human settlement patterns around the world.

By the 1980s, anthropologists and archeologists were coming to realize that the human story of the North Pacific is unique in history, and it defies closely held notions about the way human societies are supposed to behave. Instead of "Indians" and "Asians," you see a broad cultural continuum around the North Pacific, extending in a sweeping arc that extends from at least as far south as the Yurok peoples of Northern California to the Jomon and Ainu peoples of Japan. From almost the moment human beings appeared in North America, fully adapted maritime societies were present throughout the North Pacific, on both sides of the ocean. And they are among the oldest fishing cultures to be found anywhere in the story of human civilization, anywhere on the planet. Elsewhere, maritime societies developed in relation to broader economic activity, typically as parts of agricultural cultures, in close economic association with, say, wheat farmers and cattle herders. Around the North Pacific, something else was going on. A civilization emerged from the salmon-spawning beds of post-Pleistocene valley bottoms and along desperately rugged coastines, and it had few of the characteristics conventionally attributed to "hunter-gatherer" societies or other fishing cultures. North Pacific cultures were composed of self-sustaining, densely populated societies marked by rigid hierarchy and social rank, based in large, permanent winter villages. And nowhere else on earth were human societies so fully integrated within marine ecosystems. Nowhere else were people so dependent upon fish. Among some North Pacific cultures, the isotopic signature found in human remains is exactly the same as that found in dolphins.

The next thing you see is salmon.

Fom the very beginnings of human history in the North Pacific, salmon were involved. Salmon were there at the close of the last ice age, and for most of history since then, salmon — not human beings — were the species most responsible for altering the shape and form of the continents around the North Pacific. As they set about the work of recolonizing the coastlines from their Ice Age refugia, they spawned in glacier-fed rivers that were re-emerging from a Pleistocene landscape that had been covered by ice for tens of thousands of years. Almost half of North America had been covered in ice sheets that were several kilometers thick in places, and the spawned-out bodies of those first salmon provided nutrients for the first willow and alder forests, for bugs and birds and bears, and for the people who began to settle down at river mouths and at strategic fishing sites adjacent to canyons. Every year, millions of tonnes of energy was brought up out of the depths of the North Pacific and deposited deep within the continents surrounding it. In ways that science is only now taking into consideration, salmon were intimately involved, from the very beginning, in determining the form and shape of the continents' terrestrial ecosystems, sometimes hundreds of kilometers inland. Salmon were involved in the form and shape that human societies took as well.

There are other things, too, other shapes and forms that have begun to appear on the horizon. There are things that we have never seen before, and there are things we will never see again.

It is no longer the ocean that appeared in the imagination of Descartes, who saw "nature" as something apart from and at odds with humanity, something that was to be subdued, with "progress" measured as the degree to which battles against nature were won with scientific artillery. Those latitudes were behind us, as were the ideas of John Stuart Mill, who imagined the natural world as a hostile army, "her powers . . . in the position of enemies, from whom [man] must wrest, by force and ingenuity, what little he can for his own use." In those waters, Herman Melville could imagine an ocean that was evil, embodied by a ruthless and vengeful leviathan. Even Sigmund Freud claimed to see such things, and against its power he clung to a utopian vision of humanity united in the cause of "taking up the attack on nature, thus forcing it to obey human will, under the guidance of science."

It was from that sea of madness that the jangling machinery of the industrial revolution came, lubricated with oil rendered from the North Pacific's whales. There were cannery towns, logging camps, pulp mills, steam donkeys, floatplanes, Vivian diesels, and Easthope gas boats. A new, cosmopolitan North Pacific civilization rose up out of the shell middens. There were mines, and the forests were mined of trees, the high seas were mined of whales and seals, the rivers were mined of salmon, and the straits were mined of rockfish.

And then there were new ideas that gave meaning to what we saw in the North Pacific, long after the ideas of Descartes and Mill and the others had been abandoned. They came from people like the English chemist James Lovelock, who toiled in front of his computer screens at the Jet Propulsion Laboratory in Pasadena, California, and saw a nameless phenomenon in all his equations. He gave it the name Gaia and said it was a benign presence that embraced all life on earth, presiding over the movements of insects and regulating the thermodynamic properties of the atmosphere itself. In 1971, informed by these kinds of ideas, a dozen mystics and flute players from Vancouver's Kitsilano neighborhood headed into the North Pacific aboard the *Phyllis Cormack,* a seine boat they christened the *Greenpeace,* and the world changed again.

But that ocean, too, is one we have now crossed. This book was written at that moment in history when the Industrial Age had come to an end throughout much of the North Pacific. It is now an ocean into which a lone halibut fisherman setting out from Prince Rupert will venture on a calm and sunny morning and not see what Melville saw, because the ocean is where life and money comes from. But that same halibut fishermen, heading home and rounding Cape Saint James with his hold empty and a southeaster blowing 40 knots, sees nothing benign in nature either. He sees that the North Pacific wants to kill him. And when scientists with the U.S. National Oceanographic and Aeronautics Administration and Canada's Institute of Ocean Sciences see that after all these years, there is no equilibrium in things, or if there is equilibrium at all it occurs alongside chaos and disorder, the winds shift, ideas fall, and everything collapses into ghost heaps again.

That is the way things happen in the North Pacific. Malcolm Lowry suffered delirium tremens and saw a coast "of deep-forested mountains with the sunset fire lingering on their murderous peaks," and it was toward that fire that utopians from Denmark trudged, all the way to Cape Scott. They gazed out upon the Pacific and warmed themselves around a flickering light of their own imagining until it vanished and the forest crept back in again. Pacifist Finns came to Malcolm Island, where they called their colony Sointula, the Place of Harmony. The rain drowned their faith. Brother Twelve brought German aristocrats, English spiritualists, an American spy, and a woman who claimed to be the reincarnation of Isis, and then his Colony of Truth disappeared into sword ferns and thimbleberry. The Methodist prophet William Duncan and his 1000 Tsimshian disciples built Metlakatla, the North Pacific's holy city. There were Victorian houses, there was a cathedral and a printing press, a brass band, and bright, gas-lit streets. By 1887, all of it was gone, swallowed by the forest and the rain.

In these ways, the North Pacific is a haunted place, and seeing ghosts may be a necessary part of coming to terms with those disturbing forces we have come to see at work in the ocean. But in these ways, too, the North Pacific reveals itself as a thing of great fury that will not so willingly allow us to comprehend its meaning.

This book does not propose any new theory to explain the meaning of the events under way in the North Pacific, or in the imaginary ocean that is so much a part of it. From the great age of exploration to the age of sattelite scanning, from Hooper Bay in California to Port Moller in Alaska, the beaches have become littered with failed hypotheses, and the ribs of gillnet boats poke out of the mud like dinosaur bones. This book is only a contribution to the conversation, and the only firm conviction it relies upon is that the tide comes in and the tide goes out. Things change, and things stay the same. And despite the folly of all our mistakes, and all of our utopian conceits, and the lateness of the hour, it is still quite possible to decide what kind of an ocean it might be.

Up and down the coast, in the contours of the shoreline, you can still make out the shapes of ideas, the old net lofts, boardwalks, cannery buildings, and post offices, all entombed in tangles of blackberry. It is the same at village after village, at Klemtu, at Minstrel Island, and at Namu. At Goose Bay, at Butedale, and at Aberdeen. Then the tide comes in again, and through the trees, there are sometimes glimpses of older ideas, like Hokwhokw, the long-beaked thunderbird, and Komokoa, chief of the undersea world. There are new ideas, too, and there are still deep-forested mountains with sunset fire lingering on their murderous peaks. And sometimes, when the rain lingers in the cedar limbs in a certain way, it is as though the forest embraces the whole, haunted world. The tide goes out. The tide comes in again.

The world is not coming to an end.

❧ ONE ❧

The Beginning of the World

Hereabouts was all saltwater, they say.
He was flying all around, the Raven was,
looking for land that he could stand on.
After a time, at the toe of the islands, there was one rock awash.
He flew there to sit.

—from Raven Travelling, *a Haida epic,*
translated by Robert Bringhurst, in A Story as Sharp as a Knife:
The Classical Haida Mythtellers and Their World

"THE LAND WAS STRANGELY different than what it is now."

With those words, an old man who lived in a little house on the banks of the Fraser River began to tell a story. It was 1936.

The old man was Peter Pierre. When he was a boy, the story had been entrusted to him by an "Indian doctor," as traditional healers and story-tellers were known along the Fraser in the 1930s. In his childhood, Peter Pierre was regarded as a gifted boy, and in the late 1860s, before he'd reached the age of 12, he was taken by his mother to a small group of old men who had persisted in maintaining certain traditions that were dis-appearing, even then, among the remnants of the Sto:lo fishing communities along the Fraser's lower reaches. The old men took the boy under their care. They took pains to train him in a variety of skills, one of which was to recount, with precision, the elaborate histories of his community.

Peter Pierre's community was Katzie, a half-day's journey by canoe, if the tide was right, from the mouth of the Fraser. There wasn't much left

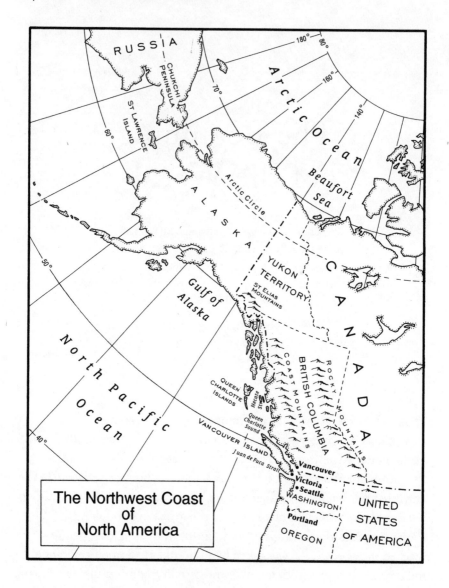

The Northwest Coast
of
North America

of Katzie in 1936. Smallpox, Spanish influenza, measles, and other introduced diseases had taken their toll, and only about a hundred Katzie people were left of a community that may have once numbered in the thousands. By the 1860s, the Katzie had come to live in three small villages. One was on the Fraser's north bank, another was on the south bank, and the third, where Peter Pierre was raised, was between these two, on Barnston Island, in the middle of the river.

Peter Pierre told his story to the anthropologist Diamond Jenness.

There were no leafy trees to cast deep shadows. The dark-green firs stood as they stand today, but they were grim and silent; no winds rocked their summits, no birds nested in their branches, no animals roamed by day or night past their motionless trunks. In the waters of the sea and the rivers there were clams and mussels, but no salmon, eulachon or sturgeon, no seals, and no sea lions. . . .

The land was indeed strangely different then.

It could be that Peter Pierre's story was a description of the kind of landscape the Katzies' ancestors encountered at the close of the Pleistocene epoch, about 10,000 years before. Shortly before that time, the great Cordilleran ice sheet had covered almost everything from Yukon Territory to a point about halfway down the Washington coast. As the ice receded, it left a coast that was a barren, glacier-scarred place. A rough picture of those early years emerges from Peter Pierre's story. It is a picture remarkably similar to the portrait of those early years sketched by geologists and paleobotanists. The valley bottoms were sparsely forested, and seawater had begun to inundate vast coastal plains that had extended from the mountains. At various places along the coast, the continent itself was rising, too, cracking and breaking, freed from the weight of kilometers-thick ice sheets. In the wake of the retreating Cordilleran ice, a meager forest of lodgepole pine and other conifers had sprung up in Washington and along British Columbia's south coast. To the north, the forest was even more sparse. Between the Queen Charlotte Islands and the Estevan Islands, where Hecate Strait is now, there was a tundra of dwarf shrubs with groves of spruce, pine, and alder scattered here and there.

Up and down the west coast, living on in the cultural memory of aboriginal societies, there are many stories like the ones Peter Pierre told. They are what might be described as records of those early years, but some of those stories might also be accounts of the geological upheavals that followed long after the close of the Pleistocene epoch. Generally, the scientific community hasn't known quite what to make of such dawn-of-the-world stories, and there is often great difficulty in "confirming" the oral tradition with archeological evidence.

Archeologists who have gathered evidence of early human settlement around the North Pacific have generally been preoccupied with human migrations from Asia to the Americas. All the delving into when, exactly, and how, exactly, and how many times, exactly, these migrations occurred has had some bothersome side effects. Many of the native people studied in this way find it too tiresome for words. Excruciating arguments erupt between various factions of archeologists whenever some graduate student comes upon an old bone and claims to have uncovered the oldest evidence of human occupation in the "New World." So far, no scientist has convincingly and conclusively shown that humans were present in North America earlier than 14,000 years ago, but the contest goes on and on. This is all very well and good, except that it tends to place an inordinate focus on a simplistic narrative in which faceless Stone Age hunters, apparently with nothing better to do with their time, are constantly trudging eastward across Asia, and if they get as far as the Chukchi Peninsula, they immediately race across the Beringian "land bridge" while the rising seas lap at their heels, eventually arriving in North America.

In that orthodox version of events, big-game hunters crossed Beringia into Alaska and then scurried down a narrow passage between North America's two great Pleistocene ice sheets, the Cordilleran and the Laurentide, about 12,000 years ago. From there, they populated all of North and South America, within about a thousand years. Not only did they make it through the Central American isthmus and get as far as Tierra del Fuego in this short time, but they also found their way over the Rockies and established a settled way of life on the Pacific coast from Northern California to southeast Alaska.

There have been good reasons to find this scenario implausible. One reason is that widespread evidence — although not definite and over-whelming, but certainly persuasive — indicates that human beings were present far south of the ice sheets, even as far as South America, around the same time they were supposed to be arriving in Alaska. Another problem with the scenario is the geological evidence. Everything seems to point to a warming period of possibly some thousands of years that would have opened up a passageway between the Cordilleran and Laurentide ice masses. But much evidence also suggests that the corridor opened up only briefly about 12,000 years ago and then snapped shut again. There is also the problem of imagining that anyone could survive the conditions in the corridor itself, which could have been much more than a thousand kilometers (600 miles) in length and may have been a horrible, freezing wind tunnel or a long and shallow fjord.

But all these problems can be at least theoretically solved, in one way or another, and Frederick West, curator of the Peabody Museum in Massachussetts and an ardent proponent of the ice-free-corridor notion, presents an articulate version of events that will probably stand as the most convincing argument for it. West sees a single Paleolithic culture, which he calls the Beringian tradition, to account for a series of astonishing similarities in the stone tool kits of hunters who were present throughout Beringia, on its Asian and North American frontiers, at least as early as 15,000 years ago. In Russia, archeologists use the term "Dyuktai culture" to describe these hunters, who first roamed throughout northeast Asia from a center of gravity in the upper reaches of the Aldan River, which is just a short jog across the Stanovoy range from the Amur River Valley. In Alaska, evidence of the same type of culture has been found in several stone-tool assemblages not far from Alaska's Bering Sea coast, and American archeologists have used the term "Denali culture" to describe it.

West says that Dyuktai and Denali people were part of the same Beringian tradition and that during a time of catastrophic ecological upheaval and rapid climate change, about 12,000 years ago, a small band of these Beringian hunters found themselves at the eastern frontiers of their vanishing subcontinent, well into present-day Alaska. West says it took perhaps a single generation to pass through the ice-free corridor, from its entrance around Yukon to its exit somewhere down in Montana. It was probably "the result of having, literally, taken a wrong turn," West says, with people "ending up in an inhospitable chute that became itself an impelling force to continue the migration. Perhaps the first peopling of America was the result of bad judgment — an accident."

The ice-free corridor had become a necessary orthodoxy among archeologists by the 1960s. It was considered the only way to explain a series of stunning revelations that followed the 1949 discovery by University of Chicago scientist Willard Libby that it was possible to measure the rate of decay in the radioactive isotope carbon 14 in organic matter. Libby's discovery meant that it was possible to figure out when things died. Archeologists soon started sending Libby bones to analyze. Libby's technique quickly proved that two specimen collections from Clovis and Folsom, in New Mexico — bones from mammals that had spear points still stuck in them — had been killed by people more than 10,000 years before. Other Clovis-type specimens were found to be 11,500 years old. In all the hubbub that followed, the ice-free corridor became an article of faith.

One can be left with the impression that the scientists who delve into the early period of the North Pacific's human history have found nothing better to do with their time than add more detail to this same, unavoidably dreary story, and to present more evidence of the soundness of their faith in the ice-free corridor. But there is no longer any consensus around the idea that all "New World" peoples descended from a single group of big-game hunters who found themselves in Alaska a few thousand years ago. There is no consensus about exactly where it all began, and there was certainly a lot more going on around the North Pacific in those early days than the standard narrative suggests. And fortunately, scientists on both sides of the Pacific have been looking into those things and telling different, more interesting stories.

One of those scientists is Carol Zane Jolles, an anthropologist at the University of Washington. What Jolles observes is something that the usual story of the "Bering land bridge" completely and utterly overlooks, which is that not all of it collapsed into the sea. There is still a piece of it left, and people have been living there for thousands of years, apparently unaware that there was some link between Asia and North America that had ever been broken in the first place.

Saint Lawrence Island is about 160 kilometers (100 miles) long and about 50 kilometers (30 miles) wide. It's only 38 sea miles from Russia's Chukchi Peninsula, and 125 sea miles from Alaska's Cape Woolley. The people of the island are the Sivuqaghhmit, who speak a dialect of Siberian Yupik. The islanders have centuries-old relationships with the Yupik and Chukchi peoples from the Russian shore, and even though the island has been American territory since the 1800s, and despite the long and dreadful period of the Cold War, many islanders have close relatives in the Russian coastal town of New Chaplino. There doesn't seem to be any point in history at which the Saint Lawrence Islanders were not perfectly aware of, and probably trading with, the Kaviagmiut and other people on the Alaskan side of the Bering Strait. The Siberian Chukchis certainly were. In 1816, Russian explorers visiting Saint Lawrence Island found the local people already in possession of European trade goods. Either those goods came across Siberia and were traded to the islanders by Ungaziq people on the Chukchi Peninsula — in exchange for gut-skin rain gear, skin boats, and walrus hides, which comprised the Saint Lawrence Islanders' usual currency — or they originated with Hudson Bay Company traders, far to the east.

There is also much to be said about Beringia itself, which was not just some spindly, precarious, and temporary overpass that is relevant only because of the access it provided big-game hunters looking for new hunting opportunities on the other side of it. Beringia was not a bridge at all. It was a very big place, and because of the warming and cooling trends that marked the later periods of the Pleistocene epoch, the portion that connected the present coastlines of Asia and North America is believed to have been submerged at least twice. The "bridge" collapsed once between 75,000 and 45,000 years ago, and again sometime after 25,000 years ago, and by 10,000 years ago, Beringia was gone for good. But during all the intervening millennia, Beringia was a real subcontinent, a low-lying plain probably about the size of Europe's Iberian peninsula, which includes present-day Spain and Portugal.

Like most northerly Pleistocene landscapes, the Beringian interior was pretty grim, unless you were a large herbivore. Even if you were a hunter skilled in hunting large herbivores, you wouldn't likely look upon Beringia's inland plains as all that pleasant. Just how the ecology of Beringia should be described is another one of those subjects about which there is heated debate among scientists. Some argue that Pleistocene Beringia was mainly a dry, windy tundra, with sedges and grasses struggling up out of the dusty ground, relieved only occasionally by swamps and bogs. Others see a more lush and productive landscape, almost like a savannah. Still others see a steppe covered by diverse forms of vegetation and grassy wetlands.

One of the greatest problems in fixing a definite date for the appearance of human beings on the shores of the North Pacific is that you can't always tell where the land was, where the shore was, how deep the oceans were, or even how high the mountains were.

It's been hard to know even where to look for the evidence, and there's not much left to look at from those early times anyway because the coast has gone though such ups and downs over the years. These ups and downs are a result of eustatic and isostatic variations in North Pacific coastlines. These changes not only put the possible locations of coastal settlements well inland of modern coastlines but also left other possible village sites at the bottom of the sea.

Eustatic variations are the changes related to the rise and fall of sea levels. During the Ice Age, so much of the planet's water was locked up in ice that sea levels were a lot lower than they are today, and as the Ice Age waxed and waned in its final years, sea levels rose and fell. Isostatic variations involve the rise and fall of the continents relative to sea level. The very weight of the ice sheets on the continents tended to flatten everything. When the Pleistocene epoch ended, the Pacific margins of the continents slowly rose back up, and isostatic changes were more dramatic in some places than in others. The Pleistocene epoch, which began about two million years ago, had run its full course only a little more than 10,000 years ago, with the final recession of the ice sheets. The final millennia of the Pleistocene, and the first few centuries of the Holocene epoch, were times of eustatic and isostatic pandemonium.

Even during the long winter of the Pleistocene, it is not as though the entire northern third of the planet were covered in a single, unchanging blanket of ice for two million years. There were warming and cooling trends. Generally, throughout Asia and North America, the continents above, say, the latitude of the Canada–U.S. border were unforgiving places. But at no point was the entire landscape completely covered in ice. There were small pockets of Ice Age refugia, where various hardy forms of life could survive the long winter of the Pleistocene, and there were also large ice-free areas, with forests, rivers, and lakes, and there were immense coastal plains. But it was still all pretty harsh by modern standards. Much of the ice-free landscape, well into the Arctic regions, was dominated by cold and extremely dry taiga or steppe. It certainly wasn't conducive to people settling down in villages, but it was well suited to grazing mammals, browsing mammals, and various ungulates and megafauna — antelope, deer, elk and caribou, camel, bisons, musk oxen, and mammoths. It was also well suited to human cultures that had adapted to hunting such animals in those kinds of conditions. And about 40,000 years ago, fully "modern" humans began appearing all over Europe and Asia, rapidly and completely succeeding Neanderthals.

Fully and anatomically "modern" humans, known as *Homo sapiens sapiens,* may well have been around for 100,000 years or more, but there's little evidence of it. Determining the date of the first appearance of fully modern humans on the planet is difficult not just because of the dearth of human bones in the early archeological record. It's also difficult because there is no clear consensus about whether the immediate ancestors of fully modern humans were Neanderthals — those low-brow cavemen of Saturday morning cartoons — or whether Neanderthals were just an evolutionary cul-de-sac down a side road branching off the great human highway. Another problem is the business of determining what is meant, exactly, by the term "fully modern humans." One characteristic is reflective consciousness, but the presence of such an abstact trait is hard to infer from the confusing collections of rocks and bones that archeologists normally have to work with. And besides, Neanderthals were capable of reflective consciousness, as the evidence of 100,000-year-old Neanderthal burials clearly shows.

The presence of fully modern humans about 40,000 years ago is undisputed. There is overwhelming evidence, around the same time, of human culture — the obvious presence of language, art, and elaborate ritual. This clear presence of modern humans coincides exactly with a period known as the Upper Paleolithic "revolution," an event marked by the complete disappearance of Neanderthals and the sudden proliferation of sophisticated hunter-gatherers who pursued game animals with intricately carved weapons. These people carved amulets and talismans, employed hundreds of different stone, bone, and wooden tools, and painted exquisite portraits of wildlife on the walls of caves.

At least 20,000 years ago, people just like this were hunting on the Stanovoy Plateau, around the shores of Lake Baikal, in the upper reaches of the Lena River, and across the Yablonovy Mountains in the Amur River watershed. This rugged and still sparsely populated region of northeast Asia stretches from the windswept terrain north of present-day Ulan Bator, in Mongolia, to the rugged Sikhote Alin Mountains, on Russia's Pacific coast, north of Korea.

The emerging evidence for the Lena-Amur headwaters area as a kind of starting point for the maritime cultures of the North Pacific, and for all "New World" peoples, cuts across several disciplines. Cross-discipline agreement on ideas like these is extremely rare. Scientists who argue that the first peoples of North and South America share a common Lena-Amur origin include archeologists, geneticists, and linguists.

Christy Turner is an an archeologist who has spent most of his career analyzing teeth. A former senior scholar at the USSR Academy of Sciences, Turner, in his laboratory at Arizona State University, has examined tens of thousands of teeth, taken from human remains found in archeological sites throughout North and South America, Asia, and Europe. Of all the microevolutionary dental traits Turner has come across, the most striking is the presence of two basic patterns, which Turner has called sinodonty and sundadonty. Sinodonts are people with upper first premolars that have a single root, lower first molars with a triple root, and a few other distinguishing features. Sundadonts, meanwhile, have front teeth with only a weak "shoveled out" area at the back of them, a congenital absence of upper back molars, and some other features not shared with Sinodonts. Aboriginal peoples in the "New

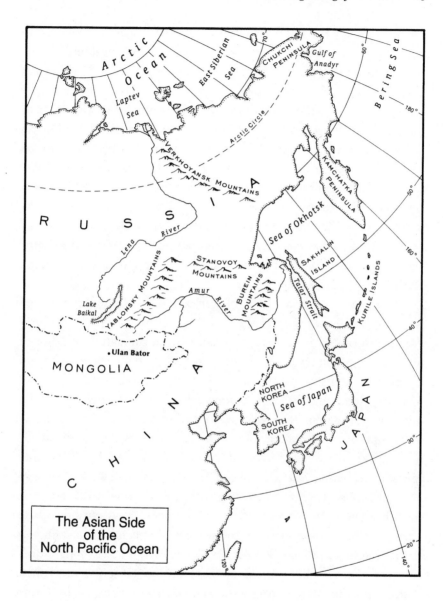

The Asian Side
of the
North Pacific Ocean

World" all share the sinodont pattern. Turner has spent decades tracking the presence of Sinodonts through Asia's archeological record. The first known Sinodonts were hunters who lived in the Amur River area of northern China, about 20,000 years ago.

Turner argues that Sinodonts may have been around a lot longer than that, maybe even 40,000 years. But it's in the Amur River headwaters that the earliest archeological record of Sinodonts can be found. To the south of them were Sundadonts. To the west of them, even as nearby as Lake Baikal, were more Sundadonts. Turner reckons that the Sinodonts were certainly present in the upper reaches of the Lena River. By tracking the occurrence of sinodonty in the archeological record, and by taking a closer look at subtle variations within the features of sinodonty, Turner sees the Sinodonts slowly making their way down the Lena River.

The Lena River is one the world's great rivers. Rising in the mountains just west of Lake Baikal, the Lena flows northeast, winding around the eastern rim of the Central Siberian Plateau through steppe, boreal forest, swamp, and taiga. The Lena then turns to the northwest, beginning a long and gentle curve around the western flanks of the Verkhoyansk Mountains. More than 3000 kilometers (1864 miles) from its headwaters, the Lena River disperses into a maze of estuarine channels that empty into the Arctic waters of the Laptev Sea, which is about halfway between Finland's Barents Sea coast and the Chukchi Peninsula on the Bering Sea. Turner sees the Sinodonts making their way down the Lena River over the course of a few thousand years. Some of them head east across Siberia. Some stay around the Asian side of the Bering Sea. Others wander over the Beringian subcontinent and end up in the vicinity of present-day Alaska. Some end up down along North America's Pacific coast, but others just keep on going east, and then south, until they have occupied every nook and cranny of the "New World."

It was the subtle variations within the features of sinodonty that allowed Turner to develop this more elaborate version of the peopling of the Americas. Within sinodonty, subtle differences in dental patterns form three distinct clusters, two of which suggest an extremely early

North Pacific maritime adaption. The first cluster, Aleut-Eskimo, produces a division that includes the aboriginal people of the Aleutian Islands, the Chukchi of the Bering Sea, "Eskimos" of Alaska and Siberia, and the Bering Sea's Koryak people. The second group Turner calls the Greater Northwest Coast division, which includes the coastal tribes between southeast Alaska and Northern California. The final division is the Macro-Indian group, which takes in all other aboriginal peoples in North and South America.

In the 1980s, Turner reckoned he'd try to compare his findings with the results of research in other disciplines. So he teamed up with anthropologist and geneticist Stephen Zegura, who specializes in evolutionary biology and physical anthropology, and with the linguist Joseph Greenberg, a member of the U.S. National Academy of Sciences and the author of the four-volume *Universals of Human Language.*

Turner's findings were generally confirmed by the archeological evidence, which supports a hypothesis of three distinct stone-tool traditions in the early human story of North America. These tool traditions are sometimes called early Aleutian, Paleo-Indian (which corresponds with Turner's Macro-Indian dental division) and the Denali tradition, sometimes called Paleo-Arctic (which corresponds with Turner's Greater Northwest Coast dental division). The genetic evidence is also consistent with what the dental and archeological evidence implies, strongly suggesting a tripartite division of Aleut-Eskimo, Paleo-Indian, and Na-Dene (which includes Greater Northwest Coast), and perhaps even more divisions, each of which emerged in Asia from a gene pool that was distinct from everything around it about 20,000 years ago. The linguisitic evidence, meanwhile, also points to three separate traditions that formed the basis of the earliest North American languages.

Turner, Zegura, and Greenberg published the results of their findings in 1986 and concluded that the most reasonable interpretation was that their three divisions of peoples, Amerind (the same as Turner's Macro-Indian group), Na-Dene, and Aleut-Eskimo, represented three migrations from Asia. Comparing their own research with the findings of others, Turner, Zegura, and Greenberg fine-tuned Turner's original hypothesis to suggest that the Amur River people had descendants not just on, say, Vancouver Island, but directly across the Pacific on the northern Japanese island of Hokkaido. They argued that the antecedents of the Northwest Coast cultures were already quite different from those of their Aleut-Eskimo and "Indian" cousins before they even left the Lena-Amur region. They argued strongly for a route for the Macro-Indian (otherwise known as Amerind or Paleo-Indian) group down the Lena River and eastward across Siberia, but they had other thoughts about the route taken by the ancestors of the Aleuts and Eskimos. They gave tacit support to archeologists who have suggested that the Aleut-Eskimo ancestors did not go up the Amur, over the Yablonovy Mountains, down the Lena, and across Siberia, but rather went down the Amur, about 15,000 years ago.

The Amur River, also one the world's great rivers, arises in the Stanovoy mountain range on the Chinese-Russian frontier, only about 500 kilometers (300 miles) east of the Lena's headwaters. But unlike the Lena, the Amur winds its way eastward, forming the present border between China and Russia. It flows down a 1000-kilometer (600-mile) course that drains vast low-lying plains on its northern banks and the Greater Khingan Mountains of northern Manchuria to the south. Then the Amur turns abruptly northward for another 500 kilometers (300 miles) or so, flowing down through a broad valley between the Burein Mountains and the Sikhote Alin range. The river finally empties into the Tartar Strait, a narrow waterway that separates Sakhalin Island from the Russian Pacific mainland.

In the hypotheses supported by the work of Turner, Zegura, and Greenberg, the Aleut-Eskimo Sinodonts made their way down the Amur from its headwaters, then headed up the Russian Pacific coast and skiffed along Beringia's southern coast until they arrived on the islands just the west of the Alaska Peninsula.

Some scientists thought the work that Turner, Zegura, and Greenberg had done was brilliant, and that they had been necessarily bold. William Laughlin, a venerable American scientist, an anthropology professor at the University of Connecticut, and the foremost authority on Aleutian archeology, ethnology, and culture, cautiously but clearly supported many of the trio's arguments. Others thought they had gone too far. Lyle Campbell, from the State University of New York, declared that attempting to reconstruct migration routes and relationships between the ancestral societies of the New World's peoples was just unreasonable conjecture. Campbell advised that "the whole speculative venture should be abandoned."

But the old orthodoxies were quickly collapsing, as surely as the imaginary Beringian land bridge had collapsed in the old orthodoxies themselves. The fixation with big-game hunters running single-mindedly across the Beringian interior in the direction of North America, then showing up almost immediately in the central U.S. plains states, came to be positively annoying to a small group of archeologists in the late 1950s and early 1960s. Those archeologists were not dissenters or schismatics, but they had their doubts, and they had some ideas of their own about the overlooked significance of early human occupation of the Pacific coast. Among those few maverick scientists was Calvin Huesser, who suggested that many archeologists were unduly ignoring evidence for early North Pacific maritime cultures and glossing over inconsistencies in the mainstream "ice-free corridor" scenario. In a 1960 paper published by the American Geological Society, Huesser presented evidence from his own years of research on the Pacific coast suggesting that the ice-free corridor was unnecessary and that a coastal route more or less around the Cordilleran ice sheet was at least just as possible.

Knut Fladmark was a pioneer in the study of early Pacific coastal archeology, early coastal geography, and the implications of ice-free refugia that existed during the Pleistocene epoch up and down the Pacific coast. He was not happy with the way Huesser had been forgotten, and he was a bit bored by all the dogmatism about big-game hunters heading east across Beringia, then south down a corridor between continent-sized glaciers, then sticking spears into mammoths in New Mexico, then settling down on the beaches of the Pacific. An archeologist with British Columbia's Simon Fraser University, Fladmark had spent the 1970s poking into crevices and gumbooting along beaches up and down the B.C. coast, and he quickly became convinced that Huesser's ideas about coastal migrations were completely plausible. Fladmark revisited Huesser's findings, conducted his own fieldwork, and reviewed the evidence about the coastal extent of the Cordilleran ice sheets that geologists had been accumulating since Huesser's time. Fladmark's own conclusion was that Huesser's hypothesis had not only withstood the test of time and new scientific findings but had started to look quite feasible.

In a groundbreaking analysis published by the Society for American Archeology in 1979, Fladmark presented evidence for a first settlement of North and South America, by a Pacific coastal migration route from Beringia's south coast, that was certainly as convincing as the ice-free-corridor scenario.

What had confounded Fladmark was that most archeologists accepted that people were capable of crossing significant stretches of open water in Asia's far northeast 30,000 years ago but still believed that these people chose an inland route through Beringia. Fladmark saw no reason that those early maritime people would not have skiffed eastward along Beringia's southern coast, which was warmed by a Japanese current that was not cooled, back then, by any infusion of Arctic water through Bering Strait. Significant portions of the outer coasts of Alaska, British Columbia, and Washington remained ice-free during the Pleistocene epoch, and those refugia supported forests and birds and were adjacent to rich marine resources. Fladmark speculated that those midcoast and north coast refugia might even have harbored salmon runs.

Fladmark challenged his fellow archeologists to ask themselves two simple questions. Why would anybody want to go running around the forbidding Beringian interior when its south coast was a much better place to be? Why had so many archeologists already reached that sensible conclusion about Beringia's south coast, "but none have taken the next step and suggested that instead of abandoning their boats on the American shore to run joyfully inland in search of 'big game,' a few of these early voyagers may simply have continued southward along the Pacific coast of North America"?

Fladmark proposed a way to address the matter of the early North Pacific without causing another fractious controversy. He was adamant that he found little sense in the idea that big-game hunters emerged from some narrow chasm in the frozen continent, somewhere south of

Alberta, and the next thing you know they've become fully adapted fishing cultures a couple of thousand kilometers to the northwest, almost back where they started, on the coast of southeast Alaska, on the Queen Charlotte Islands, and on British Columbia's central coast. But he made it plain that the proponents of the ice-free-corridor scenario could coexist with those who supported a late Pleistocene Pacific coast route. He said the absence of old coastal archeological sites, which could easily be a consequence of rising and falling sea levels and coastlines, should be taken as just that — an absence of something, and certainly not proof that there was no coastal route to look for.

Fladmark proposed: "Instead of despairing of ever dealing sensibly with the archeological significance of submerged land surfaces, we should carefully examine all available evidence, including cross-areal comparisons and the nature of the oldest visible archeological remains found above sea level along the now drowned coastline, in order to reconstruct that part of the sequence lost to air-breathing researchers."

These quandaries have never been worrisome to the coast's aboriginal societies. Over the years, many aboriginal leaders have publicly despaired over all the scientific curiosity about Asian origins and scientific uncertainty about the antiquity of coastal aboriginal cultures. The oral traditions of practically every coastal society assert a completely local origin. In Peter Pierre's stories, the Katzie and their neighbors descended not from Beringian hunters or North Pacific voyagers but from the first people placed on earth, in the Katzie territory and the adjacent countryside, by He-Who-Dwells-Above, at the very beginning of time. In those same stories might be found "that part of the sequence lost to air-breathing researchers" as well.

Aboriginal mythologies are often interpreted in ways that are, to say the least, a bit overly creative. But the record found in the oral tradition often accords quite neatly with what geologists and paleoecologists have to say about what was going on, all over the coast, at the dawn of the Holocene, about 10,000 years ago. The stories from the oral tradition tend to be charged with tremendous emotional energy. They often involve ghosts and the persistence of great sorrow and terror associated with specific landforms and named landmarks. In the paleoecological and geological renditions, there are great floods, localized advances of ice sheets in final bursts of Pleistocene fury, earthquakes, and rapid ecological and climate change.

Harry Assu was a respected chief and elder of the Kwagewlth people of Cape Mudge, about 150 sea miles north of Katzie. In the early 1980s, Assu told his stories to Joy Inglis, a specialist in coastal native art, culture, and myth. In one story about the early days of the Kwakwala-speaking people, there is an account of a great chief, Wai-Kai. For years, Wai-Kai had been warning of a great flood that would change everything. When it came, the people of Topaze Harbour rafted their canoes together and tied them fast to a rock on the mountain behind the village. In the great storms and upheavals that followed, the canoes were swept to Smith Inlet, Knight Inlet, Blunden Harbour, Village Island, Harbledown Island, and other places. That is how the Kwakwala-speaking people came to be where Europeans found them, Assu explained.

The story was a lot like one told by Peter Pierre, in which Katzie people survive a great flood by anchoring their canoes to a mountain above Pitt Lake, the Katzies' ancestral home, where He-Who-Dwells-Above had put the Katzies' ancestors on the earth at the beginning of time.

About 60 kilometers (40 miles) up the Fraser from Katzie, there is another mountain, and another story. On Sumas Mountain there are a series of caves below a rocky outcrop, known as Kilgard Bluffs, where the ancestors of the Sto:lo people are said to have retreated during a great flood. The Sto:lo say their ancestors landed in canoes on Sumas Mountain, at Spider Peak, when the entire Fraser Valley was beneath the waters of a huge inland sea. Geologists also say the the Fraser Valley was entirely under water in the early years of the Holocene. Ray Silver, a Sto:lo elder who grew up at the base of Sumas Mountain, says that he has never gone near the caves because the old people used to tell him to stay away from them, and it had something to do with the spirits of the people from the time of the flood. Ray's nephew, Dalton Silver, feels the same way about the caves. "I've hunted deer up there," he told me during a visit to the mountain. "I've been above them and below them, but it's like there's something there that stops you. You can feel it." Ray Silver says that when he was a boy, the old people said that songs would come out of the caves in the wintertime, the kind of songs that come out of initiates when they are first overcome by *syowen*, the spirit possession that occurs during the winter dance season. "Years ago, I went to sleep after work, and I dreamt I was out hunting ducks on the flats," Ray remembers. "I was hunting and I heard one of those songs coming from there. It got louder and louder. It was going south, and then it faded away."

To the north and east of Katzie, above Harrison Lake, in the valley of the lower Lillooet River, there is another mountain. The valley is home to the local In-Shuck-ch people, who take their name from the mountain, which is said to have been the only mountain in that part of the country that remained above the waters during the time of the Great Flood. It is a story just like the one told by Chief Assu, by Peter Pierre, and by the Silvers. Just to the north of the In-Shuck-ch territory, above Pemberton Meadows, there is another mountain, known as Smimele. In the Smimele story, a man named Ntci'nemken took one child from each of the local villages into his canoe, and when the floodwaters receded he landed on the terraced slopes of Smimele, which is just northeast of Pemberton Meadows.

In the Upper Skeena Valley, the ancestral home of the Gitxsan people, the landscape is marked by a variety of geological events that form the basis of clan names, crests, songs, and sagas. There are floods, long winters that bury entire villages, and ecological upheavals. In one story, a great Bear Spirit arose from the bottom of Seeley Lake. The bear, known as the Medeek, came crashing down out of the high country to the south of the Skeena River, uprooting trees as he went. Mountains collapsed, lake levels rose and fell, and creeks changed course. In 1985, geologist Allen Gottesfeld conducted a survey of Chicago Creek, which drains Seeley Lake, and concluded that about 3500 years ago, a massive torrent of debris crashed down the creek, uprooting trees as it went. In 1986, Simon Fraser University professor Rolf Mathewes analyzed sediment samples from the bottom of Seeley Lake and concluded that an ecological upheaval had raged through the countryside about 3500 years ago. Mountainsides collapsed, lake levels fluctuated wildly, and creeks changed their courses.

About halfway between Katzie and Alaska, up the narrow inlets toward Bella Coola, there is a place known in the Nuxalk language as Kwatna, Place of Many Boulders. There are no boulders there. The archeologist Phil Hobler, who began his studies on the coast in the 1960s, went to work at Kwatna in 1969. He spent his career in trenches, mainly in the Nuxalk country, where he spent season after season screening fish bones, bifacial points, and bits of adze blades from various dig sites. After decades of talking to old people about what these things meant, his conclusions are humbling. "It's taken geology about 120 years to discover what was already there in the oral traditions of the coast," he says. It was something he guessed, when he first started working at Place of Many Boulders, where there are no boulders. A few meters below the surface, among the detritus of a community that was thriving around the time of Christ, there were boulders strewn everywhere.

But it was a few sea miles up the coast from Kwatna, in the Heiltsuk territory, that Fladmark's insistence that maritime peoples had been present on the Pacific coast from the earliest times was justified, based solely on evidence that conformed to the rigid rules required of conventional archeology. The proof came at Namu, an old Heiltsuk village, situated in a small bay about halfway up Fitz Hugh Sound, about 70 sea miles north of Vancouver Island. Namu had long been known to archeologists. James Hester of the University of Colorado carried out the first excavations at Namu in 1969. By 1977, one of Hester's assistants, Roy Carlson — a colleague of Fladmark's at Simon Fraser University — was heading up the Namu field studies, which continued into the 1990s. In 1978, the same year that Fladmark challenged archeologists to start taking the Pacific coast more seriously, at Namu, Carlson's crew unearthed a 9000-year-old, tool-worked, egg-shaped stone, which was to become a treasured piece of a museum collection at Simon Fraser University. It isn't much to look at. It's just a small stone, smaller than an egg, but about the same shape, with a carved groove encircling it. It's most likely a sinker from a fishing line. If it is, it is the oldest known piece of fishing gear in British Columbia. It probably dropped, unnoticed, out of some fisherman's tackle box, about 9000 years ago. The stone was one of the few things left of a flourishing little fishing village, and beneath the

9000-year level was more detritus that hinted at a village occupation going back 11,000 years. The antiquity of the site established Namu as one of the first fishing villages anywhere on earth.

It wasn't just the age of Namu that mattered, although that was striking enough, since it seemed to put human beings on the Pacific coast almost at the same time they were present at Clovis and Folsom, and the Clovis-Folsom hunters had been considered the first human beings below the northern fringes of the Pleistocene ice sheets. It was also that the people at Namu were nothing like big-game hunters. They were remarkably dependent on marine life — sea mammals, shellfish, and a variety of finfish. People went trolling in small boats, harpooned porpoises and seals, gathered mussels and barnacles from the beaches and plants and berries from the land.

Through the 1970s and 1980s, archeologists were pushing back the earliest date of human presence all around the North Pacific. On the North American shore, evidence for human settlements was being found at time depths that had been exclusively reserved for Clovis-Folsom big-game hunters, well inland. It was becoming obvious that during those early days at Namu, fully adapted maritime cultures were emerging around the North Pacific, roughly from Japan to California, that had little if anything to do with whatever it was that "Indians," "Paleo-Indians," "Amerinds," or "Macro-Indians" may have been doing in the North American interior. Fishing cultures as ancient as any on the planet were developing throughout the North Pacific. Beringian hunters, the ice-free corridor, and Clovis-Folsom spear points didn't really figure into it at all.

Meanwhile, the combined efforts of Aleut communities, archeologists, linguists, and geneticists had finally established the lineage and history of the people of the Aleutian Islands. That lineage and history turned the standard narrative, featuring eastward-moving Beringian hunters, completely upside down. Aleuts, it turned out, had practically nothing to do with that story. By 1980, at the University of Connecticut, the archeologist William Laughlin had summarized his life's work with the Aleuts, which began in 1938. Russian, French, and Danish scientists assisted, and Aleut people volunteered for blood tests, cranial-size

surveys, and dental analyses. Laughlin managed to construct a comprehensive historical portrait of the Aleuts, a people renowned for their
longevity (before contact with Europeans, Aleuts commonly lived more
than 100 years), their good humor, their astonishing physical strength,
and their proficiency as mariners.

Aleuts had always been a bit of a problem for the Beringian-hunter
scenario. From the earliest times, they lived in cavernous, semi-subterranean houses, some of which were more than 80 meters (260 feet) long.
They wore colorful clothes made from the skins of tufted puffins, cormorants, and seals. Almost all their food came from the ocean, and the
Aleuts flourished in a marine environment that was as rich and productive as anywhere on earth, teeming with salmon and halibut, whales
and herring, seabirds, seals, and sea lions. Albert Harper, also from the
University of Connecticut, worked with Laughlin to assemble a genetic-
divergence map of the Aleuts' origins that showed that they didn't really
have anything to do with "Indians" at all.

About 15,000 years ago, the Aleuts were already genetically distinct
from the population that included the ancestors of the people who came
to be called Indians. Almost 9000 years ago, Aleuts were already distinct
from the people Americans ended up calling Eskimos and Canadians
ended up calling Inuit. A migration was involved in the Aleutian story
— as there is, ultimately, in the story of every human society on the
planet. But the Aleuts' journey had nothing to do with the Beringian
plains, and it had nothing to do with walking, and it didn't even involve
much eastward movement. In remarkably seaworthy skin boats known
as baidarkas, the Aleuts moved east for a little while, but they also traveled south, and after settling on the Alaska Peninsula, some headed back
to the west. Gradually, over thousands of years, their territory extended
to a point almost 1000 sea miles west of the present-day Alaska Peninsula. It had been like moving, over a 9000-year period, in a big circle,
around the brow of Beringia's south coast and the necklace formed by
about 100 islands in the Aleutian chain.

Before contact with Europeans, at least 16,000 Aleuts occupied the
archipelago, forming the longest east-west distance occupied by a single
language and racial group anywhere on the planet. The Aleutian islands

begin a short jog by kayak from the present-day Alaskan mainland. They sweep in a broad and curving southwesterly loop that dips down into the North Pacific to a point roughly the same latitude as the northern tip of Vancouver Island. From there, the islands curve gently away to the northwest, and from Attu, the final island in the Aleutians, it is almost possible, on a clear day, to see Russia's Commander Islands, 180 sea miles away. From the Commanders, it is only 97 sea miles to the Kamchatka Peninsula, on Russia's Pacific coast.

On the Russian coast, at about the time that people were settling down at Namu, people were doing much the same thing at river mouths and at lagoons around Peter the Great Bay. They were using tools like those in use at Namu, and they were developing into a comfortable culture based on salmon, oysters, and rockfish. Russian archeologists know these people as the Yankovskaya culture. The people lived in large longhouses and buried their dead in shell middens, practices strikingly similar to those that developed on North America's Northwest Coast, except the Yankovskaya people had pigs and ceramic pots. To the south of Peter the Great Bay, the same kind of communities were springing up on the island of Yokchido, off the coast of Korea, and at the mouths of mainland rivers. The shell middens were growing higher every year behind their pit houses — semi-subterranean houses of a type found in the Aleutians and in the early villages of North America's Northwest Coast.

At the same time, around Japan, sea levels had risen high enough to submerge a coastal plain that was once so vast that Hokkaido, Sakhalin Island, and the Asian mainland were all joined by it. At Natsushima Island in Tokyo Bay, people were harvesting shellfish and paddling around in small boats, using hook-and-line gear to catch deep-water fish, just like at Namu. On the nearby Noto Peninsula, instead of huge timbers of the kind found in rectangular formations that comprised the superstructure of Haida houses, archeologists were uncovering the foundations of huge timbers arranged in circles.

On Hokkaido's Pacific coast, a closely related fishing culture had established itself that maintained elaborate ritual relationships with dolphins. One burial at the site featured dolphin skulls arranged in a circle, facing the skeleton of a whale. Across the Pacific, at Port Moller, on the north shore of the Alaska Peninsula, Japanese archeologists Atsuko and Hiroaki Okada were surprised to find a similar burial at a village that eventually grew to be probably the largest pre-European settlement in the Bering Sea. In the Port Moller burial were the remains of three men and four children, encircled by the skulls of ten beluga whales.

On the Queen Charlotte Islands, in the South Moresby archipelago, conclusive evidence of a completely maritime economy had come to light that was at least 9000 years old — roughly the same vintage as early Namu. Skilled boatmen were harvesting the marine resources throughout the archipelago's Gwaii Haanas island chain at a time when a vast plain extended from the islands almost to the mainland. The seascapes of those days, sketched by paleoecologists, look as if they were meant to illustrate the stories Nuxalk people used to recount from their epic, known as *Wanderings of Cormorant,* about a vast coastal plain to their north. The geological record was producing a picture that similarly reflected the Haidas' oral traditions of a time when the countryside was all grass, islands rose out of the sea, and people walked on the open ocean. During those times, to the north of the Queen Charlotte Islands, people in boats were arriving in the islands and mainland inlets that now form southeast Alaska, which was then a country of open forest, parkland, and shrub tundra. At Heceta Island, 130 sea miles north of the Queen Charlottes, archeologist Robert Ackerman and two of his colleagues from Washington State University completed a survey of the island for the U.S. Forest Service in 1985 that uncovered evidence of a marine-oriented society that may have been just as old as the village at Namu. The finds clearly show that at least 8000 years ago, people were living on Heceta Island, harvesting shellfish and using hook-and-line gear to catch lingcod, rockfish, flounder, Pacific cod, and greenling. While Heceta Islanders were cutting up their fish with razor-sharp microblade knives, people just like them were fishing and digging clams on the Alaskan coast, at the tip of the Chilkat Peninsula. A bit farther north and to the west, also about 9000 years ago, people were living on Baranov Island, apparently doing much the same kinds of things.

From beginnings such as these, the Japanese anthropologist Hitoshi Watanabe, at Tokyo's Waseda University, argues that a maritime cultural continuum evolved all around the North Pacific from scores of founding societies, some of which were closely related and some of which merely shared some ancestors. They came to take on their own distinct cultural patterns down through the years, but despite the long years that passed, they held on to a whole range of common elements. The societies that shared those same features, Watanabe argues, were as varied and diverse as the Jomon of early Japan, the Ainu of Sakhalin Island, the Gilyak of the Lower Amur River in the Russian far east, the Nuu-chah-nulth of Vancouver Island's west coast, and the Quinault of the Washington coast. From the early Yurok to the Jomon, Watanabe argues, there existed what should be understood as a single culture zone.

Among the common features Watanabe proposes for the maritime societies that eventually developed around the North Pacific are: a tendency to "sedentism," which is the occupation of permanent villages in patterns similar to those of agricultural societies, but in contrast to the norm among hunter-gatherer societies; social stratification, often involving elaborate and fairly rigid class systems; a general pattern of quadrangular house pits, buildings constructed of posts that supported a central ridgepole, linear settlement patterns, fortifications, and warfare; seagoing vessels, along with elaborate fishing gear and fishing methods; a heavy reliance on dried fish and a taste for fish eggs, sea urchins, and seaweed; and an elaborate economic and ritualized relationship with salmon that includes the "first salmon" ceremony.

By 1989, the significance of North Pacific maritime "prehistory" was being taken seriously enough for several academic, cultural, and government institutions to convene an international circum-Pacific conference. The conference, at the Seattle Center, was sponsored by Washington State University, the USSR-Smithsonian-Canadian Crossroads of Continents International Exhibition, the Washington state government, and the Pacific Northwest Archeological Society. More than 150 scientists from several disiciplines gathered to present evidence about the human heritage of the Pacific Basin.

One of those scientists, Clement Meighan from the University of California at Los Angeles, went straight to Calvin Huesser's overlooked studies of the possibilities of human movement around the North

Pacific. Meighan also acknowledged Fladmark's challenge from a decade before. Meighan had been one of the archeologists who had been satisfied by the ice-free-corridor scenario and conceded that he himself, in the 1950s, had been guilty of assumptions about the age of coastal settlements that had proved ludicrous. Meighan reported that he had since revisited much of his own earlier work and found that it should be, in his words, "entirely discredited." By rethinking the conventional hypotheses about the way human societies are supposed to evolve, and the way people are supposed to have settled the Pacific coast, an entirely different kind of story could be told, Meighan said. That story appeared to reach as far back as Clovis and Folsom, and Meighan said it wasn't confined to the coast north of Washington. It could be found as far south as the islands off Southern California.

Meighan and several other archeologists, with the help of more than 100 UCLA students, had been revisiting old shell middens on the islands of San Miguel and San Clemente, 55 sea miles from the California coast, and on San Nicolas Island, which is more than 80 sea miles offshore. These sites had not been subject to the same isostatic and eustatic changes that had caused such scientific trouble on the Northwest Coast. California sea levels were in more or less the same place as they had been thousands of years before. The islands' old villages were still more or less the same short stroll to the beach. The kelp beds just off the villages were still there, and so were the shellfish beds and most of the fish species that the early people had relied upon, quite comfortably, for their sustenance.

Meighan said that new evidence showed that probably on San Nicolas, but definitely on San Miguel and San Clemente, people had established fishing villages as much as 10,000 years ago. On San Miguel Island, people had probably been fishing and gathering clams for at least that long. These were peoples whose way of life was totally maritime from the outset, almost entirely dependent on fish and shellfish. There was absolutely no reason to believe that they had descended from the Clovis and Folsom mammoth hunters, Meighan added. The Pacific maritime culture was probably present on the California coast at the same time that the first Clovis-Folsom hunters appeared in the North

American interior. Meighan then said that if anyone thought it necessary to attempt to locate the islanders' ancestors, they should probably
look in the early shell middens of Japan and the northeast Asian coast.

There was also an interesting point that Meighan impressed upon the
delegates to the Seattle conference, and it had to do with the awkward
business of "ethnocentrism" as an explanation for the way the North
Pacific's human history had been treated so casually, by scientists and
historians, for so long. "Our perception of maritime developments in the
New World," Meighan said, "has undoubtedly been influenced by
unconscious analogies to the European sequence: Paleolithic hunters to
mesolithic shell-midden dwellers, the latter of no great antiquity in
northern Europe. Such a European analogy is not appropriate for North
American developments."

A decade after Meighan's presentation at the Seattle conference,
archeologists in California were pondering the possibility that the people who settled California's islands may have actually arrived there as
much as 2000 years earlier than Clovis and Folsom. The first radiocarbon dates for the bones of a woman discovered on Santa Rosa Island
in 1959 suggested she had died 10,000 years before. The results weren't
taken seriously, however, because they didn't fit the prevailing archeological orthodoxy. But in 1999, Don Morris, an archeologist with the
Channel Islands National Park, and John Johnson, anthropology
curator at the Santa Barbara Museum, had a section of the soil layer
surrounding the 1959 bones radiocarbon-dated; it showed a 13,000-year
time depth. Because archeological evidence indicating a human
presence south of the great Pleistocene ice sheets earlier than 12,000
years ago is never the result of confirmed radiocarbon dates for human
remains, but is always inferred, it is also always contentious. Neverthe-
less, Morris and Johnson's results did shake things up. At the time, the
oldest skeletal remains found in North America south of the great
Pleistocene ice sheets were from an Idaho gravel quarry, in 1989. Those
bones came from someone who had died more than 10,600 years before.

Despite the findings of scientists such as Fladmark, Watanabe,
Meighan, Laughlin, and the rest, and despite the stories told by North
Pacific peoples themselves, the idea that human beings have been deeply

involved in the marine ecosystems of the North Pacific for such a long time is still not widely understood or appreciated. It is no longer just a problem associated with the absence of evidence, although physical evidence does become scarce as humans go about the work of altering North Pacific coastlines, with increasing ferocity, as the years pass. Sometimes it's just a simple problem of not looking for the evidence. Sometimes it's a problem of looking directly at the evidence but not seeing it. It's just something that happens, right around the North Pacific.

On the Korean coast, small rivers still support runs of masu and chum salmon that directly descend from the salmon runs that supported societies of shell-mound builders and pithouse dwellers that laid the first foundations of the present-day city of Pusan. But South Korean archeologists have ignored these early fishing cultures because of what Seoul National University archeologist Seonbok Yi calls "paradigmatic" academic blinders that distort any view of South Korean history that doesn't reflect a simple story of big-game hunters retreating northwards from an advance of early farmers. In North Korea, the situation has been far worse. The prevailing ideology there, which arises from a mix of Stalinism and personality-cult autocracy, has insisted on a single, completely dogmatic narrative in which Korean society is said to have evolved in a direct line, within the country's present borders, over the past 500,000 years.

On the Canadian side of the Pacific, about 120 kilometers (75 miles) up the Fraser River at a place known as the Milliken site, archeologists in the 1960s uncovered evidence of about 9000 years of continuous human occupation. In the lower layers of the site were charred pits of the wild cherry, which become ripe around the same time as the Fraser's sockeye runs are moving through the canyon. Not far from the Milliken site, there is is a thing you can look at, but not necessarily see at all, even though the thing stands in plain sight, at the water's edge, on a point of land that juts into the river from the east bank. You can look at it from a point on the west bank of the river, about a five-minute drive north of Yale and down a rutted dirt road. The thing stands at a place known as Xelhalh, where the river channel is less than 100 meters (300 feet) wide. It's not like it should have gone unnoticed. It is a stone wall, perhaps 20 meters (65 feet) long and a couple of meters (6 feet) high. But it is the kind of thing you would expect to see at Dun Conor on the island of Inishmaan, off Ireland's west coast, or maybe in the Anasazi country of New Mexico, but not in the Fraser Canyon. It wasn't supposed to be there, so officially, at least, it hadn't been seen. Archeologists had long maintained that British Columbia's aboriginal people didn't build things like that, so it never ended up registered as an official archeological site.

The first time I saw it, it was pointed out to me by Sonny McHalsie, a member of the Popkum community and a Sto:lo cultural historian. The place where we were standing, across the river from Xelhalh, is called Tatxlis, which means Gritting His Teeth. The name comes from a story about Xa:ls, the Great Transformer.

It was Xa:ls who first taught people how to harvest salmon in great numbers, and it was Xa:ls who brought order to the world. Xa:ls is said to have arrived on the earth several thousand years ago at what is now Point Roberts, a peninsula just south of the mouth of the Fraser River that juts below the 49th parallel to form a tiny, isolated piece of the United States appended to British Columbia's mainland coast. From there, Xa:ls traveled up the Fraser, performing many supernatural feats, and when he came to Tatxlis he is said to have been confronted by a powerful shaman named Qewxtelemos. A battle began, involving various kinds of medicine powers and lightning bolts. During the battle, Qewxtelemos sat across the river, on the east bank, at Xelhalh. The place on the west bank of the river where Xa:ls sat was at our feet, on a rock, indented with grooves Xa:ls is said to have worried into the surface with his thumb, weakening his enemy with each scratch. Xa:ls transformed Qewxtelemos to a stone.

Upriver from Tatxlis, at a place called Eayem, another rutted road leaves the highway. After a short walk down a trail, directly in front of Rita Pete's fishing cabin and just above the roaring river, there is another wall, tangled in the salmonberry bushes. I walked right through a collapsed section of it without noticing. All that was left of it was a section a few meters long and about 2 meters (6 feet) tall. Some of the stones were as big as people and probably weighed 500 kilograms (1100 pounds). Another couple of kilometers upriver, we visited the old fishing stations of the village known as Lux'ts'owquom, down a rickety staircase off the highway, a jaunt across the CN rail line, a dubious footbridge over a creek, and a slog through stinging nettles. At least that was the way in when I first visited. There's a road in there now.

Lux'ts'owquom means Always Skunk Cabbage. Below an especially dark and formidable cataract, the stone wall there was also in remnants, in three sections suspended between rocky outcrops. Archie Charles, the Seabird Island chief whose fishing site is nearby, could still remember when a bunch of college kids wrecked the wall in the 1940s. The old Sto:lo people with fish-drying racks around Lux'ts'owquom said the wall was once about 80 meters (260 feet) long, and there were baseball-sized, carefully rounded stones stacked in piles behind it, like caches of cannon balls on a castle parapet.

Archeologist Dave Schaepe, who started work with the Sto:lo Nation in 1998, said there was no cause to be surprised by the canyon's stone walls. From Massachusetts by way of New York University, Schaepe had done fieldwork in the Amazon, Illinois, and Idaho. He said the walls, if you think about them as fortified defensive checkpoints, make perfect sense. At the height of the salmon-fishing season, a flotilla of coastal Indians, the Euclataws, say, could promptly be obliged to turn back downriver or suffer a fusillade of sling-propelled shotputs.

In 1808, when the explorer Simon Fraser came down through the canyon, he was brought to Tatxlis. Fraser was shown the Gritting His Teeth scratchmarks that Xa:ls is said to have worried into the rock with his thumb. In the notes Fraser made in his journal of the day's events, there is this passage: "At the bad rock, a little distance above the village, where the rapids terminate, the natives informed us, that white people like us came here from below; and they shewed us indented marks which the white people made upon the rocks, but which, by the bye, seem to us to be natural marks."

Simon Fraser made a simple mistake about what it was he was being told. You could say Fraser's mistake came from the kind of "unconscious" assumptions that UCLA's Clement Meighan talked about, or from wearing "paradigmatic" blinkers of the kind Seoul National University's Seonbok Yi talked about. Fraser didn't know he'd made any wrong assumptions about anything until two days after he stood at Tatxlis, when he made a truly tragic discovery. The river he had been following was not the Columbia after all. It was another river that emptied into the sea at a latitude near 49 degrees north, which meant the quest he'd begun five years earlier had been in vain. Disheartened, Fraser turned back from the river's mouth, at Musqueam, and began the long return journey back up the river that came to bear his name. Eventually, he returned over the Rockies.

Xa:ls continued upriver, too. Old Secwepemc people say Xa:ls himself became transformed into a stone that can still be seen near the Fraser River at Pavilion, above Lillooet. The Nlaka'pamux say that once Xa:ls completed his work on earth, he ascended into the sky and became a star.

TWO

The Order
of Things

The sea is an unknown — and enormous — land;
if its water were evenly spread, the whole world would be
drowned a mile deep. The oceans are filled with mystery
and may hold from half a million sorts of animals
to twenty times as many.

— *Steve Jones*, Darwin's Ghost: The Origin of Species, Updated

IN 1736, A 24-YEAR-OLD Moscow geography student by the name of Stephen Krasheninnikov found himself on the rainy Pacific coast of Kamchatka, 6000 kilometers (3700 miles) away from home. Her Russian Imperial Majesty, Anna Ivanovna, Empress of all the Russias, had instructed the Russian Academy of Sciences to conduct a thorough scientific assessment of her far eastern possessions; the academy's professors, who were not particularly enthusiastic about the Kamchatka part of the assignment, had sent Krasheninnikov ahead to get the lay of the land. Almost as a postscript, Stephen's instructions obliged him to stay in Kamchatka until he could provide a thorough description of the flora, the fauna, the geography, the geology, the local peoples, their customs and their languages, and whatever else might be interesting about the place. Kamchatka is about the same size as California.

Krasheninnikov found the people interesting enough, though "as wild as the country itself." In the northern part of the Kamchatka Peninsula were people he called the Koreki. Some of them were reindeer herders, and others were settled along Kamchatka's rivers. The Kamchadals were mainly coastal people who lived in permanent villages, fished, and hunted sea mammals. To the south of the Kamchadals, the "Kuriles" — relatives of the Hokkaido Ainu — occupied the peninsula's southern cape and the Kurile Islands. Krasheninnikov preferred the company of the Kamchadals, "their manners being more civilized."

The Kamchadals' favorite food was dried fish, "which they use instead of bread." Their second favorite food was fish eggs, which they prepared in a variety of ways. Their third favorite food was smoked fish. Their next favorite food was something called *huigul*, which, by the way Krasheninnikov described it, sounds exactly like the grease rendered from rotting oolichans that is still so prized among many native communities on British Columbia's coast. This menu is followed, in Krasheninnikov's report, by a series of recipes that include an enormous list of ingredients from whale fat to dried berries. A curious entry in Krasheninnikov's notes on the Kamchadal diet describes the practice of occasionally enlivening the boredom of the winters with a liquor brewed from hallucinogenic mushrooms. Krasheninnikov recounts an incident in which a Russian soldier tried some, then decided it would be a good idea to go for a nice, brisk march. The soldier kept on walking until he died.

In the section of his report titled "Of Fishes," Krasheninnikov clearly struggled to describe Kamchatka's various species in the dry and descriptive language expected by his professors back at the academy in Saint Petersburg. But when he wrote about salmon, the fish the Kamchadals relied upon as heavily as Russians relied upon cattle and grain, Krasheninnikov abandoned the slightest pretense of dispassion. The Kamchadals named the months of the year after the different salmon runs and erupted in rejoicing upon seeing them return. They venerated salmon in solemn ceremonies. The salmon of Kamchatka were "wonderful proofs," Krasheninnikov wrote, "of the Divine Providence, and the goodness of the Creator." Krasheninnikov continued: "The fish come from the sea in such numbers that they stop the course of rivers, and cause them to overflow the banks; and when the waters fall there remains a surprising quantity of dead fish upon the shore, which produces an intolerable stink. At this time the bears and dogs catch more fish with their paws than people do at other places with their nets."

Krasheninnikov attempted to describe the broad categories of the salmon that choked Kamchatka's rivers. There were "red fish" that the Kamchadals called *narka*. There were "white fish," and when they returned to spawn, "the young ones . . . accompany the old to take care of the roes and convoy the young fry down." The Kamchadals called others *chavitsi*, the *keta* or *keoko*, and the *gorbusche*.

Back in Europe, 29-year-old Carl von Linné, a Swedish medical student, had already mounted two of his own specimen-gathering expeditions, but they hadn't been nearly as arduous as Krasheninnikov's. Linné's ramblings across Lapland were the result of his own fascination with plants and flowers. Linné's parents wanted him to be a Lutheran minister, and they'd hoped he would at least keep his nose to the grindstone at medical school. But Carl had a good excuse for roving around the top of Scandinavia gathering shrubs: In those days, doctors had to prescribe all sorts of plant-derived remedies, and Linné reasoned that he should at least know a little bit about the remedies he would be prescribing. The truth was that not unlike the Kamchadals and their veneration of salmon, Linné believed that by comprehending the structure of the natural world, one might see God's divine order of the universe. And there's nothing wrong with that.

Taxonomy, in the broadest sense of the term, is one of the oldest and most fundamental pursuits of philosophy. Attempts at zoological classification systems can produce a wide range of results, depending on who's making the attempts and the culture within which those attempts are made. The French philosopher Michel Foucault makes this point in his book *The Order of Things*, and he presents as an example an ancient Chinese system of comprehending order among animals: "a) Belonging to the Emperor, b) embalmed, c) tame, d) suckling pigs, e) sirens, f) fabulous, g) stray dogs, h) included in the present classification, i) frenzied, j) innumerable, k) drawn with a very fine camelhair brush, l) et cetera m) having just broken the water pitcher, n) that from a long way off look like flies."

There were a variety of rudimentary systems of taxonomy known to Europeans in the early 18th century, but Carl von Linné wanted something more — a system expressed in terms familiar to his own time and place in the world. The same year that the Russian Academy of Sciences was drawing up Krasheninnikov's instructions for Kamchatka, Linné graduated from Holland's Harderwijke medical school. He had just published the first slim edition of his *Systema Naturae,* under the Latinized form of his name, Carolus Linnaeus, in which he proposed a way to organize humanity's understanding of all the living things on earth. The Linnaean classification system soon became the standard way to comprehend God's divine order of the universe. It remains the most fundamental way that Western science allows us to see order in nature. Various terminologies have been used to give meaning to Linnaean order, but its hierarchies remain largely unchanged: kingdom, phylum, class, order, family, genus, species.

It would take almost six decades before the Linnaean worldview was relied upon to make sense of the salmon that Krasheninnikov had observed among the Kamchadals.

In 1792, the Empress of all the Russias was Ekaterina Alexeevna. She came to Russia from Poland, in 1744, as Sophia Augusta Frederica, the 15-year-old child bride of the heir to the tsar's throne, Peter Feodorovich. But to be a tsar's wife you have to be baptized by the Russian Orthodox Church, so Sophia Augusta Frederica received the sacraments of the Eastern rites and was christened Ekaterina Alexeevna. A few years later, after she deposed her husband with the help of the Russian Imperial Guard, she became known as Catherine the Great. She was a fierce bit of business, and historians say she brought Russia quickly out of its doldrums. She enjoyed the company of intelligent people, and she was curious about the Pacific. After several nervous-making reports from Irkutsk suggested that Spanish ships were becoming a too-frequent site off Russia's unguarded Pacific coast, the Imperial Court revived its interest in Kamchatka.

It was in 1792 that the German naturalist Johann Julius Walbaum found himself in the employ of Catherine the Great, back where Krasheninnikov had been, in Kamchatka, all those years before. Since

Krasheninnikov's time, the Linnaean way of seeing the world had evolved into the science of taxonomy, and Walbaum was skilled in its methods and techniques. It was with Walbaum's arrival in Kamchatka that Pacific salmon first began to swim within the Linnaean imagination. What Walbaum saw, when he looked at Pacific salmon, were obviously in the order Salmoniformes. According to Linnaean rules, the fish would have to be assigned to a family, and that family would have to be Salmonidae, which includes all trouts and salmons. Walbaum assigned Pacific salmon to the broad genus known to the Linnaean system as *Salmo*. The hard part came next, because there were apparently several kinds of salmon in the Pacific, and all of them were unknown to the Linnaean imagination. These salmon were "new" species, so Walbaum's work came to be about "discovery." What followed upon Walbaum's initial effort was an arduous business of specimen collecting and analysis that resulted in the classification of five new "species." Walbaum classified Krasheninnikov's red fish as *nerka*, so in the Linnaean nomenclature it became *Salmo nerka*, or more completely, *Salmo nerka* (Walbaum), after the fashion of adding the name of the species' "discoverer." On North America's coast, some native communities called the same fish *sukkai*, so eventually, the narka that Krasheninnikov saw became generally known as sockeye. The "white fish" — the ones that Krasheninnikov believed were accompanied to the spawning grounds by their nephews and nieces, who then stayed to escort the fry back into the ocean — Walbaum called *Salmo kisutch*, known later to Americans as silver salmon and to Canadians as coho. *Keta* was christened *Salmo keta*, known widely as chum salmon, and *gorbusche* became *Salmo gorbuscha*, known commonly as pink salmon.

In these ways, just as the child bride Sophia Augusta Frederica became Ekaterina Alexeevna by the sacraments of the Russian Orthodox Church, Walbaum christened each Pacific salmon by the sacraments of the Linnaean faith.

As it turned out, Walbaum had placed Pacific salmon in a genus they would occupy only temporarily. It took decades of arguments among icthyologists before Pacific salmon were assigned a satisfactory place within the Linnaean cosmology. Eventually, Pacific salmon were classified not as members of the genus *Salmo* — the genus of Atlantic salmon, with which Europeans had been long acquainted — but as species within the genus *Oncorhynchus*, which most taxonomists now consider an elaboration upon the more primitive *Salmo* genus.

It wasn't until the late 1980s that Pacific steelhead salmon, known widely as steelhead trout, were transferred from *Salmo gairdneri* to *Oncorhynchus mykiss*. Then there are masu and amago salmon, which spawn only in some southerly Asian rivers, and these fish are still in a bit of a limbo, because they are only tentatively treated as two species. Some biologists suggest that they should be seen as one species. Other biologists say masu should be separated into two species, the sea-run masu and the lake-dwelling yamame. Still other biologists say amago is really two species, the lake-dwelling biwamasu and the sea-run amago. By the time biologists find some agreement on these matters, masu and amago may well have evolved into different species entirely, the schism will have resolved itself, and there will be other things to discuss.

These uncertainties may seem a bit like theological controversies among medieval Christian monks, but they have real-world consequences in industrialized societies, where order is considered so necessary. In British Columbia, salmon fisheries management is a federal jurisdiction, but trout fishing falls under the province's authority under a delegation of federal constitutional powers from early in the 20th century. When the Linnaean rules determined that steelhead "trout" had become steelhead salmon, there was a time when deputy ministers and fisheries bureaucrats in Ottawa and Victoria were completely unsure who was in charge (steelhead fisheries management ended up remaining with provincial authorities). In the United States, legal acknowledgment of a species' distinctiveness under the Endangered Species Act can mean the difference between survival and extinction. By the late 20th century, North American fisheries agencies were obliged to elaborate further upon the Linnean system to structure conservation efforts and defend necessary action to protect salmon habitat. Thus began the identification of even more orders of organization, well below the species level, which was necessary to comprehend what salmon are like in the real world, and not just in the world of the Linnaean imagination. These efforts produced the awkwardly described "evolutionarily significant units" that U.S. scientists rely on and the similar "conservation units," described as "aggregates of spawning populations," that some Canadian fisheries bureaucrats imagined.

This is the way science comprehended salmon by the 20th century. It is the way we *see* Pacific salmon. But for all we can say about what we understand about salmon, and for all our rigorous methodologies and sophisticated technologies, our comprehension of salmon is still, at its most fundamental level, an elaboration upon an idea of God's divine plan for the world developed by a 18th-century medical student whose botanical classifications depended upon notions of "public" and "clandestine" relationships between plants, and who saw "legitimate" and "illegitimate" marriages between flowers. Linnaeus also believed that the Garden of Eden had been a mountain island somewhere near the equator, with arctic species near the summit, temperate species on the hillsides, and tropical vegetation down on the beach.

To be fair, Linnaeus was brilliant, and the science of taxonomy is, after all, a bit more rigorous in its pursuits than the forms of logic that gave rise to the European conceptions of hierarchy, class, and gender that so defined the imagination of taxonomy's founder. But the Linnaean way of finding order in the universe still cannot account for the story of the genus *Oncorhynchus*. It is still not known whether the story is about a freshwater fish that went to sea or about a saltwater fish that went inland to spawn. Taxonomists who favor the former argument see an evolutionary ladder for Pacific salmon that is a complete, mirror-image opposite, in every respect, of the evolutionary ladder seen by taxonomists who favor the latter argument. It is one of those rare scientific controversies in which one side can actually say, without intending any offense, that the other side has everything completely backwards.

It has been only two centuries or so since Pacific salmon first entered the ocean of the Western imagination, but the story of *Oncorhynchus*, regardless of whether the story began with a freshwater fish or a saltwater fish, has been unfolding for a lot longer than that. It is certain that Pacific salmon have been around for at least a million years, and perhaps as long as 15 million years. During the Pleistocene epoch, salmon survived in Ice Age refugia, as far away as the Lake Chapala basin in Mexico. Rapidly — at least in evolutionary time — salmon recolonized the coastal regions of the continents on both sides of the Pacific. It took only a few thousand years. The circumstances that allowed this to happen are complex.

Pacific salmon are almost exclusively anadromous, which means they spend their lives in both fresh water and salt water. They are also almost exclusively semalparous, which means they get only one chance to mate, because they die right after they reach the spawning grounds. Also, Pacific salmon almost always return to the streams where their lives began, sometimes to exactly the same spot in exactly the same corner of exactly the same creek. There is an enormous amount of diversity and variation within these rules, but within each separate spawning population, the rules tend to be extremely rigid. And within each spawning population there is also almost always at least a tiny minority of dissenters who insist on imagining that the stream just up the coast would be a better place to spawn, or that if everyone just tried a little bit harder to get over that waterfall, the world would be a better place. Those adventurous minorities within salmon populations had a lot to do with how it came to pass that almost every river and creek that was accessible to salmon, after the ice sheets receded, ended up with salmon, before the onset of the Industrial Age.

While the Linnaean system may be a perfectly brilliant means to achieve perfectly brilliant ends, it doesn't do what it wasn't intended to do, and it wasn't intended to explain all the functions an animal performs within the world. Understanding Pacific salmon in that way — trying to understand the *meaning* of salmon within nature — has not been something that fisheries biologists have been exactly preoccupied with. To understand something about what Pacific salmon mean, and to understand something about the story of salmon in the Pacific, it helps to remove the same kind of "paradigmatic blinkers" that Korean anthropologist Seonbok Yi says has so encumbered our ability to understand the story of the people of the North Pacific. When scientists remove those blinkers, they begin to look at the relationships salmon have developed with other species, and to look at all those things that happen in the world salmon occupy. To do these things, it is not enough to look in the ocean. You have to look in the forest. And what you see there is an animal that science has only recently begun to understand. It is not just a freshwater fish that goes to sea, or a saltwater fish that spawns inland. It may be both, but it is also a lot more than that.

It is often observed that the great salmon runs of North America's Northwest Coast, as they had evolved here, would not have been possible without that protective arboreal cloak of redwood, cedar, hemlock, spruce, and fir known as the temperate rain forest. That forest once extended from a point a few sea miles north of San Francisco to the northwestern shores of Alaska's Cook Inlet. But it can also be observed that the forest, as it evolved through the millennia, would not have been possible without salmon. Nowhere else on earth do forests play so crucial a role in the survival of a creature of the sea, but at the same time, nowhere else on earth does a marine species contribute so much to the survival of forests. It's true that Atlantic salmon made enormous contributions to the terrestrial ecosystems around the North Atlantic, but Pacific salmon runs have always eclipsed the biomass of Atlantic salmon. In the North Pacific, salmon are at the heart of a relationship between fish and trees, and between aquatic and terrestrial ecosystems, that is unique on the planet.

As salmon set about the long process of recolonizing the coastal landscape from their Ice Age refugia, the first trees to spring up from the glacial till of the valley bottoms took root in the spawned-out bodies of the first salmon. It took cedar 5000 years to make its way to Alaska. It took several thousand years to create the forests that so intimidated the first European explorers who skiffed along the coast in their ships in the late 1700s. Just as there isn't a forest on this coast that has not been home to salmon, there isn't a month of the year when salmon are not spawning somewhere on the coast. Salmon are there, always, in the forest.

What the forest provides in its relationship with salmon is food, shelter, and a fairly stable environment. The forest regulates the violent hydrology of the ragged landscape in an elaborate set of arrangements involving deep tree root systems, porous soils, and the steady release of sediments and cobbles from substrates, allowing a controlled recruitment of spawning gravel to stream systems. Forest canopies trap moisture, establishing cool and wet microclimates. The trees themselves provide cover against predators and distribute organic debris through stream systems that provide a fecund environment for salmon alevins — those first, tiny eruptions from salmon nests — half-egg, half-salmon. Fallen trees, exposed root wads, and snags create riffles and back eddies that act as a kind of hydraulic control valve that slows stream velocity, forming stable and oxygen-rich water for salmon fry. Leaf litter and detritus form microecosystems of benthic invertebrates, algae, and insects that provide a food source for salmon fry and for juvenile salmon in those final weeks before they swim downstream to the sea.

The forest also contributes to the productivity of estuaries and other types of rearing habitat vital to juvenile salmon. The dynamics of the relationship between the North Pacific Ocean, the North American continent, and Northeast Asia play themselves out deep into the salt-water environment and far into the mountains. Marbled murrelets forage at sea but require old-growth forests for their nests. Seals are common inhabitants of estuaries and coastal marshes, and some seal populations, in large river systems, are adapted to what are essentially interior-type ecosystems, having established niches for themselves sometimes more than 100 kilometers (60 miles) from salt water. The great brown bears of Kamchatka's Kuril Lake, which gather in the densest concentrations of bears on the planet, are almost wholly dependent upon salmon. Analyses of the bones of grizzly bears from the Upper Columbia watershed, more than 1000 kilometers (600 miles) from the sea, show that up to 90 percent of the carbon and nitrogen in the bears' diets came from salmon.

The contribution that salmon make to terrestrial ecosystems deep within the continents surrounding the North Pacific has never been fully acknowledged by science. It has never been taken into account in fisheries management regimes. It was only in the final decade of the 20th century that scientists began to seriously consider the ecological significance of salmon. The picture that emerges is of animals that arise from the depths of the Pacific to make journeys that take them inland, often far beyond the coastal landscape, and that do not stop migrating when they spawn and die. Instead, they continue on through the countryside, wraithlike, and long after death they remain key participants in an ongoing conversation occurring throughout terrestrial ecosystems.

Animals that rely directly upon the flesh of spawning salmon for food include mink, weasels, wolves, coyotes, red fox, deer mice, shrews, red squirrels, flying squirrels, marsh hawks, red-tailed hawks, gulls, crows, ravens, Steller's jays, wrens, and dippers. Even herbivores such as deer have been known to eat spawned salmon carcasses. Other coastal animals feed on salmon eggs. These animals include Canada geese, robins, goldeneyes, and a surprising variety of fish, such as Dolly Varden trout, sculpins, suckers, grayling, and even juvenile coho. Seaward-migrating juvenile salmon, meanwhile, fall prey to another host of animals from the moment the salmon emerge from gravel as alevins. Those predators continue their pursuit of salmon fry, smolts, and juveniles, well into the salt water. These creatures include many of the same species that rely on spawning salmon, as well as river otters, loons, mergansers, kingfishers, and magpies. A surprising variety of fish target juvenile salmon as prey, including pollock, sculpins, herring, cutthroat trout, and even adult chinook, coho, and steelhead salmon.

Mary Willson, a biologist with the Forestry Science Laboratory in Juneau, Alaska, is one of the few academics who have attempted to follow the salmon through the landscape in their afterlife. She chafes at the narrow understanding that has been prevalent in fisheries management agencies down through the years. The rain forest should be seen as a series of elaborate, ongoing relationships between marine and terrestrial ecosystems, Willson says, and salmon perform "ecological interactions between these two ecosystems [that] are central to regional ecology." When salmon runs are lost, either by overfishing or habitat degradation, ripple effects will eventually run throughout terrestrial ecosystems, but fisheries scientists rarely even wonder about these kinds of things. "The loss or severe depletion of anadromous fish stocks could have major effects on the population biology of many species of wildlife consumers, and thus, on terrestrial animal communities," Willson says, "but these possibilities have not been examined and indeed have seldom been addressed at all."

In a paper Willson and her colleagues Scott Gende and Brian Marston wrote for a 1998 edition of the academic journal *BioScience,* the case for the importance of the salmon's contribution in its relationship with the forest is expressed this way: "We suggest that anadromous and inshore-spawning fishes constitute such an important prey base for terrestrial wildlife that conventional ecological and management dogmas need to be revised." They go on to conclude: "We think that these fish provide a resource base that supports much of the coastal ecosystem."

Sometimes the contribution that marine protein makes to terrestrial ecosystems is so obvious as to be overwhelming. Black-tailed gulls, often wholly dependent on small finfish and other forms of sea life, have been known to create entire island ecosystems simply by ingesting and defecating, transferring marine protein from the sea to the land. In a study of black-tailed gull rookeries in the North Pacific, scientists Hiroshi Mizutani and Eitaro Wada, from Tokyo's Mitsubishi-Kasei Institute of Life Sciences, determined that the volume of nitrogen, phosphorus, and potassium in rookery-island soils was far greater than even that of the world's most fertilizer-intensive agricultural industries. On some small islands where the gulls roost, Mizutani and Wada found "the plant community would not exist if the birds were absent."

At other times, the role marine nutrients play in the population dynamics of a single bird species is dramatic enough by itself, if only because the result supports bird populations from the very heart of North America. One vantage point from which this phenomenon can be directly observed is on the banks of the Squamish River, about 75 kilometers (46 miles) north of Vancouver.

Every year, in early November, bald eagles begin to appear above the Squamish Valley as little black specks against the snowcapped peaks of the towering Tantalus Range to the north and east. Some of the eagles come from as far away as Wyoming, Saskatchewan, and Arizona. The birds begin appearing in the cottonwoods along the banks of the Squamish, and on the nearby Cheakamus, the Ashlu, the Mamquam, and the Cheekeye, when the air has become heavy with the full, rich smell of spawned-out chum salmon. By Christmas, there are thousands of dead salmon strewn among the river boulders. There are coho and chinook, but mostly they are winter chums, their bodies split open, their spines protruding, and their eyes gone, pecked out by the crows and the gulls. It is the smell of the place that draws the eagles down into the cottonwoods, that timeless and familiar smell of winter on the coast, and by New Year's Day, bald eagles perch motionless in roosting trees within calling distance of the ancient Squamish smokehouse villages and fishing stations of Seaichem, Aickwucks, Zookwitz, Skowishum, Kowtain, and Yekapsum. The eagles rest in the trees with their talons wrapped around branches barely able to hold their weight.

A lot of eagles visit the Squamish River every year, often more than 3000 birds. In 1994, volunteers counted 3769 eagles, a number that easily exceeded the human population of Brackendale, a bohemian backwoods village on the banks of the Squamish River where annual eagle-count efforts are coordinated. The 1994 count broke the world record for eagle counts set at the Chilkat River in Alaska ten years earlier.

In late fall and winter, the salmon runs returning to the coast's myriad creeks, streams, and rivers cause British Columbia's bald eagle population to swell from perhaps 12,000 resident birds to about 30,000 birds — almost half the bald eagles on the continent. Most of the eagles that come for the salmon on the Squamish are from the north, from British Columbia's northern interior and from the north coast, the Nass River, and the Skeena, from Alaska, Yukon Territory, and the Queen Charlotte Islands. For as long as anyone remembers, the Squamish River has been visited by clouds of eagles during the winter, and they come for the salmon.

To get to the Squamish River from the north, the eagles ride thermals and updrafts, following ridges and mountainsides down the coast during the autumn months. They glide as much as they can at speeds of up to 80 kilometers (50 miles) an hour, stopping in at spawning rivers along the way. Their arrivals coincide with the north-to-south spawning sequence of late-running salmon species such as coho and chum. They end up at the Squamish Valley, and to a lesser extent, the Harrison River, the Cowichan, the Nanaimo, the lower Fraser River, and dozens of smaller rivers.

Almost half the wintering birds are juveniles and subadults. They are the ones without the distinctive white caps, and the whiteheads that haven't yet paired up and staked out a section of home turf around a nesting site. Nesting pairs don't travel much. They stake out a crook of an old-growth Douglas-fir or another old coniferous tree, although a big old cottonwood will do. They build huge nests that have been known to reach 4 meters (13 feet) across and more than 3 meters (10 feet) in depth, weighing close to 5 tonnes. Building material usually consists of dead branches, sticks, and driftwood, although sea lion bones have been found in nest construction material, along with eelgrass, bull kelp, and cow parsnip, and even plastic tarpaulin and nylon rope. Nesting pairs will hang around the same nest, year after year, producing one to three eggs a year, and they can be fiercely territorial. They are notoriously inhospitable to interloping eagles, and as summer turns to fall, young adults and the single birds start in search of spawning salmon, migrating to rivers such as the Squamish.

To survive the winter, eagles — particularly the juveniles and subadults that don't have the skills or the seniority to harvest locally abundant prey — require secure food sources. Apart from things like road kill, that leaves spawning salmon — mainly chum salmon, which tend to spawn late in the year in the lower reaches of big rivers, or in the myriad small rivers that flow through steep and heavily forested terrain to empty directly into the sea.

Although science has clearly demonstrated the importance of salmon to eagle populations, you don't have to be a scientist to make reasonable assumptions about what would become of eagles if there were no salmon. In 1995, Lefty Goldsmith, who was the 72-year-old treasurer of the Squamish Estuary Conservation Society, made the point clearly, and Lefty was never a scientist. He was a union organizer with the Mine, Mill and Smelter Workers, and a machinist with the Britannia mine just south of Squamish between 1947 and 1972, when the mine shut down.

Over the years, Lefty Goldsmith — Britannia's first and only left-handed machinist, which is how he got his nickname — had developed a unique expertise about the Squamish, its salmon, and the eagles that come every year because of the salmon. He had made meticulous observations of the birds over the years, but he was cautious about his conclusions. There were certain things, though, that Lefty was confident about, like what would happen to the eagles if salmon stopped coming back from the sea, if the salmon spawning beds were wrecked by logging or industrial development. "The eagles will slowly migrate away," Lefty told me.

And that is precisely what the eagles have done at dozens of rivers south of the Squamish.

There are still significant chum salmon populations that spawn in the final 150 kilometers (90 miles) of the Fraser River and in tributaries to the lower Fraser River such as the Harrison and the Lower Stave. Sometimes the eagles that come to the Squamish for the winter fly over the mountains to the Harrison for a day or two and then come back again to the Squamish. But a report prepared in 1994 by federal fisheries biologist Brian Riddell for Pacific Biological Station in Nanaimo noted that in British Columbia's southwestern corner, "one third of the spawning populations known since the early 1950s have now been lost or decreased to such low numbers that spawners are not consistently monitored."

By the time an eagle flies as far south as Puget Sound, there's hardly any natural habitat left. Three-quarters of the sound's tidal marshes and riparian habitat have been lost, especially around the estuaries of rivers such as the Puyallup, Duwamish, and Snohomish. The Skagit River still supports large wild chum populations, but to the south and the west, all the way to California, the winter pickings are slim. Every year, another salmon run finds itself listed under the U.S. Endangered Species Act. By the 1990s, in southern Puget Sound, most chum salmon stocks either had become severely depleted or had vanished entirely. Logging, urban encroachment, and overfishing had left many streams barren of any salmon. The hardest-hit streams were generally the streams that provided prime chum salmon habitat, which translates into prime eagle wintering habitat. When the salmon go, the eagles go.

What all this meant was that the Squamish Valley remained one of the last great feastbowls for wintering eagles in North America. It had become a significant southern terminus for migrating eagles that would otherwise keep moving to spawning rivers along the coast as far south as the mouth of the Columbia. It meant that the Squamish, by the end of the 20th century, had become vitally important for almost half the bald eagles on the planet.

You could say, ecologically speaking, that the Squamish is in relatively good shape. Squamish-bound steelhead salmon had taken a beating during the last half of the 20th century, but by the 1990s, they were showing signs of recovery. Chinook salmon numbers stabilized around the same time, but coho returns were falling off the charts, as they were in almost all of British Columbia's south coast rivers. Abundant pink salmon — never a hot item in either the sports or the commercial fishing industry — were returning to the Squamish in odd-numbered years only, and they were holding their own after decades of decline. So were the river's midwinter chum salmon runs.

You could also say, demographically speaking, that the Squamish eagle population exhibited all the tragedy of a refugee camp. By the 1990s, the number of resident eagles in Washington State had declined to about 500 nesting pairs. The wild salmon were mostly gone, and state wildlife officials were dumping the skinned carcasses of road-killed coyotes and beavers in strategically situated farmers' fields, trying to divert migrating eagles away from urban areas.

Lefty Goldsmith's firsthand observations of the way salmon support eagle populations are as persuasive as any scientific study. And there are others like Goldsmith, long-time residents of British Columbia's north coast, who will tell you that they can discern, on a clear day, from the window of a de Havilland Beaver, at 1500 meters (5000 feet), which creeks have salmon in them and which creeks have a waterfall at their outlet that's just a bit too steep for salmon to climb. It's the color of the trees. The salmon creeks are shrouded in trees that are a darker shade of green. Salmon creeks just seem to have bigger trees along their banks, and salmon valleys just seem to have more "stuff" in them. The foliage is thicker, the tangle more intense. Even if these anecdotal accounts were verified by science, such subtle differences between creeks with salmon and creeks without salmon would not show the difference between what the coast ended up being like and what the coast would have been like without salmon. That's because the presence of a single salmon creek nestled somewhere within a vast stretch of landscape, over thousands of years, could easily alter the nature of all the other non-salmon creeks and the landscape itself. Birds move around, bears move around, wolves move around, and so on. To get precise about these matters, you have to look a lot closer than the view provided from a floatplane at a very high altitude.

You've got to hang on as the floatplane bumps its way down through the clouds and follows a flight path in the shape of a bent corkscrew until Whale Channel emerges just below the floats, at the last minute, and the plane splashes down in Barnard Harbour, at Princess Royal Island, on British Columbia's north coast. That was the way I met Tom Reimchen, a biologist who specializes in the relationships between salmon, bears, and a whole range of species found in coastal rain forests. He was just coming out of the forest after a morning up a creek, collecting core samples from hemlock, cedar, and spruce trees to analyze for marine-derived nitrogen — the heavier nitrogen that salmon bring back with them from the deep ocean. With his rain-soaked red hair and piercing blue eyes, he looked like some sort of forest tribesman from Norse myth, certainly not what one might expect a 53-year-old biology professor from the University of Victoria to look like. Reimchen had spent much of his academic life in the field studying bears. He especially enjoyed being with them at night. Bears catch most of their salmon at night, a fact that Reimchen himself uncovered in the Queen Charlotte Islands.

As Reimchen clambered out of a ragged old inflatable dinghy, he shook my hand with his left hand. A camera lens cap was taped to the palm of his right hand, to protect a wound he'd suffered a few days earlier. He'd fallen on a broken branch, and a tooth-sized chunk of the branch was still stuck inside his palm somewhere. It didn't seem to bother him at all. It had been rough going, collecting core samples that morning, and he and his crew had already thrashed up and down about thirty salmon streams over the previous three weeks. Reimchen looked preposterously vigorous.

I found myself thinking about Reimchen's stamina three days later when I was sitting in a creek, cowering against the rain under the root wad of a giant fallen spruce tree, with water pouring into my gumboots. I was watching pink salmon pulsing by like dozens of little shadows on the water, and on the far side of the creek a bear was paying close attention to the same fish, but all I could think about was all the horrible little devil's club puncture wounds that covered my hands and my forehead. Everybody else on Reimchen's expedition seemed to have avoided being ravaged like this, and some of them had been thrashing through the brambles for more than three weeks. This was only my third day. The bear glanced over at me, so I held up my scratch-covered hands and muttered some complaint under my breath. The bear ignored me. We were about a mile up from salt water in the tangled undergrowth of an unnamed creek that flows down from the mountains of Gribbell Island, which is just north of Princess Royal Island, which is about two-thirds of the way between Cape Caution, at the northern tip of Vancouver Island, and Prince Rupert. The bear was a Kermode bear, but not one of the white bears that have made the Kermode population so famous. Its fur was black, but it was still impressive, that close.

The point of Reimchen's fieldwork was to determine the extent to which salmon contribute marine-derived nitrogen, in the form of their own spawned-out bodies, to coastal forest ecosystems. The main idea was to get a picture of how much of the famously insane fecundity of the rain forest results from the presence of salmon, and especially salmon-eating bears, which act as a kind of transit system through the forest for all the nitrogen and nutrients that salmon bring back from the sea. In his earlier work on the Queen Charlotte Islands, Reimchen found that during a single spawning season, each bear would haul as much as 1600 kilograms (3500 pounds) of salmon out of a creek, carry it into the forest, and leave half on the forest floor. Those leftovers provided crucial nutrients for everything from ravens and weasels to bugbane and huckleberries and cedar trees.

An annual nutrient load of that magnitude, over thousands of years, will obviously affect the landscape. But the extent of that impact is often a lot more subtle than the eagle-filled sky above the Squamish River. Crows dart from the forest canopy, snatch bits of salmon that bears have left behind on the forest floor, and cache their meals in the crooks of trees, under mounds of grass, and sometimes under rocks. Mink, among the most secretive of forest animals, appear to delay the timing of their breeding cycle so that pregnant females will be lactating during the salmon runs, when food is abundant. Invertebrates and plankton in lake systems flourish with abundances of sockeye, which deposit enormous amounts of nitrogen and potassium in interior lakes with every spawning. At Alaska's Iliamna Lake, returning sockeye, which have been known to number 24 million, contribute about 170 tonnes of sockeye to the lake every year. At Karluk Lake in southeast Alaska, a comparatively small sockeye run routinely contributes more than 20 tonnes of phosphorus to that lake's annual nutrient budget. This amount of phosphorus covering the lake surface is about the same as the recommended application of standard commercial fertilizer for evergreen trees raised in nurseries. The bears around Karluk Lake, meanwhile, carry tonnes of fish into the forest, which provides the forest floor with an estimated 6.7 kilograms of phosphorus per hectare (6 pounds per acre) every year.

Reimchen wanted to know how deeply the marine-derived nitrogen from salmon carcasses is involved in the elaborate web of relationships that make up the coastal rain forest's ecology. Figuring out this sort of thing meant trudging up coastal creeks to where salmon spawn, and to where the bears are, to collect samples of wood and leaves and hemlock needles and whatnot for later analysis. Reimchen had lost count of all the black bears he and his fellow researchers had encountered since the season's fieldwork began. But the grizzlies were easier to remember. In the days before I met up with him in Barnard Harbour, Reimchen found himself greeting a grizzly at a distance of three paces on the Lockhart-Gordon River. There was another that walked out onto the beach at the Ashlulum, just to have a look at everyone, and the one that swam across the estuary of the Nootem, and the one that bluff-charged one of the crew on the Kwatna. They had seen black bears on Goin Creek, Salmon Bay River, Packe Creek, and Cornwall East Creek, and it was on the Nius River that they saw their first white bear, which was actually sort of amber colored. It was one of those ghostly creatures that have come to be called spirit bears, genetic variants that occur within the coastal Kermode bear population, which is centered on Princess Royal Island.

Every day, Reimchen and the others would get up at dawn, eat a light breakfast, climb into their rain gear and hip waders and head off to bushwhack their way up another creek. Reimchen and Dan Klinka, a 25-year-old student from the University of Victoria, spend their time drilling holes in old-growth hemlock, cedar, and spruce, while Deanna Mathewson, a 30-year-old graduate student, gathers leaves of sword fern, deer fern, black huckleberry, bugbane, false azalea, salmonberry, false lily of the valley, and the ubiquitous devil's club. You'd think each creek would have blurred into the next after a while, with the study routine becoming a floating tangle of underbrush and moss-covered rocks, and evenings going over the day's events in the galley of the 20-meter (60-foot) *Blue Fjord*, a 60-year-old former coastal police cruiser that served as the project's floating base camp. But there was nothing monotonous about it. At night, when the *Blue Fjord* was at anchor, salmon would swim around the hull, setting off explosions of biolumi-nesence. During the day, between bear encounters, there were hump-back whales, Dall's porpoises, and Pacific white-sided dolphins to remind us all that humans are not necessarily the pinnacle of evolution among vertebrates, despite what Linnaeus might have thought, and despite the brave impression I was trying to leave the bear that ignored my complaints about the effects of devil's club.

Even if all this would eventually get monotonous to a lot of people, Reimchen was not like a lot of people. After getting his degree at the University of Alberta, Reimchen moved to the Queen Charlotte Islands to study things like sticklebacks, particularly those distinct types of sticklebacks endemic to the Queen Charlotte Islands, where Reimchen ended up known as "Stickleback Tom." After teaching biology for a while at the University of Alberta, Reimchen returned to the Charlottes to continue his studies for a few years before taking up a full-time teach-ing post at the University of Victoria.

The Queen Charlottes archipelago, which is coming to be known as Haida Gwaii, the name given the islands by its aboriginal people, is one of the few places in the northwestern quarter of North America where the ice sheets of the Pleistocene epoch did not call all the shots. There are strange little pockets of wildflowers on the island that shouldn't really be there, and there was the Dawson's caribou, a dwarfish version of the woodland caribou that was hunted to extinction early in the 20th century. The islands had become home to about 250 populations of endemic sticklebacks, including one bizarre species that distinguishes itself by having no spiky little stickles at all, and no armour, and is covered with a strange and gooey sort of gelatin. The odd thing about the islands' sticklebacks is that although they are not all that far removed in evolutionary time from sticklebacks anywhere else in North America, there are some little populations of sticklebacks on Graham Island's Argonaut Plain that are completely different from any other. The Argonaut Plain sticklebacks are a million years removed from all the other sticklebacks on earth, except for a small population in Japan and two populations in southeast Alaska. The only way to account for such a thing is the survival of relic populations of sticklebacks in Ice Age refugia.

The thing that connects Argonaut Plain sticklebacks with the salmon-eating bears of the coast is that coastal black bears have similar isolations in their ancestry. The black bears of the Queen Charlotte Islands, and the Kermode bears of the B.C. north coast and its adjacent maze of islands, are from a different lineage than the rest of North America's black bears. The coast's bears — the "salmon bears" that range from Vancouver Island to southeast Alaska — share a postglacial ancestor with the rest of the continent's black bears, but they've been apart for several thousand years. To find a common ancestor between black bears and grizzly bears, you have to go back about a half a million years, which sounds like a long time ago, until you remember that Pacific salmon have been around for at least a million years.

By the late 1980s, analysis of mitochondrial DNA — that genetic fingerprinting that comes down through the maternal line — was beginning to make great strides in answering questions about how long ago different animal populations, and different species, began to evolve in different directions from each other. Reimchen got excited by all of this. He started to look into the mitochondrial sequencing of other endemic coastal species, particularly bears. "I realized then," Reimchen recalled one night over a glass of rum in the *Blue Fjord*'s galley, "that I had to go molecular."

When the federal and provincial governments agreed to establish the Gwaii Haanas National Park Reserve in the southern section of the Queen Charlotte Islands, Reimchen began eight years of research to establish the significance of the relationship between the Pacific coast's marine species — particularly salmon — and terrestrial ecosystems. Reimchen first determined that although human beings were taking about 9 million kilograms (20 million pounds) of fish from the waters around Gwaii Haanas, another 3 million kilograms (6.6 million pounds) were being directly consumed by seals, sea lions, bears, eagles, ravens, and other creatures. With the support of the Canadian Parks Service, Reimchen embarked on an exhaustive study of the importance of salmon to all these animals. At Bag Harbour, Reimchen awoke one night in his tent to a lot of noise coming from a nearby creek. When he went to investigate, he was surprised to see bears everywhere, fishing for salmon. It was not surprising to find bears fishing for salmon. What was surprising was that they fish at night, and that they get most of their salmon at night — 80 percent, it turned out. It's not that bears have particularly good night vision. They don't. It's that salmon have even poorer night vision, and salmon in a spawning creek tend to hold still in one place during the night. All a bear has to do is stand there and wait to feel a fish nudging up against a paw, and whack. Dinner.

But the bears, Reimchen found, leave about half their dinner on the forest floor, where it becomes food for a range of scavengers, from eagles down to beetles and fly larvae. But it doesn't end there. It continues on, into devil's club, false lily of the valley, cedar, spruce, hemlock, and on and on, comprising an annual infusion of nutrients into practically everything that grows, creeps, and crawls in the adjacent forests.

Marine-derived nitrogen is the evidence of the contribution that salmon make to the forest, and it's handy to study because it's discernible from "ambient" nitrogen. It's heavier. In some trees at Bag Harbour, Reimchen found that nitrogen from salmon comprised fully 50 percent of the nitrogen in trees near spawning streams. And marine-derived nitrogen shows up not just along the banks of a creek but throughout a salmon-stream watershed. So, with every collection of plants and shrubs and tree cores Reimchen, Klinka, and Mathewson gathered and analyzed, they also had to collect the same suite of specimens from a control area nearby, to compare the nitrogen content in the foliage near a salmon stream with the ambient nitgrogen content in foliage away from the stream. But finding a tree in the forest that has not been directly influenced by salmon is not easy. In research conducted by other scientists, marine-derived nitrogen was found in trees 50 meters (164 feet) from a salmon stream. "So we went to 100 meters (328 feet)," Reimchen says. "Then we went to 150 meters (492 feet), and we were still getting anomalies." To find a good control site, Reimchen and his crew had to find the closest patch of forest that wasn't within a salmon watershed at all. Reimchen doesn't like collecting things from the control sites. No bears. This is a man whose idea of an enjoyable night is to spend it standing dead still among a group of bears, in the dark, while the bears go about the business of catching fish.

In the middle of a rainy night, in a creek, just up from tidewater on Princess Royal Island, you can't see much in the dark. But Reimchen can still make out a creature that is wholly different from the fish that Johann Julius Walbaum saw, or the fish that swam in the imaginary ocean of conventional fisheries management throughout the 20th century. The salmon Reimchen sees, and the fish that Lefty Goldsmith saw on the Squamish River, is a creature deeply involved in ancient and important relationships with bears, trees, eagles, and just about everything that grows or crawls or walks across the landscape.

Throughout the 20th century, fisheries-management agencies saw absolutely no value in those ancient relationships, and in fact regarded them with hostility, as though they were on the order of the "illegitimate" marriages Linnaeus imagined between certain flowers. Whatever benefit salmon provided to bears, eagles and seals was regarded as a loss of production to industrial salmon fisheries.

In Alaska, between 1917 and 1953, state fisheries officials paid a bounty for every eagle killed by state residents. Over the years, the bounty ranged from 50 cents to $2 a bird. In southeast Alaska, where eagles routinely congregated along the banks of more than 2000 salmon spawning streams, the bounty produced carnage. More than 100,000 eagles were shot down through the years. Alaskans also used high-powered rifles and dynamite to kill salmon-eating seals in the Copper River delta, and Alaskans also experimented with a variety of technologies to keep bears away from spawning salmon, including electric fences, chemical repellants, and noise-making devices. On the B.C coast, in the 1920s, fisheries patrol vessels were fitted out with machine guns to kill salmon-eating seals and sea lions, and Oregon fisheries managers followed suit, killing about 7000 seals and sea lions in 1923. In Canada, "merganser control" programs were developed to reduce predation on juvenile Atlantic salmon in east coast rivers, and until the 1960s, federal policy required fisheries officers conducting salmon-spawner surveys on the B.C. coast to shoot any bears they found in salmon streams.

There was nothing necessarily "irrational" about such responses, each of which were carefully considered, generally implemented within the most reasonable scientific parameters, and perfectly consistent with the Linnaean view of the world. Eagle bounties, bear eradication programs, and the slaughter of salmon-eating marine mammals were attempts to bring a sort of order to nature. Indeed, many of the earliest salmon-fisheries managers considered nature to be irrational, in the way it let such bounty go to waste on mere bears and birds. Others, like Living-stone Stone, considered the father of salmon-fisheries management on the U.S. west coast, saw evidence of a divine plan in salmon. Just as Stephen Krasheninnikov saw in salmon "wonderful proofs . . . of the Divine Providence, and the goodness of the Creator," Stone also saw God's hand at work. In 1884, Stone wrote that he had reached the conclusion that Providence had anticipated the arrival of white people in North America, and the exponential growth in the continent's human population. The presence of thousands of unutilized eggs in every female salmon was evidence of it, Stone believed.

> Nature, perhaps more aptly speaking, Providence, in the case of fish . . . produces great quantities of seed that nature does not utilize or need. It looks like a vast store that has been provided for nature to hold in reserve against the time when the increased population of the earth should need it and the sagacity of man should utilize it. At all events, nature has never utilized this reserve, and man finds it already here to meet his wants.

Like Linnaeus, Livingstone Stone had an ecclesiastical bent. In fact, he began his adult life as a preacher. After he got a job on the Miramichi River in New Brunswick, stripping Atlantic salmon of their eggs for transport to New England rivers, Stone soon became obsessed with the possibilities presented by intervening in natural processes, particularly by the artificial propagation of fish in hatcheries. Stone believed not only that salmon were unnecessarily wasted by nature but that salmon didn't even need rivers. Rivers could be put to more practical uses, such as impoundments for agricultural irrigation, Stone reckoned. Restraints on salmon fleets were unnecessary as well — all that was necessary was the construction of salmon hatcheries. Then, humanity could tap nature's storehouse in perpetuity by harvesting the bounty of artificial salmon runs, each of which would begin and end their ocean journeys at a hatchery's temple gates. In the 1870s, Stone was put in charge of the U.S. government's Pacific salmon hatchery program. His messianic vision was adopted by generations of fish culturists across the United States and Canada and became the official policy of the U.S. Fisheries Commission.

By 1930, seventy-three hatcheries had been constructed between California and Alaska. There is nothing inherently evil about salmon hatcheries, but on North America's west coast, they were established in the belief that under laboratory-type conditions, natural predation upon salmon eggs could be eliminated and domesticated salmon runs could produce far greater numbers of salmon than wild populations could. This ideology allowed no room for salmon as a keystone species that was a vital structural component of the ecosystems of the northwestern third of North America.

As it turned out, there is no evidence that hatcheries can produce more salmon than nature produces. Decades of experience with hatcheries suggests that the opposite is probably true. Hatchery fish tend to be genetically weaker than wild salmon and often exhibit lower survival rates than wild salmon. But hatchery fish also tend to displace wild salmon by competing with them for food in the ocean, and hatchery fish also attract heavy fishing, which often results in the overfishing of comigrating wild runs of salmon.

A century after Livingstone Stone built the first Pacific salmon hatchery on California's Sacramento River, hatcheries had come to consume the lion's share of public funding for salmon-enhancement projects in both Canada and the United States. On the Columbia River, hatcheries had failed to replicate that once-wild river's natural production, despite annual expenditures exceeding $500 million. In some years returns fell to 673,000 salmon — one-twentieth of the Columbia's former production. Along the Oregon coast, hatchery managers despaired as coho returns fell from about four million salmon in the 1970s to only slightly more than 300,000 in 1997 — the year that all the remaining wild coastal coho in Oregon were declared threatened under the U.S. Endangered Species Act. In 1994, Canada's federal government initiated an evaluation of hatchery programs and found that rather than producing a net gain in salmon production, public investments in hatcheries produced a net loss. Hatchery fish were replacing and supplanting wild runs, and fisheries conducted upon hatchery stocks were eliminating wild salmon. In 1995, the U.S. National Marine Fisheries Service reached the same conclusions and found that the Columbia's remaining wild coho salmon were being significantly harmed by hatchery coho programs.

Sorting out the ecological consequences of removing wild salmon from the landscape is a difficult task, but in a 1999 study, prominent U.S. salmon biologist Jim Lichatowich and his colleagues, Ted Gresh and Peter Schoonmaker, attempted to quantify those consequences south of the 49th parallel. The study estimated that a pre-industrial biomass of salmon, ranging between 160 and 226 million kilograms (between 350 and 500 million pounds), returned every year to the rivers of Washington, Oregon, Idaho, and California. By the 1990s, that biomass had declined to 13.7 million kilograms (30 million pounds), about 7 percent of salmon's pre-industrial contribution of nutrients to the terrestrial ecology of the U.S. northwestern states. This nutrient deficit in terrestrial ecosystems explained, in part, the broad-scale ecological damage done throughout the U.S. Pacific Northwest. Because of the critical role salmon carcasses play in the long-term survival of salmon — the nutrients they contribute to spawning streams create ideal conditions for salmon fry — it also helped explain "the downward spiral of salmonid abundance and diversity in general."

The consequences of removing salmon from an ecosystem can have immediate and dramatic effects. Villagers in the small community of Oweekeno, about 400 kilometers (250 miles) north of Vancouver, observed those consequences firsthand during in the autumn months of 1999.

The local Rivers Inlet sockeye salmon runs, which once supported the second-largest sockeye fishery on the B.C. coast, had collapsed. From a total stock size of more than three million sockeye, which had been routine in the 1950s, Rivers Inlet sockeye had declined precipitously over the years. Commercial overfishing, habitat destruction as a consequence of logging, the use of fish-killing herbicides by forest companies, and changing ocean conditions are all cited as likely culprits. The sockeye fishery was closed in 1995. In 1999, a mere 3500 sockeye spawners were counted in the Rivers Inlet spawning grounds at Oweekeno Lake.

The first starving grizzly bears began to make their way into Oweekeno village in late September. The local grizzly bears, which rely on salmon for as much as 70 percent of their diet, had coexisted with the people of Oweekeno for untold generations. Every autumn, bears walked through the village, fat and sated from their sockeye fishing, making their final rounds before the winter's hibernation. But in September 1999, the grizzlies had come to the village looking for food. Children were kept indoors for weeks. Some bears tried to break into houses, other bears took up residence in basements. The situation became untenable, and provincial wildlife officials were called in to assess the situation. They shot six grizzly bears and relocated three others.

By December 1999, thirteen grizzly bears had been shot and killed in Oweekeno. The villagers had no fish for the winter, and the skies were empty of ravens and eagles.

THREE

From Sea Cows to Civilization

The human ecologist will never neglect
the belly of the people.

— *Frank Fraser Darling, "The Ecological Approach
to the Social Sciences,"* American Scientist

WHEN WE FIRST ENCOUNTERED them, we were heading eastward through heavy seas at a latitude roughly halfway between Hawaii and the Aleutian Islands. They were like tiny, sloop-rigged, blue-hulled sailboats, skiffing across the sea surface in flotillas of a hundred or more. It was before breakfast, and we'd only just concluded the two-hour morning routine of sliding around the trawler's slimy deck, pulling ink-squirting, 2-kilogram (4½-pound), meter-long squid out of the mesh of the gill net we'd set the night before. I was standing on the forward deck, cradling my morning coffee, when the sailboats appeared out of nowhere. Each was about the size of the palm of a man's hand.

Known as vallellas, they have come to be called by-the-wind sailors. They are related to jellyfish, but they are really three distinct colonies of animals. One colony forms the sail, rising amidships on a hard-ridged mast that holds the sloop to the wind. Another colony forms the translucent blue hull, which serves as a digestive system. The third colony, composed of hanging stingers, forms the tiny ship's keel. Little is known about how vallellas work. There is also the matter of why they do what they do, and how it happens that three types of organism can find each other in the ocean, arrange themselves in such a way as to construct something that behaves like a sailing ship, gather together in fleets, and then sail off together, in the same direction.

This was not an easy thing to ponder from the bow of a trawler on one of those days when moving across the ocean meant a Ferris wheel ride through heavy fog and sea spray, with flying fish soaring in flocks above the waves, and schools of diving birds darting through the water below them. It was disorienting enough just trying to stand upright as the *Arctic Harvester,* a 50-meter (160-foot) trawler with a crew of scientists from Canada and the United States, and fishermen from Newfoundland and British Columbia, rolled toward an unseen horizon. And then, through the middle of it all, came the little blue sailboats.

For the next few days, the seas swarmed with them. And then one morning they were gone, as though the ship had rounded some invisible cape that separated one ocean from another, sometime during the night. On the long journey between Honolulu and Vancouver Island, the ocean changed abruptly like that several times. For days, the skies would be thick with tropic birds and frigate birds, and then one morning the horizon would be broken by flocks of storm petrels from the Kurile Islands, tossed around in the sky like barn swallows scattered by gusts of wind. After several days of Cook's petrels and Leach's petrels, the skies would suddenly give way to fork-tailed petrels and red phalaropes. Shearwaters, jaegers, Laysan's albatross, and black-footed albatross were always there, appearing out of nowhere, diving for food on the surface or just below it. Their prey was mainly lanternfish, bioluminescent comb jellies, shrimp, and other small fish that erupted at dawn and at dusk from a solid layer of color that showed on the *Arctic Harvester's* depth sounder at an otherwise constant depth of about 11 fathoms.

The reason we were out there was to contribute to a research effort headed by Canada's Department of Fisheries and Oceans, involving the Canadian Wildlife Service, the U.S. National Marine Fisheries Service, and the U.S. National Oceanographic and Aeronautics Administration. The research was a response to the alarming expansion of the Asian driftnet fleet, an aggregation of several hundred deep-sea fishing vessels, mainly from Japan, Korea, and Taiwan, that fished with lethal driftnets, mainly for squid. Each of their nets was up to 50 kilometers (30 miles) long, and by the late 1980s, some estimates suggested that the driftnets of the Pacific, tied end to end, would have circled the planet at the equator with a third left over. Quite apart from the effects of the fleet on target species such as squid, the $1.5 billion North Pacific driftnet fishery was responsible for a harvest of an unknown amount of North American salmon, along with the incidental death of 50,000 marine mammals and 500,000 seabirds annually.

The extent of the squid driftnet fishery's impact on high-seas ecosystems was largely unknown, so the *Arctic Harvester* had been assigned to the mid-Pacific squid grounds to help fill in the blanks by fishing with long line gear, as well as a 3-kilometer (2-mile) driftnet, at various coordinates across the North Pacific. The daily routine consisted of fishing, recording the catch, taking note of sea surface temperatures and weather conditions, and recording our sightings of birds, marine mammals, ships, and debris. The birds were a delight, and of those that became entangled in our fishing gear we managed to release, alive, all but three — two sooty shearwaters and a fork-tailed storm petrel. At times, the sea was seething with Dall's porpoises, common dolphins, Pacific white-sided dolphins, and striped dolphins. We once came across a pod of twelve rare northern right-whale dolphins, and among the dozens of whales we encountered were several sperm whales, minke whales and humpback whales. Thankfully, only two marine mammals were killed on the *Arctic Harvester*'s voyage, a male and a female common dolphin. They had been seen fishing together in the hours before they were hauled aboard. They drowned after getting tangled in our net.

The driftnet ships we came across were often rusting hulks, stained by squid ink. The Korean vessels were the worst, and reports from Seoul suggested the Korean fleet was little better than an armada of floating prisons. Despite being about as far away from land as it's possible to get on the planet, it was a rare day when we didn't come upon garbage of some kind. Our debris-sighting log contained entries for plastic pop bottle cases, hundreds of fishing floats, dozens of balled-up chunks of driftnet, light bulbs, a blue tarpaulin, a cooking pan, a plastic milk bottle, a 45-gallon drum, a pair of rubber gloves, glass balls, Styrofoam blocks, and a small skiff. Unsightly as these floating piles of garbage were, each mass of debris formed the core of a distinct floating ecosystem. In one tangled mass of fish net, rope, and plastic we found a self-contained, kelp-shrouded galaxy comprising gooseneck barnacles, crabs, and mussels, with twelve bottles of Japanese whiskey, Suntory brand, at its nucleus. Each bottle, sadly, was empty.

But it would be wrong to think that the Asian driftnet fleet was the first time human beings had involved themselves so deeply in the North Pacific's ecosystems as to pose the threat of extinction and broad-scale extirpation of marine species. The mid-Pacific squid grounds were being mined by whaling ships, sealing schooners, and trawlers long before the Asian driftnet fleet showed up. To fully explore the history of human involvement in the North Pacific's ecosystems, however, is to make a voyage through a netherworld every bit as disorienting as those mornings on the bow of the *Arctic Harvester,* when fish fluttered through the air and birds swam below the waves. Part of the difficulty in sorting it all out is simply the time scales involved. Another problem is that by relying on the charts conventional histories provide, a voyager will encounter things, in the real world, that are not supposed to be there.

It is fairly certain that the first documented victim in the long story of humanity's involvement in the North Pacific's ecosystems was a huge, herbivorous sea mammal that came to be called the Steller's sea cow, after the naturalist Georg Steller. The sea cow weighed more than 7000 kilograms (15,000 pounds) and reached lengths of 9 meters (30 feet). It was encountered by Vitus Bering in 1741, when he and Steller and fourteen of Bering's crew were shipwrecked on a remote island at the western end of the Aleutian archipelago, where Bering eventually died. The creature was a member of the order Sirenia, which includes relic populations of only four species — three manatees (West African, West Indian, and a freshwater species in the Amazon Basin) and the dugong. After centuries of unyielding slaughter, large herds of dugongs remain only in the Persian Gulf, where, long after the 1991 Gulf War was over, the population was still suffering from the effects of massive oil spills that resulted from the war.

The Steller's sea cow is believed to have been confined to the waters around the island where Bering and his crew were shipwrecked — now known as Bering Island — and nearby Copper Island. Because the islands had never been occupied by humans, the sea cows had no fear of people and tended to loll about in shallows and kelp beds, swimming up beside ships. Although reports of sightings have persisted down through the years — including a fairly persuasive 1962 account from the crew of a Russian whaling ship in the Gulf of Anadyr, on Russia's Bering Sea coast — sea cows are believed to have been hunted to extinction by 1768.

The second recorded human-caused extinction in the North Pacific also involved Bering's 1741 shipwreck. The spectacled cormorant was a huge, nearly flightless bird that weighed as much as 6 kilograms (13 pounds). Steller, Bering, and the rest of the shipwrecked crew may well have been the first humans ever to see a spectacled cormorant, and the crew members kept themselves alive by hunting and eating the slow-moving birds, which, like sea cows, had no ingrained fear of humans. In later years, the spectacled cormorant became prized by fur traders, whalers, and Aleut hunters, who hunted them for their feathers until about 1850, when there were none left to hunt.

But the story might be a bit more complicated than that.

Although no sea cow remains have been unearthed at any archeological site in the North Pacific, Daryl Domning, a paleontologist at the University of California at Berkeley, has speculated that the isolated occurrence of the sea cow on the Commander Islands by the time of their discovery by Vitus Bering's 1741 expedition may be the result of pre-industrial overharvesting. Speculating that aboriginal whaling in the North Pacific may have begun with sea cow hunting, Domning notes that sea cows were present, thousands of years ago, in the waters off Japan and Kamchatka, and an 18,000-year-old sea cow skull fragment was dredged from Monterey Bay in California in 1970.

There may well have been many instances of massive overfishing throughout the North Pacific, long before the 19th and 20th centuries. On the Fraser River, pink salmon return almost exclusively in odd-numbered years, a situation that has led some biologists to speculate that overfishing in the distant past may have prevented pink runs from even-numbered years from reestablishing themselves. Also, the spectacular abundances of salmon that early Europeans observed in west coast rivers may not necessarily have indicated anything "normal" about salmon in its imagined natural state. Those early "superabundances" were likely anomalous, at least partly a consequence of the smallpox holocaust that so dramatically reduced aboriginal fishing immediately before European coastal exploration. Analyses of shell mounds in Japan, meanwhile, have allowed archeologists to document a pattern of overharvesting of clam beds during the Jomon period. Archeologists from Washington State University have documented similar patterns of overfishing in their studies of shell mounds along the American side of Juan de Fuca Strait — patterns that appear to have resulted in an emphasis on territorial circumscription and the emergence of a "managerial class" in tribal society.

If there is a beginning to the story of humanity's intensive participation in the ecological life of the North Pacific, then it starts around the time of Xa:ls, the Great Transformer, whose thumbprints are worried into the rocks at Tatxlis, in the Fraser Canyon. The Sto:lo say they have lived on the Fraser forever. There's an old story associated with almost every back eddy, and every bluff carries some mark of the human hand. For reasons that the roaring river and the twisting gorge of the Fraser canyon still make obvious, Tatxlis, where Xa:ls sat and scratched his thumb into a rock, was a key portal to a civilization based on salmon. It is also a place that marks the end of the early period of human societies on the Pacific coast, and the beginning of something else, about 6000 years ago.

Human societies were about to become an important part of what went on in the North Pacific. Salmon were about to become the way it would all happen. Until this point in history, people had participated only in the most tentative, localized ways in the North Pacific's ecosystems. People had already hunted whales, seals, and sea lions. They had integrated porpoises, rockfish, and dolphins into their own innermost longings about a ritualized order to the universe. They had already put down roots in coves and bays, lived long lives as small-boat handliners, and spun yarns about big fish around their home hearths. They had conformed with traditions and complied with customary fishing laws that had settled disputes that even their grandfathers had forgotten. People had walked with their children along sweeping beaches where clams lay in thick beds that supported large villages through long winters.

People had already been fishing salmon for thousands of years, but the very nature of the relationship between people and the ocean was about to change.

About 6000 years ago, all around the North Pacific, the coastlines had stopped their violent, post-Pleistocene crumpling and unfolding. Sea levels were becoming more stable, changing more slowly. With each passing year, greater numbers of salmon arose from their Ice Age refugia and headed into the North Pacific. And every year they returned to the continents, colonizing ever-broader stretches of the coast, and pioneering deeper and deeper into the interior, replenishing the ice-scarred landscape with an annual infusion of life-giving nutrients, nitrogen, and phosphorus for the forests, and food for bears, eagles, and just about everything else. In human societies, salmon became the abundant, predictable, and renewable resource that gave rise to a revolution not unlike the transition from hunter-gatherer economies to agricultural economies elswhere on the planet. About 6000 years ago, artifact assemblages in the archeological record show abrupt transitions in cultural features that are often as obvious as the changes brought on by the Upper Paleolithic revolution, 40,000 years ago.

Something starts happening. It shows up on Hokkaido, and it shows up in the old Ainu villages along the small chum salmon rivers of the Kurile Islands, which range, like a north-south copy of the Aleutians, from Hokkaido's Nemuro Bay to the southern capes of the Kamchatka Peninsula. It shows up among Kamchatka's Kamchadal peoples, on the islands around the Gulf of Alaska, at least as far south as the Chinuk people's fishing sites on the Columbia River, and as far inland as the Carrier people of the Upper Fraser, on the Rockies' western slopes. The "early period" was ending. In the ecological history of the North Pacific, and in the history of the Pacific's coastal terrestrial ecosystems, a new horizon had been reached.

Every year, millions of tonnes of marine protein rose up from the depths of the Pacific to form into thick columns and crowd through the Fraser's narrow canyon. But the strategic importance of the place wasn't just about abundant harvests. The dry winds that pour out of the sage desert upriver meant that huge volumes of salmon could be preserved through the year by wind-drying. That's why Tatxlis was so important. The most conservative estimates put the Fraser canyon's pre-smallpox human population at about 20,000 people.

There has been a tendency among North Americans to imagine the North Pacific's aboriginal peoples within the "noble savage" mold, after the ideas of Jean-Jacques Rousseau. Alternatively, following the lead of Enlightenment thinker Thomas Hobbes, North Americans have often regarded aboriginal peoples as so barbaric that salmon runs would have been quickly fished into extinction had aboriginal fishing communities only possessed the technology to do so. But neither view reflects the reality of Northwest Coast culture.

By the late 20th century, archeological research, aided by advances in electronmicroscopy, revealed that throughout the Northwest Coast, aboriginal societies had been engaged in industrial-scale harvests of salmon that sorely test romantic notions of aboriginal life before European settlement. Northwest Coast societies clearly defy the standard definition of hunter-gatherer societies in several ways, including the extent of their salmon fisheries, which produced volumes of fish at a scale comparable to those of the commercial fisheries of the Industrial Age. Also, Northwest Coast aboriginal societies deployed the most productive salmon-fishing technologies — weirs and traps — which could easily have wiped out all the salmon on the coast. But they didn't.

Just how many salmon were caught in the North Pacific's pre-industrial salmon fisheries is difficult to determine, but by the end of the 20th century it was becoming clear that pre-industrial aboriginal harvests took more fish, by orders of magnitude, than most anthropologists and historians had imagined. The extraordinary volume of salmon harvested by North America's aboriginal peoples first came to a light in a little-known study conducted by Gordon Hewes, a doctoral student at the University of California at Berkeley in 1947. Hewes was still trying to confirm his first findings more than a quarter of a century later. In a 1973 analysis published by Northwest Anthropological Research Notes, Hewes provided an estimate of the annual per capita consumption of salmon among the salmon-fishing peoples of northwestern North America, based on some of the most conservative population estimates.

He concluded that the tribal fisheries of the pre-smallpox period accounted for a staggering 57.6 million kilograms (127 million pounds) of salmon annually. To put that figure in context, it amounts to slightly more fish than the average annual commercial catch of sockeye on the British Columbia coast during the 20th century.

More than a decade later, at Simon Fraser University, archeologist Brian Chisholm attempted to reconstruct the pre-contact diet of aboriginal peoples in British Columbia by analyzing carbon 13 molecules in human remains. Chisholm was analyzing remains from 187 sites along the B.C. coast to determine, among other things, the relative importance of marine and terrestrial protein in aboriginal diets. Chisholm used techniques similar to those used by Reimchen and other scientists studying salmon's contribution to terrestrial ecosystems. Protein from land mammals bears a different isotopic signature from that of marine-derived protein sources — finfish, shellfish, and marine mammals. Chisholm determined that give or take 10 percent, 89 percent of the protein in coastal peoples' diets, going back close to 6000 years, came from the sea. Another study, with archeologist Erle Nelson and McMaster University geologist Henry Schwarcz, Chisholm examined the carbon 13 in thirty-eight skeletons that had been recovered over the years by archeologists from sites as far afield as Crescent Beach, near the British Columbia–Washington border, and Greenville, in the Nisga'a territory. The results showed that the protein in almost every individual's diet was at least 90 percent marine derived.

The size of the human population supported by the distinct maritime economy of the Northwest Coast remains a subject of great conjecture. But but by the end of the 20th century, just as estimates of the salmon catch by aboriginal people had to be radically revised upward, the human population in the pre-contact period was also proving to be greater, by orders of magnitude, than most anthropologists and historians had reckoned. It is certain that even by the time the first Spanish and English explorers arrived in their ships, some coastal societies had already been depopulated by epidemic diseases that originated in Europe.

Captain George Vancouver and his botanist, George Menzies, were both convinced that some cataclysm had been visited upon the coast in the years before their arrival in 1792. As Vancouver's ship, the *Discovery*, made its way through the portal of Juan de Fuca Strait, its officers and crew came upon an eerie landscape of deserted villages, sometimes littered with skeletons. The strait's waters were plied only by small parties of local people, fishing from canoes. There were the remains of towns, overgrown with nettles and brambles, scattered with the bones of the dead. Although Vancouver could not find "direct proof of extensive depopulation," Peter Puget, a ship's officer aboard the *Discovery*, noted that "the Small pox most have had, and most terribly pitted they are; indeed many have lost their Eyes and no Doubt it has raged with uncommon Inveteracy among them but we never saw any Scars with wounds, a most convincing proof in my mind of their peaceful Disposition."

Cole Harris, a cultural geographer at the University of British Columbia, reckons that the pre-European population of British Columbia was in the neighborhood of "well over 200,000" people. In one of the greatest tragedies in human history, much of the Northwest Coast culture area, from Northern California to southeast Alaska, was extensively depopulated by introduced diseases that had spread across the continent in the years before the first explorers arrived on the Pacific coast with their diaries and notebooks. The disease that wreaked the greatest havoc was smallpox. It was more devastating to the Northwest Coast than the Black Plague in medieval Europe. From the Salish towns along Juan de Fuca Strait to the Haida towns of Skidegate and Tanu, a civilization was reduced to remnants. Between the tumbled-down walls and roof beams of collapsed longhouses, young trees emerged out of the devil's club to join cedars that had stood for a thousand years.

Whatever the coastal population might have been before the effects of epidemic diseases, it is accepted among anthropologists and archeologists that British Columbia's coast, and its coastal valleys and river corridors, supported what was probably the densest population in North America, north of the Valley of Mexico and west of the Mississippi River.

Using data derived from marine-protein content analyses of the type that Chisholm had conducted, and population estimates of the type that Harris developed, anthropologist Randall Shalk came up with estimates of the pre-industrial aboriginal harvest of salmon in the Columbia River basin. Shalk was working with much better population data than were available to Hewes and others before him. Using new data, along with estimates of protein and carbohydrate requirements, knowledge of salmon migration patterns, and estimates of salmon abundance, Shalk estimated that the aboriginal peoples of the Columbia River basin caught in excess of 18 million kilograms (40 million pounds) of salmon annually. This production level is comparable to industrial salmon harvests during the peak years of the Columbia's commercial fisheries, between 1883 and 1919.

In the Fraser River basin — which was always a much more significant salmon producer than the Columbia — a similar picture emerges. Pre-smallpox population estimates vary quite widely, but if the aboriginal population of the Fraser River basin was somewhere in the middle of the various estimates — say, 60,000 people — one is still left with estimates of an annual average salmon harvest that range from 13.6 million to 27.2 million kilograms (30 million to 60 million pounds). Volumes of that magnitude come close to the annual average catch of Fraser River sockeye salmon in the commercial fisheries between the 1890s and the 1990s.

The picture that emerges from all this new scientific knowledge is something that can be described, without hyperbole, as civilization. It was a complex of cultures — Heiltsuks and Oweekenos, Nuxalk, Sto:lo, Kwagewlth, Haisla, Tsimshian, Gitxsan, Nisga'a, Haida, and so on — all built upon fish. And the way such full-fledged, broadly based marine economies developed involves events under way throughout the North Pacific about 6000 years ago, during the time of X:als on the Fraser River, Wiigyet on the Skeena, and Coyote on the Thompson and the Columbia Rivers.

During that time, the eustatic and isostatic tumult of the post-Pleistocene years had come to an end, allowing salmon to recolonize the continents surrounding the Pacific. It was also a time of rapid climate change throughout the North Pacific. But the story of the Northwest Coast is not so simple as salmon, then people, then civilization. A lot more is required for a civilization to develop, and it involves abundance, technological innovation, natural resource management, elaborate social organization, division of labor, trial and error, and plain old serendipity. Around the same time that salmon were reestablishing themselves as a dominant species of the North Pacific's ecosystems, geological stability was allowing gradually sloping beaches to form, all along North America's west coast and along the Japanese and Asian mainland coastlines, exposing broad tidal flats and clam beds. Intensive shell harvesting became possible, and the presence of such easily harvestable sources of protein as clams and oysters contributed to the development of the permanent and semipermanent winter villages that so distinguished North Pacific societies from hunter-gatherer societies.

In the San Juan Islands off the Washington coast, shellfish harvesting occurred on a scale that is not unreasonably described as aquaculture; at a place known as Elelung, on Orcas Island, clams were intensively cultivated on tidal flats protected by a series of stone hedgelike structures built at the extreme low-water mark around the bay.

On the Asian side of the North Pacific, a similar story was unfolding. About 6000 years ago, salmon had begun to transform coastal ecosystems and coastal cultures, and the emergence of gradually sloping beaches was allowing intensive exploitation of shellfish resources. The Sea of Okhotsk, which had been a vast coastal plain linking Hokkaido, Sakhalin Island, and most of the Kurile Islands with the Asian mainland, had become a vast, shallow sea. Like the Straits Salish cultivation of clam beds on Orcas Island, tribal communities associated with the Yankovskaya culture, which extended along the Sea of Japan and the Sea of Okhotsk from Korea to Peter the Great Bay, were engaged in what Russian anthropologists have described as aquaculture, or at least "an elementary technology of oyster-breeding."

It was also about this time, when the planet was gradually warming and salmon were providing much-needed nutrients to newly formed valley bottoms, that cedar began establishing itself as a dominant tree species throughout North America's Northwest Coast. After a long migration north, cedar eventually found a foothold as far north as Alaska's Baranov Island. Cedar became the raw material for clothing, oceangoing canoes, great works of monumental art, and a lumber supply for large cedar-planked houses that also served as fish-processing and storage plants, as well as "banquet halls, theatres and temples," according to the anthropologists Wayne Suttles and Kenneth Ames. Construction on this scale required, and allowed for, the development of complex social organization and elaborate division of labor.

Just as the northward march of cedar and the reemergence of major salmon runs parallels the development of the Northwest Coast culture pattern, the northward expansion of the temperate rain forest on the Asian side of the Pacific had similarly profound cultural implications. But instead of cedar, the northward trend in Asian maritime cultures can be followed through ceramics. The earliest pottery making known in any human civilization occurred on the Japanese island of Kyushu, at least 12,500 years ago. Cord-marked pottery (the Jomon people of early Japan were given the name because it refers to the distinctive cord-marked ceramics they were known for) begins to appear among the sea mammal hunters of coastal Japan in a pattern that parallels the poleward expansion of temperate forests.

But what destined the cultures of the North American side of the North Pacific to make their own distinct way in the world involved the development of fishing technology designed to harvest known abundances of specific and fairly predictable runs of salmon. Although a dizzying array of "gear types" were employed in aboriginal salmon fisheries, the most efficient, and the type that probably accounted for the lion's share of production, was the fish trap. In 1992, Roy Carlson — the pioneering archeologist who pushed back the time depth of Northwest Coast culture to 9,000 years — conducted an overview of British Columbia's archeological sites and came across 455 reports of sites with weirs, fish traps, or "probable fish traps" in the files of British Columbia's Archeology Branch. Of these, 231 are the remains of stone fish traps, and 41 sites contain the stubs of stakes and pilings from old wooden-built weirs. The remaining 183 were too vaguely described in the archeological reports to be clearly identified, but even firsthand, eyewitness encounters with these complexes have left observers at a loss for words: Alexander Mackenzie settled on the term "machines" to describe the complicated salmon-fishing technology he came upon during the final days of his trek across the continent to the Pacific in 1793.

Mackenzie passed several dam-and-trap complexes operated by the Nuxalk people on the Bella Coola River, on British Columbia's central coast. At "Friendly Village," about 50 kilometers (30 miles) above salt water, Mackenzie found a permanent or semipermanent structure of logs and gravel that constricted about two-thirds of the river and forced the current through a narrow opening in the middle. "Beneath it the machines are placed, into which the salmon fall when they attempt to leap over," Mackenzie wrote. "On either side there is a large frame of timber-work six feet above the level of the upper water, in which passages are left for the salmon leading directly into the machines which are taken up at pleasure. At the foot of the fall, dipping nets are also employed."

What resulted from these spectacularly productive salmon fisheries and this overwhelming reliance on marine resources was something that was unique in the history of human societies. Unlike other highly organized fishing cultures around the world, Northwest Coast societies were self-sufficient, in that they did not develop their fisheries in association with agricultural or mercantile societies with whom they traded their fish. On the Asian coast, the coastal Jomon and Ainu peoples lived side by side with interior cousins who engaged in forms of horticulture. The Kamchadals were fishing peoples who also tended crops and raised pigs. The maritime Chukchi were marine oriented, but the inland Chukchi were also reindeer herders, like the Sámi people of Scandinavia. On the North American side of the Pacific were cultures that were not composed of "hunter-gatherers," but they weren't agricultural societies, either — although with certain practices that at least verge on aquaculture, some coastal societies might be said to have fit somewhere in between. The point is that for every attempt to characterize the distinguishing features of Northwest Coast societies, exceptions tends to come along that call all the rules into question.

Northwest Coast societies were long believed to have been easily distinguished from their Asian counterparts by being strictly nonagricultural, without even a trace of horticulture, and by being separated from any cultures that engaged in agriculture or horticulture. But several cases of Northwest Coast horticulture confound that characterization, further illustrating the distinctiveness of Northwest Coast culture in human history.

One question that has vexed historians and anthropologists is how it came to pass, exactly, that as early as the 1850s just about every native community within sight of Mount Baker — that towering, dormant volcano in Washington State, just south of the Canada–U.S. border — was growing potatoes.

The first potatoes planted on the Northwest Coast were almost certainly the potatoes Russian traders planted in soil fertilized with seaweed at Sitka in the late 1700s. By 1814, the Pacific Fur Company had planted enough potatoes on the Columbia River, near Astoria, to harvest fifty bushels' worth. In the Strait of Georgia area, potatoes were being planted at the Hudson Bay Company post at Fort Langley by the 1830s. By 1857, potato growing was known among the Semiahmoo, Duwamish, Samish, Snoqualmie, Snohomish, Skagit, Katzie, Port Townsend, Dungeness, Port Discovery, Sooke, Songhees, Cowichan, and Nanaimo peoples, among others. The Duwamish people had 12 hectares (30 acres) under cultivation near the mouth of Lake Washington in 1855, and a chief at Saanich, on southern Vancouver Island, owned potato fields cultivated and maintained by slaves.

Various types of potatoes were harvested on the coast. There was the "no-eyes" potato cultivated by the now-extinct Snokomish people of the Boundary Bay area. There were big, round red potatoes grown by Straits Salish people on San Juan Island. There were kidney-shaped potatoes cultivated by Lummi people.

Some people roasted them and ate them with dried fish. Others liked them boiled. Still others preferred them steamed. Some preferred to sell them — in 1852, the Katzie, at what is now Pitt Meadows in suburban Vancouver, sold a substantial quantity of potatoes and cranberries to two traders, Cooper and Blankhorn, for resale into the produce markets of San Francisco.

The alleged leap from a hunter-gatherer way of life to intensive agriculture is conventionally held to be an epochal event in human social evolution, carrying with it all sorts of upheaval and disruption. But potato cultivation caused no such transformation of North Pacific coastal societies. One reason this is so might be that although potatoes quickly became popular, crop cultivation was simply no big deal. Potatoes were just another crop.

Around the time of the potato's arrival in the Strait of Georgia, the term for potato was "wapato," which applied to both *Solanum tuberosum* — the potato — and to the indigenous *Sagittaria latifolia*, commonly known as arrowhead, which grows in marshy areas and sloughs. Its leaves are like those of the calla lily, and its tuber looks and tastes a lot like the common white potato. Apart from the term "wapato," there were several ancient names for *Sagittaria latifolia*. Halkomelem-speaking peoples called it *ska'us*, and so did the northern Straits Salish. Puget Samish called it *ska'wic*. But generally, throughout the coast, whatever term was used for the potato was also the name people used for the *Sagittaria* tuber, and cultivation of *Sagittaria* occurred on a massive scale. In the autumn months of 1827, Hudson Bay Company officials who had recently arrived on the Fraser River, observed "as many as 5,000 Indians, gathered along the Lower Fraser for salmon, assembled at the Pitt River to dig 'skous,' a tuber that grew in pools and swamps, and which was considered a delicacy."

The Pitt River country is the home territory of the Katzie people, who were famous throughout the Strait of Georgia area for their *Sagittaria* crops. Some "wapato ponds" were owned by the Katzie collectively, while other ponds were owned and carefully managed by individual families. Ponds and sloughs were cleared in large tracts — some several hundred feet long — and when the *Sagittaria* was ripe, families would spend the month-long harvest season, usually in October or November, picking *Sagittaria* from canoes or by "dancing" — wading through the shallows and treading on the plants until the roots floated to the surface. It was a labor-intensive process, often requiring several hundred harvesters in each pond.

Another plant cultivated throughout the Strait of Georgia area was camas, a herbaceous perennial. *Camassia quamash* and *Camassia leichtlini* both produce big potatolike bulbs, and it was most likely the practice of camas farming that allowed the peoples of the strait to adopt the potato so enthusiastically. Unlike the potato, camas was harvested in the spring when it is in flower, and unlike *Sagittaria*, it was used the way Europeans and Asians used cereal grain; it was dried, ground into flour, and mixed with berries and other foods to make cakes or kneaded into loaves for storing. On Jarman Prairie, east of the hills above Bellingham Bay, Nuwhaha women were cultivating camas and other indigenous bulbs in small plots surrounded by high pole fences secured with cedar rope long before they incorporated potatoes into their fields. The women of Nooksack did the same thing. The women of Semiahmoo, at what is now White Rock, near the Canada–U.S. border, and the Songhees, whose territories enclosed the Victoria area, maintained "camas prairies" behind their villages.

Camas production, like the production of *Sagittaria*, was women's work, which may explain why European observers failed to appreciate the significance of plant domestication and cultivation in the economic life of coastal peoples. To be unobservant of the contribution women make to the economy of societies is a habit that may explain why the prevailing North American perspective was — and remains — that aboriginal peoples of this coast were hunter-gatherers only, albeit subsistence peoples in an especially favorable environment. But camas cultivation wasn't merely foraging. Among the Lummi,

> the women usually gather the bulbs with digging sticks, a task which involves strenuous work for many days. The diggers lay out little plots in the shallow soil where camas grow, cut the earth in small sections, lift the soil with the sticks and collect the bulbs in their baskets. They crush the soil directly afterwards and plant the seeds broken from the stems. Small sections are lifted consecutively until the whole plot is finished.

Camas thrived on the alluvial marshes at river mouths, on the small inland "prairies" around the strait, on Whidbey Island in the San Juans, and in the Garry oak savannah of southern Vancouver Island. But it was the grassy, south-facing slopes of the smaller islands in the southern Strait of Georgia that appear to have made the best growing sites. The Samish maintained a well-known camas field on a small island off the south shore of Lopez Island in the San Juans. The Semiahmoo traveled as far as Waldron Island, south of Saturna Island, to their camas grounds.

The Saanich community of Tsartlip farmed camas on a small islet just south of Sidney Island and on D'Arcy Island. One particularly productive growing site was on Mandarte Island, shared by the Saanich of Tsartlip and Patricia Bay. Several families camped on Mandarte for the camas harvest — the women digging the bulbs and tending the fields while the men went out fishing. On these smaller islands, fires were set to burn the fields after planting.

The anthropologist Wayne Suttles, whose work with the Coast Salish peoples stands as one of the greatest contributions to Northwest Coast anthropology, made note of the association between camas farming and the incipient aquaculture prevalent in the Strait of Georgia area:

> Among the Straits people, whose territory extended into the San Juan and Gulf Islands, families owned not only camas beds but clam beds as well. In both cases they took some care of their property. In camas beds they kept the ground loosened up so as to make digging easier, and one informant spoke of burning off the bed after digging. In clam beds they sometimes took out the bigger rocks; one old Samish woman supervised the digging in her horse-clam bed, not allowing anyone to leave broken shells in the sand. Such beds and patches were the property of upper-class families. Ownership was through inheritance, but I suspect that an investment of labor helped maintain it.

Far to the north, meanwhile, the Haida people, who became famous for their extensive 19th-century potato fields, also cultivated tobacco plantations, long before the arrival of Europeans. The "Haida tobacco," as it was known, was *Nicotiana quadrivalvis,* a variety of tobacco indigenous to the southwestern United States.

Throughout the North Pacific, tobacco smoking was a habit coastal societies picked up quickly from Russian, English, and American fur traders, and tobacco addiction had become rampant by the early 1800s. On the North American coast, sea otter pelts sometimes went for small amounts of tobacco, and by the mid-1800s, the maritime Chukchi people of the Gulf of Anadyr, on the Russian side of the Bering Sea, routinely paid ten red fox pelts for a 56-kilogram (120-pound) bundle of tobacco leaves.

But long before the fur trade period, the Haida and Tlingit were already cultivating crops of tobacco, and it wasn't for smoking. It was chewed with lime and used as a narcotic stimulant. Along with the Kamchadals' affection for hallucinogenic mushrooms, Haida tobacco was one of the few instances of narcotic use among North Pacific peoples. There is no doubt about the antiquity of Haida tobacco. In the Haida oral tradition, tobacco was a gift from Raven to Cloud-Woman of the Eagle clan. It was used to bribe Old-Man-Great-Blue-Heron and to bribe spectators to participate in a gambling game in the "Sound Gambling Sticks" story. Tsimshian stories contain accounts of tobacco being used to bribe a sky-being. The Tlingit explain the tobacco plant's origin as a gift to the Chilkat people from Raven, who taught people how to cultivate it and manufacture tobacco from it. The first Russian explorers found that the Tlingit were carrying on a lucrative trade in locally produced tobacco, and references to the meter-high plant show up in journals from the voyages of George Dixon in the 1780s and George Vancouver in the 1790s. As a consequence of contact with European traders, tobacco cultivation came to an end among the Haida and the Tlingit, and *Nicotiana quadrivalvis* is now believed to be extinct in the wild — the only known specimens of the species are those preserved by the Royal Botanical Gardens at Kew, in London, England, and in the herbarium of the British Museum.

But all of these instances of agriculture or horticulture or forms of aquaculture by themselves do not mean that Northwest Coast societies were "agricultural," and they are not what made Northwest Coast culture so distinctive. The heavy reliance of North Pacific peoples on marine protein was a key feature that set them apart from other peoples on the planet. In many cases, human beings were carrying a nitrogen-isotope signature in their bones that was exactly the same as that of dolphins. But even among North Pacific peoples, the Northwest Coast cultures stand apart. In her 1982 study, "Northwest Coast Traditional Salmon Fisheries: Systems of Resource Utilization," the historian Patricia Ann Berringer observed that Northwest Coast culture was wholly anomalous in the story of human civilization, so much so that social scientists should be obliged to rethink their classifications of nonindustrial societies altogether. What made Northwest Coast culture so distinctive, in Berringer's view, was that it wasn't agricultural, but at the same time, "it had a complex social structure, rigidly hierarchical with ranked social groups, a relatively dense population concentrated especially at river confluences and outlets, living in permanent winter villages from which user-groups emerged on seasonal excursions of resource exploitation."

The story of the Northwest Coast just doesn't fit with the way hunter-gatherers are supposed to evolve — in fact, there was nothing much "hunter-gatherer" about it at all. Exhibiting traits almost exclusively associated with cultures engaged in intensive agriculture, the Northwest Coast culture was unique: Nowhere else on earth was fishing so crucial to the development of such sedentary, self-sustaining, and complex societies. So, making sense of Northwest Coast cultural patterns is something that the usual anthropological and sociological terminology tends to stumble over a bit. Knut Fladmark, the archeologist whose pioneering work so effectively challenged orthodox thinking about Clovis mammoth hunters, coastal migration routes, and the antiquity of North Pacific maritime societies, gave it a try in 1975. Fladmark argued that the best way to understand the classic Northwest Coast culture pattern was to see it in its broad ecological context. By looking at the history of Northwest Coast cultures in "paleoecological" terms, Fladmark found: "The elaborate superstructure of Northwest Coast societies, exemplified in the winter village settlement pattern, provided a regulatory or homeostatic mechanism for the equalization and stabilization of energy levels within the cultural component of the ecosystem by the expenditure and redistribution of seasonal energy surpluses." Granted, that's a bit of a mouthful, but the point is that Northwest Coast cultures had managed to integrate themselves, with almost unprecedented success, into the ecosystems with which they had co-evolved. The result, in Fladmark's words, was an "overlay of flamboyance and seemingless boundless energy; massive size and incredible complexity, extravagance in art, architecture and social behavor." That's what "cultural complexity" is.

Northwest Coast culture was about the regulated harvest of whales, seals, sea lions, halibut, herring, flounder, rockfish, oolichan, sole, greenlings, tuna, shark, wolf fish, crabs, clams, mussels, skate, sturgeon, and cod. It was also about cedar, "Long Life Maker," and everything that it allowed from its manufacture. But the primary ecological relationship at the heart of Northwest Coast culture was between people and salmon, and it must be said that there was something about the pattern of aboriginal salmon fisheries management in the Northwest Coast culture area that produced sustainable fisheries, unlike the industrial fisheries that followed.

There are several important differences between the aboriginal salmon fisheries that persisted for so many centuries throughout the Northwest Coast and the industrial fisheries that emerged in the late 1800s. A key feature of the aboriginal salmon fisheries was that fishing was spread out along the salmon's migratory route, usually well within the coast's river systems, where trap-and-weir complexes were the central mode of harvesting. Despite popular belief, comparatively few salmon of any species were caught in the ocean. In fact, apart from the Straits Salish reef net fisheries, it appears unlikely that there were any fisheries directed upon sockeye salmon, in salt water, anywhere on North America's west coast.

Because of the vast cultural and spatial diversity of the Northwest Coast, which featured dozens of unique societies dependent upon site-specific resources, salmon-management regimes tended to contribute to the maintenance of the genetic and spatial diversity so necessary for the survival of salmon runs. The most productive trap-and-weir fisheries were directed upon specific runs of fish, managed and regulated according to customary laws that required adequate escapement for fisheries upriver and for spawning returns. As a result, salmon fisheries tended to be stock-specific and run-specific, and harvests tended to be confined within the sustainable limits of familiar salmon runs. Fisheries were managed according to strict rules arising from a variety of myths within the aboriginal oral tradition, in a local and decentralized way. Rights of access were clearly and rigidly defined, and the benefit of salmon fisheries accrued directly to fishery participants and to those authorities vested with fisheries management responsibilities. Perhaps most important, a simple management rule prevailed: You screw up, you starve to death.

In these ways, the main features of salmon fisheries management on the Northwest Coast were remarkably similar to the management patterns that evolved in the Japanese inshore fisheries. By the medieval period, Japan's coastal fisheries — dominated by specific villages with rights of access to specific fishing grounds — had developed into a management system based upon fishing village guilds. After American and European merchants forced Japan to open its markets in the 19th century, it set out to emulate what it found to be the best in the industrialized world. Japan's military patterned itself after the German military, Japan's schools followed the lead of the British school system, and so on. After attempting to replicate central-state and open-access fisheries management along North American lines, however, the Japanese government declared the experiment a disaster. In 1901, a modernized version of the old village-guild system was reintroduced, and local controls were further strengthened during the late 1940s.

The commercial salmon fisheries that emerged in the North Pacific in the mid-1800s exhibited an eerie, mirror-image opposite of aboriginal salmon fisheries management patterns. Fishing became increasingly concentrated at river mouths and in the ocean, in mixed-stock areas where the consequences of fishing were practically impossible to predict. Small runs comigrating with large runs were fished into extinction, diminishing biological diversity within salmon species, and focused increasing pressure on fewer and fewer salmon populations. Fisheries were managed by state agencies unfamiliar with local conditions and the varying productivity rates of different salmon runs. Open-access fisheries were the norm until well into the 20th century, but the greatest benefits of the salmon fisheries accrued to a small number of industrialists with little stake in the health of any particular salmon run. As in aboriginal fisheries, mythology played a part in industrial fisheries management, especially the myth of a superabundant ocean and the all-powerful capability of science and technology to fix the messes made by hydroelectric dams, lousy forestry practices, and overfishing. The primary rule of engagement in the business: You screw up, you open a cannery farther up the coast, you get the public to pay for hatcheries, or you reinvest your capital, once the salmon are gone, in another industry altogether.

§ FOUR §

Spectral Flotillas
and Lost Colonies

Where have I been ? Where shall I go, and what values
will I pack for the trip? What culture of knowledge allows me to know
what I know, which is often another way of knowing where I am?
And what pattern, what grid of wisdom, can I impose
on my accumulated, idiosyncratic geographies?

— *Stephen S. Hall, "I, Mercator,"* Orion

THE MARITIME HISTORY of the North Pacific is littered with apocryphal voyages and legendary armadas. It is a story of lost colonies, fabled portals through continents, disputes, and controversies.

In the North Pacific, as the Saint Lawrence Islanders, Yupiks, Chukchis, and others well know, there never really was an "Old World" and a "New World." In the North Pacific, there was no solid barrier between the two great stories of humanity's wanderings, at least not of the sort that the Atlantic Ocean presented. People were venturing eastward from Asia and ending up in North America at least 10,000 years ago, and it is not certain when that eastward movement stopped. The North Atlantic, however, remained a solid barrier to human migration until 1492. It's true that Inuit peoples with origins in Alaska had skirted the northern defiles of that barrier and settled in Greenland more than 4000 years ago, beginning a subtle eastward trickle of human movement that didn't end until the mid-1800s. It's also true that about 1000 years ago, the descendants of those first Inuit encountered Norse settlers —

Europeans from Iceland who had established a settlement in southern Greenland — and shortly afterwards, voyagers from that same Norse culture settled temporarily at what is now L'Anse Aux Meadows, on the Newfoundland coast. Down through the ages, there have been many fanciful accounts of early trans-Atlantic crossings, but it wasn't until 1492 that Christopher Columbus finally and completely breached the barrier for good, ushering in a gruesome and spectacular chapter of the human story, characterized by bloodshed, disease, conquest, and empire. Whatever might be made of the Vinland sagas or the voyages of Brendan the Navigator, the year 1492 clearly and certainly ended thousands of years of Atlantic separation between the peoples of the so-called Old and New Worlds.

Attempting to establish such historical certainties in the North Pacific leads the voyager into the strangest waters, infested by dispute, controversy, vested political and economic interest, and fable. Even the leaders of the great scientific expeditions of the 18th century, at the vanguard of the Age of Enlightenment, were merely chasing ghosts that haunted European kings. Just as Livingstone Stone used science in his attempts to unlock the mythological storehouse of wealth Providence had put away in salmon, the preeminent object of scientific inquiry, at its dawn in the North Pacific, was about mythology. That is how "science" arrived in the North Pacific. It came in search of the fabled Northwest Passage. It was busy with the work of folklore and myth.

But long before the Age of Exploration, voyage myths were being told and retold down through the generations, on both sides of the Pacific. In the old stories, sometimes the mariners return, and sometimes they don't.

One who returned was Swaneset. In the stories Peter Pierre of Katzie told to the anthropologist Diamond Jenness, Swaneset was one of the first human beings placed on earth by the Creator. Swaneset was said to have made a voyage by canoe down the Fraser River, out into the ocean, and on to the lands of the salmon people, where each day lasted a year. Swaneset's voyage is said to have occurred in the days before people and animals were made distinct, so the men that accompanied him on his journey were also various animals.

At the first two villages Swaneset visited, he won piles of blankets in gambling games, but at the third village he was challenged to a diving contest by people who would later become diving birds, and Swaneset was obliged to compete with western grebes, cormorants, and loons. One of Swaneset's crew, a man who would later be changed to a mink, won the diving contest. The fourth village Swaneset visited was the home of the people who would become chum salmon. Their blankets bore red and black stripes, and their houses were similarly painted, bearing the marks that spawning chum salmon would later bear on their spawning migrations up the Fraser River. At the next village, the men were all hunchbacked, but the women were pretty, and the people took to their canoes only every second day; these people became pink salmon, which, unlike other salmon species, return to the Fraser River only every other year.

Swaneset then came to a beautiful, haze-shrouded coastline where girls were playing shuttlecock and boys were shooting arrows through rolling hoops. At this village Swaneset settled in, and he married the chief's daughter, giving her family the blankets he had won at the first two villages as marriage presents. During his stay, Swaneset learned the first salmon ceremony, but he also learned something about his bride's people that accounted for their peculiar manners relating to fish bones.

Swaneset was instructed that it was the custom of the people to neatly set aside the bones of the fish they ate at mealtimes. After each meal, Swaneset watched his mother-in-law carefully remove the bones from the house to place them gently in the sea. Every morning, the old woman came up from the beach, cradling a fish in her arms as though it were a baby. Every evening, when she returned to the house after carrying the bones down to the sea, she was accompanied by a dancing boy. One day, Swaneset decided to break the rules, to see what would happen. Instead of setting the fish bones carefully aside during his meal, he kept a bone in his mouth. That evening, the boy that came back from the beach with Swaneset's mother-in-law was crippled. When Swaneset's father-in-law restored the hidden bone, the boy became whole again. It was after this incident that Swaneset's bride confided that she and her people were really sockeye salmon and that every year, at a certain season, they left their village to travel in the sea.

Swaneset eventually returned to Katzie with his bride, passing the villages of the pink salmon and chum salmon on the way. The chum salmon followed right away, but the pink salmon waited a day. In this way, the salmon people learned the way to Swaneset's village, and after Swaneset's bride bore him a son, the sockeye, pink, and chum salmon began their annual migrations to the Fraser, and the first salmon ceremony, along with its ritual return of the salmon-boy's bones to the water, became a central part of the cultures of North America's west coast.

One mariner who did not return from his high-seas sojourn was Hsu Fu. At least, not the second time.

Ninety years before the birth of Christ, the Chinese historian Ssuma Chhien wrote that a mariner named Hsu Fu had been dispatched by the Chinese emperor, Chhin Shih Huang Ti, more than a century earlier, to travel across the Pacific. Like Swaneset before him, Hsu Fu encountered people endowed with magical powers. The emperor sent him to a place known as the Land of the Immortals to find out what medicines the people there used to achieve eternal youth. Hsu Fu returned with fantastic stories about his travels, but he reported that the wizard who ruled the Land of the Immortals refused to divulge his secrets about longevity. Hsu Fu managed to persuade the emperor to provide him with a retinue of young men and women, including China's best tradesmen, and a fleet of ships. Hsu Fu said he would return to the Land of the Immortals, confident that one day he would come home with the magic potions the emperor wanted. Off Hsu Fu went. He was never seen again.

About 1000 years before Columbus, another fabled mariner appears in the North Pacific. Like Hsu Fu before him, Huishen reportedly sailed from China and returned with fabulous stories about his journey. In the *History of the Liang Dynasty*, written by Yao Silian in the 6th century, Huishen, a Buddhist monk, is reported to have arrived in the city of Jingzhou, in China's Hubei Province. He claimed that he had sailed across the Pacific to the Land of Fusang, which he named after a tree that grew there. The fusang tree was said to bear a red, pear-shaped fruit, and the people of the country reportedly built their houses from fusang timbers, wore clothes made from the tree's bark, and inscribed records on a sort of paper taken from the tree. Various Chinese scholars have asserted that the story of Huishen is an account of something that actually happened. Some scholars say Huishen was actually describing Japan, but others have been convinced that the Land of Fusang was Mexico.

Huishen, who is said to have arrived in the Land of Fusang in the year 458, returning to China after forty years abroad, appears to have been more than merely a character of fiction. His name appears in a volume of *The First Collection of Biographies of Famous Monks,* where he is identified as 5th-century monk of some renown. But that doesn't mean he sailed to Mexico, and in 1983, Luo Rongqu, a professor of Latin American history at Beijing University, caused a bit of a stir by dismissing some of his colleagues' enthusiasms for Huishen's purported travels to North America. This was no small matter, since some Chinese historians had won favor in Chinese government circles by postulating a Chinese discovery of North America. One of the historians Luo challenged was Deng Tuo, a favorite in the People's Republic, whose *Evening Talks in the Yan Mountains* contained the hypothesis that Huishen's fusang tree was the cactuslike "century plant" that was an important source of food, drink, and clothing in Aztec Mexico. Luo asserted that if Huishen existed at all, he wasn't even Chinese, but most likely a Buddhist convert from Kashmir, and that the story about his voyage simply strained credibility a bit too far. Luo's findings, published in the state-owned *China Reconstructs* magazine in 1983, prompted suggestions that his behavior was something less than patriotic. One unnamed Chinese academic at the time told the *Los Angeles Times:* "Why couldn't a Chinese have discovered America? Why does it have to be a European? This does not prove that we were not there first."

What prompted Luo to challenge the popular story about Huishen was an annoyance with what he called "wild speculation" based on convenient interpretations of legend and the archeological record. But Luo didn't dismiss the idea that Asians had traveled by sea to North America. The idea has been around for a long time, and not just in China and Japan.

It was a European, the French sinologist Joseph de Guines, who first popularized the Huishen story in his 1761 work, *Chinese Voyages to the American Coast.* Among Europeans and North Americans, for every bit of anomalous flotsam that has ever washed up on some lonely Pacific beach, there is a dusty old theory to explain it that involves, in its orbit, a voyage across the sea. The reasons for this are complicated.

From the moment Europeans reached the North Pacific and looked out upon its far horizons, the ocean was viewed according to European ideas about how to find order in the universe, and according to a presumed devine edict to remake the world in their own image and likeness. Imposing a European sense order on the Pacific came naturally to North Americans, even in developing the first salmon-fishing regulations on the Fraser River, which were word-for-word replications of fishing regulations on east coast rivers, which themselves had borrowed heavily from fishing regulations on English Rivers. The construction of the idea of the "Indian" was central to the work of imposing order upon the world Europeans encountered in North America. Despite all those things that made Northwest Coast peoples so different from the hunter-gatherers of the continent's hinterland, North Americans tended to view all indigenous North Americans, from the beginning, as "Indians," with everything that such an ideological construction implies. But the distinctiveness of Northwest Coast cultures was impossible to ignore, particularly for academics, and the brightest anthropologists of the late 19th century and early 20th century went to great lengths, formulating the most embarassing ideas about relatively recent Asiatic influences, in order to account for that distinctiveness. The same sorts of ideas had been used for centuries to explain the classic civilizations of Mexico and Peru. In 1542, at a time when Europeans were engaged in much fevered speculation about the ancestors of the people of the New World (they weren't supposed to be there because the Bible didn't account for them), a certain Hugo Grotius wrote a lengthy dissertation arguing that the Inca were relatively recent emigrants from China: "This is confirmed by the remains of Chinese ships, which, according to the reports of the Spaniards, have been discovered on the shores of the Pacific sea."

Complicating matters further was the persistent disbelief among many mainstream scholars, well into the 20th century, that mere "Indians" could have been responsible for the great civilizations of the Valley of Mexico, the Yucatán Peninsula, the Mississippi Basin, the

Anasazi country of New Mexico, and so on. There was the exasperation many anthropologists encountered, throughout the 1900s, in their attempts to make Northwest Coast cultures "fit" within conventional theories about Paleo-Indians, Macro-Indians, and other terms used to describe the descendants of the subcontinent of Beringia.

From the earliest times, the matter of "who got here first" also had important economic and political implications for European powers. If the Russians were here first, Spain's claims of sovereignty held no standing in international law. If the Spaniards stuck a cross into the ground, said a prayer, and uttered the name of the Spanish king, the land was considered Spain's. If the English could show that they had hoisted the Union Jack in the same remote corner of the coast, before the Spanish, then that would trump a Spanish claim.

Then there is the matter of Asian shipwrecks on North America's west coast. There has been no great shortage of Asian "stuff" in west coast archeological sites and no dearth of apparently Asian references in the ethnographic record. Speculation about Asian voyages to North America persists, as does speculation about early Asian settlement on North America's Pacific coast and Asiatic influence in New World cultures. Such speculation tends to be extremely contentious. For at least a century, it has been a favorite pastime of kooky avocational historians, and even the most sober hypotheses tend to become embroiled in debates among archeologists and anthropologists about "cultural diffusion" versus "independent invention."

In the most extreme case, diffusionists will argue that a single spark was the source of all civilization, which eventually brought light throughout the planet, uniting Chinese, Egyptians, Toltecs, Romans, Assyrians, and Aztecs. Independent inventionists, in contrast, are known to be bitterly contemptuous of any theory that proposes a common antecedent among cultural traits shared by peoples significantly separated from each other in space and time. In discussions between these two camps, any mention of Thor Hyerdahl — famous for his romantic notions about great sea voyages, and more famous for his attempts to reconstruct those voyages in rickety watercraft with names like *Ra* and *Kon-Tiki* — is enough to cause otherwise reasonable people to come near to blows.

For these reasons, the antiquity of high-seas Pacific voyages has always been disputatious. The proposed evidence for Asian influence in North American cultures is dubious at best. But such speculation persisted through the 20th century, and not without cause.

In 1979, the trawler *Beaufort Sea*, based in Ucluelet, on Vancouver Island's west coast, was bottom-dragging about 15 sea miles off the mouth of Juan de Fuca Strait when something became tangled in the vessel's net on the ocean floor, at a depth of about 90 fathoms. Skipper Mike Tyne ordered the net hauled back up, and in it were several shards of wood and a large urn, which was later identified as Asian and probably about 300 years old. It wasn't the first time nets had become entangled on the ocean floor in the area — the location was marked on the charts as a shipwreck, and it came to be known in Vancouver Island's fishing ports as the Asian Pot Wreck. The Underwater Archeological Society of B.C. tried to raise enough funds to examine the wreck, to no avail. The society also issued public appeals for information about other such sites, but the only response was from a diver who showed up with pieces of another 300-year-old Chinese urn. The diver refused to identify himself or the location of the wreck where he found the urn, apparently afraid that the government would interfere with his clandestine archeological activity.

These were not the first objects of apparently Asian origin to turn up on the west coast. In 1918, an object later determined to be a Korean burial urn was found on a beach at Pavlof Harbor in southeast Alaska. In 1956, on Saturna Island, in British Columbia's Gulf Islands, a young boy discovered a piece of earthenware in the shape of a human head, with a tuft of human hair still in place but the jaw missing. Provincial archeologist Don Abbot theorized that the artifact was Asian and may have been 2000 years old. In the spring of 1960, several large urns started showing up on Washington beaches. All were empty but one, which contained a "syrupy" liquid that may have once been wine, and the prevailing theory at the time was that the urns had long been trapped in the hull of a sunken ship and were released all at once as the ship's timbers suddenly gave way in a storm. The following year, an object that B.C. Provincial Museum director Clifford Carl believed was a Korean burial urn was discovered by a fisherman on a beach near Cape Cook on Vancouver Island's west coast.

Then there are the coins. An October 25, 1882, edition of the *Victoria Colonist* reports the discovery of "30 brass coins . . . at a depth of several feet" in the vicinity of Cassiar in northern British Columbia. The coins were clearly Asian, and the find set off quite a stir. Various authorities were consulted, each of which concluded that the coins were at least 1500 years old. Eight years later, not far from Cassiar, local native people were reported to have found several bronze ceremonial dishes with apparently Buddhist inscriptions on them at the base of a tree, as well as a bronze medallion. In 1952, archeologist Charles Borden came upon an 800-year-old Sung dynasty coin at the Chinlac village site in British Columbia's central interior. A Nisga'a dance apron, which ended up in a collection of the B.C. Provincial Museum's ethnology division, is decorated with a fringe of rawhide strips decorated with twenty-six Chinese coins from the K'ang Hsi period (1662–1722). And on it goes.

But all these things, by themselves, don't necessarily mean anything much. They certainly don't prove that Asian mariners preceded the Russian explorations of the North Pacific in the mid-1700s. Neither do they prove that Asians were present on North America's west coast before the period of English and Spanish exploration in the late 1700s. By the 1790s, Europeans were buying sea otter furs along North America's Pacific coast, for sale directly to Chinese buyers at various Chinese coastal ports, and Chinese coins were among the trinkets that exchanged hands in the early days of the maritime fur trade. Even firm evidence of Asian artifacts predating the maritime fur trade period, showing up at shipwreck sites on the coast, would not conclusively prove that the wrecks themselves predated the arrival of Europeans on the coast.

Still, it is plausible that Asians mariners crossed the Pacific before the period of European exploration — at least by mistake. From the early 1600s to the early 1800s, Japanese mariners were bound by the policy of *sakoku,* an isolationist edict that prohibited deliberate voyages to foreign shores. But accidents happened. Japanese ships were dismasted and mariners found themselves adrift. Chinese coastal fishermen were also highly skilled mariners. The first European explorers found coastal peoples already in possession of iron, and while some iron was likely traded south from Russian sources, an Asian presence on the west coast, from the earliest days of the maritime fur trade, is undeniable.

In 1782, Russian fur traders found the survivors of wrecked Japanese junk that had foundered on the rocks in the Aleutian Islands. In 1805, another Japanese junk came to grief near Sitka, and the survivors were returned to Japan on a Russian ship the following year. In 1813, about 250 nautical miles off the mouth of Juan de Fuca Strait, the American brigantine *Forrester* came upon a dismasted Japanese junk that had been floating aimlessly at sea for eighteen months. All but three of the thirty-five crew members had starved to death by the time the *Forrester* found the ship. Three years later, the *Forrester* came upon another Japanese junk, off Santa Barbara, California. It was another Japanese coastal trader, and it had been dismasted in a storm seventeen months earlier during a short voyage from Osaka to Tokyo. There had been seventeen on board, but, as on the Japanese vessel the *Forrester* had encountered, only three crew members had survived.

In 1834, stories about an unusual trio of captives — shipwreck survivors who were not white people — began making the rounds of Hudson's Bay Company forts on the Northwest Coast. The captives were said to be with the Makah people at the mouth of Juan de Fuca Strait. At Nisqually House, in Puget Sound, stories about the captives were dismissed, as was a report of a shipwreck said to have occurred a few hours' walk south of Cape Flattery. At Fort Vancouver, on the Columbia River, factor John McLoughlin decided to send William McNeil in the company ship, the *Llama,* to investigate the reports. When McNeil arrived at the Makah village at Cape Flattery on June 1, 1834, he was introduced to three Japanese mariners, two men and a boy. Although they were being treated "kindly" by the Makah, they were being held as slaves after having been rescued in January of that year when the ship carrying them was washed up on a beach south of the village. The three mariners were released to McNeil, who brought them back to Fort Vancouver.

The mariners' story was a grim one. In November 1832, their 200-ton ship had set sail from a Japanese coastal port in the prefecture of Owori, bound for Tokyo, 150 sea miles to the north, carrying mainly rice and porcelain as a tribute to the emperor. The ship encountered rough seas, and after it lost its rudder and its mainmast, the crew drifted aimlessly in the currents of the North Pacific for fourteen months, with one crewman after another starving to death until eleven men had perished. After the ship was wrecked south of Cape Flattery, the Makah salvaged its remains and the three sailors were held as slaves for five months, until Captain McNeil's arrival. The trio was eventually returned to Japan.

How often this sort of thing happened has been the subject of much conjecture. Charles Walcott Brooks, a member of the California Academy of Sciences, assembled files on sixty such incidents that occurred while he served as the Japanese government's official representative at the Port of San Francisco between 1858 and 1875. Walcott also collected accounts of dozens of similar reports for the period before 1858. After studying the history of Japanese maritime technology, Walcott concluded that "many thousand" Japanese fishing boats and coastal trading vessels could well have become disabled and drifted across the Pacific in the centuries before European exploration. More than a century after Brooks, George Quimby of the University of Washington was equally fascinated with the subject but came to much more conservative conclusions. Quimby reckoned that at least 180 Asian vessels might have washed up on North America's west coast in the 1000 years prior to European exploration. "Bad storms with high winds and heavy seas could easily disable coastal merchant and fishing vessels. Once a junk was helplessly adrift without masts, and usually without rudder, the Kuro Siwo [Japanese] Current, the North Pacific Current, and prevailing westerly winds destined the vessel for a trans-Pacific voyage," he concluded. Quimby also reckoned that Asian wrecks were the source of the iron chisels, blades, and spear points found among coastal peoples by the first Europeans in the 18th century.

Apart from the physical evidence that is at least suggested by bits of iron, one would think that the routine landfall of so many unfortunate Asian seafarers on the wrong side of the Pacific, as Brooks and Quimby postulated, would have left more of a mark.

On the Northwest Coast, the most persuasive argument for physical evidence of actual Asian settlement is a peculiar society of potters that appears quite suddenly near the southern Washington coast, around AD 1400, and then disappears just as suddenly, about 300 years later. Along the shores of Lake River, in a narrow valley between Vancouver Lake and the Columbia River, archeologists have unearthed hundreds of ceramic artifacts, including figurines, pipes, pendants, small sculptured heads, and decorated bowls. Some of these ceramics have been found in what appear to be the remains of kilns, and a noticeable absence of surface burning on the objects distinguishes them from the ceramics technology used in the U.S. Southwest. Alison Stenger of the U.S. Institute for Archeological Studies, after a lengthy comparative analysis of the Lake River ceramics, found they most closely resembled ceramics produced in Japan, on Alaska's Bering Sea coast, on the Russian Pacific coast, and in Korea. The ceramics appear to have been produced locally, and the archeology of the Lake River area shows no evidence that ceramics technology evolved over time. The potters seem to simply arrive, and after a few generations, they're just not there anymore.

In the oral traditions of coastal peoples, there are a variety of stories that hint at the possibility of "precontact" Asian voyagers. On Vancouver Island's west coast, there were stories of mariners in ships preceding white people who were said to eat "maggots," which has led to speculation about rice-eating sailors. And at the mouth of the Columbia River, a story persisted well into this century that may be an account of an Asian shipwreck. In that story, the ship was carrying a bride who never arrived at her wedding.

"Asiatic influence" in New World cultures has been postulated for societies as far afield as Ecuador and Peru in ways that stretch credibility, but there is at least one hypothesis, tested by scientific methodology in a variety of disciplines, in which credibility isn't stretched at least completely to the breaking point. That hypothesis involves the Zuni people of New Mexico.

The Zuni have always presented an enigma to academics, and Nancy Yaw Davis, an American anthropologist, argues that upheavals in the Zuni culture that occurred in the 13th century may well have resulted from the arrival of Japanese pioneers, and not just shipwrecked seafarers who, for some reason, headed deep into the North American interior. According to Davis, they may have been Buddhists who deliberately left Japan in search of the "middle of the world." What separates Davis's hypothesis from various pop anthropology theories about Asian voyages to North America is her reliance on solid academic studies in history, ethnology, and biology. And the Zuni themselves, whose origin mythology includes a detailed story about a terrifying ocean voyage, seem to have an open mind about the theory Davis presents.

Yaw's hypothesis begins with events in 13th-century Japan, when Asian shipbuilding technology and navigational expertise had flowered, and the Japanese archipelago convulsed with military, religious, and political upheavals. In 1274, Kublai Khan sent 450 ships and 30,000 warriors against Japan. The invasion was repelled, but the following year, the Chinese emperor mobilized the Korean military against Japan with 15,000 warriors in more than 900 ships. In 1281, Kublai Khan dispatched a navy against Japan again, and while all this was happening, Japanese Buddhism became embroiled in schism and controversy. A prominent feature of the religious upheaval was a resurgence of "Pure Land" Buddhism, which, among other things, was characterized by charismatic leaders and an obsession with finding the center of the world. Monks were continually heading off on pilgrimages into the mountains, sects were engaging in ambitious journeys to find the earth's mythical center, and the religious controversies that ensued sometimes meant that sects were banished, en masse, from Japanese cities. Davis argues that it is quite likely that during all this hubbub, with thousands of Chinese and Japanese mariners floating around the western Pacific, some could easily have ended up on North America's west coast with the middle of the world on their minds.

While these events were unfolding in Japan, something tumultuous was beginning to change the course of the Zuni pueblo culture. The archeological record suggests the arrival of small-statured people and an apparent mixture of two distinct populations that set off a period of dramatic cultural transition. Suddenly, in the 13th century, glazed pottery begins to show up in Zuni villages, not unlike the ceramics found in

Japan during that period. The Zuni oral tradition explains these events in ways that involve a bifurcated origin myth, with one tradition based in a typically local origin and the other involving a voyage across "the ocean of the sunset world" by mariners searching for the middle of the world.

It's all pretty speculative, but at least Davis's theory, with all the parallels she draws between Zuni and Japanese cultural traits, presents an intriguing explanation for a number of puzzling anomalies about the Zuni. These anomalies include distinct blood-type characteristics, a distinct language that doesn't clearly fit into any other broad language family, and a religious tradition that stands in stark contrast to other aboriginal belief systems.

But of all the theories about pre-Columbian Asian seafaring that rely on analysis of the aboriginal oral tradition, the most elaborate, and without doubt the most entertaining, are the theories of Ethel G. Stewart. As a graduate student at Queen's University in Ontario in the 1950s, Stewart became convinced that she had uncovered definite evidence of Asiatic influence in North American aboriginal cultures. Her conviction was firmly established in her study of the Dene people of Fort Hope in the Northwest Territories. Stewart's initial revelation led her to a lifetime's worth of research. Although her theories found no academic acceptance, she did cause the occasional sensation in the popular press, and she capped her career with an opus, published in 1991, titled *The Dene and Na-Dene Indian Migration, 1233 A.D.: Escape from Genghis Khan to America.*

Whatever might be said of Stewart's ideas, the 566-page tome is impossible to put down.

Stewart's ideas are based upon her interpretation of an epic narrative in the Dene oral tradition that in many ways is similar to the story of Swaneset's voyage. The Dene story, first recorded by the Oblate father Emile Pettitot in the 19th century, follows the travels of a culture hero, known in Pettitot's version as the sailor, who travels down a great river. Like the Swaneset story, characters in the Dene epic have both animal and human characteristics and carry animal names, such as Crow, Mouse, and Otter. From this story, and a generously liberal interpretation of various linguistic features among the Dene and other Athapascan peoples, Stewart constructs a complex and wide-ranging epic of her own. The story begins with Genghis Khan's rampages across Central Asia.

As Stewart sees it, the Dene people of the Northwest Territories are the descendants of a group of refugees from the Mongol siege of the northern Chinese kingdom of Hsi-Hsia in 1207. From a Gwi'chin flood story, in which all but one man is drowned because of Crow's vengeful nature, Stewart discerns remnants of the Hsi-Hsia refugees' memory of their flight to the city of Chung Hsing. In Stewart's view, Crow is really Genghis Khan, who also shows up in Dene stories as Big Mosquito and Big Porcupine.

Eventually, the Hsi-Hsia refugees make their way to the Chinese port city of Liao-tung. From there, Stewart tracks them on a voyage by ship, skirting the Sea of Japan, to an Amur River fur-trading port, just east of Sakhalin Island, in what was then the Jurchen Empire. From this port, a great voyage across the Pacific is mounted, perhaps one of several, and that's how the Dene ended up, Stewart argues, in the Northwest Territories.

Stewart's theories also account for the Tlingits of southeast Alaska, who "came from the region north of the Gobi desert" around the same time. The Kaigani Haida and the Chilkat Tlingit descended from Tatars and were related to the Uighurs of the Lake Baikal area, Stewart writes. Capilano Canyon may have got its name from the Nicola Athapascans of the B.C. southern interior, whose ancestors "preyed upon the caravans of the Southern Silk Road," where the Carrier Indians of the B.C. northern interior once worked "in the transport business" and spoke an Italo-Celtic language, Stewart concludes. The Yurok people of Northern California, meanwhile, "were a Turkish tribe of Central Asia, some of whom found their way westward with the Ottomans and ended up across the Bosporous in Europe."

Although all this would have made the basis for a fabulous work of speculative fiction, Stewart's basic ideas, to be fair, are not so radically different from "Asiatic origin" theories proposed by some early eminent anthropologists and experts on Northwest Coast culture. Marius Barbeau himself once suggested that the ancestors of certain Tsimshian clans may have been refugees from Genghis Khan's depredations. Charles Hill-Tout, one of British Columbia's most prolific early ethnographers and an accomplished linguist (when he wasn't conducting seances or writing a column for the daily *Province* newspaper in Vancouver), held several theories about the Asiatic origins of B.C. coastal peoples. Hill-Tout found similarities between the Squamish and the Hawaiian languages and argued for an "intercourse or relationship of some kind between the Kwakiutl-Nootka and Salish stocks and the Malay-Polynesians, between the Haida-Tlingit and the Japo-Corean, and between the Dene, or Athapascan, and the Chinese and cognate races." Hill-Tout would likely have been heartened to hear of Stewart's ideas, at least from the standpoint of the linguistic evidence, which Hill-Tout believed was in support of a Chinese origin for the Dene. "Of the Dene tongue," Hill-Tout wrote, "it is no exaggeration to say that 50 per cent of its radicals are pure archaic Chinese."

In the 1890s, the Royal Society of Canada was happy to publish Hill-Tout's theories, along with a treatise by the language scholar John Campbell, who claimed that his studies were "sufficient to make it morally certain" that the Haida people of the Queen Charlotte Islands were the descendants of Melanesian mariners who had crossed the Pacific only a few centuries earlier. Campbell proposed that sometime between the 13th century and the 16th century, a band of Melanesian rebels had been driven into the sea by "Hindoos" that had colonized the Malay archipelago. The rebels, Campbell wrote, "offered their choice between death and expatriation, and, spurned from every intermediate landing-place, at last found refuge on the uninhabited islands of the far east."

From 13th-century monks fleeing war-ravaged Japan and refugees from China fleeing Genghis Khan around the same time to Melanesian refugees sailing across the Pacific as recently as the 16th century, there isn't that much of a lull in the North Pacific's spectral regatta before more mariners start showing up. These sailors were also originally refugees, fleeing a tyrant every bit as nasty as Genghis Khan, and the legend that built up around them influenced events around the top of the North Pacific until the early 1800s. Their story begins with Ivan the Terrible and his siege of Novgorod in 1571.

It is certain that Russians had reached the Pacific, at the shores of the Sea of Okhotsk, by the mid-1600s. How they got there is a story that parallels the evolution of the North American fur trade. After the fur-bearing regions of the European coast had become exhausted by the 16th century, French and English capitalists invested in expansions into the North American continent from the Atlantic seaboard. Russian entrepreneurs, meanwhile, headed east.

During the medieval period, furs were a significant source of trade wealth throughout Europe. By the 14th century, London merchants were importing 300,000 pelts a year from various Atlantic sources, not the least of which were Ireland and Scotland. Fur-trade companies based in Novgorod, Moscow, and Kiev, meanwhile, relied upon extensive trade networks that extended far to the north and to the east. Before the end of the 15th century, Novgorod was exporting half a million squirrel pelts annually, obtained from trappers as distant as the Ural Mountains, 1600 kilometers (1000 miles) away. By the 1600s, more than a third of the income of the Russian state came from the fur trade. Down through the years, as fur-bearer populations became exhausted, Russian trappers began an eastward movement across Siberia, in tandem with the eastward and northeastward expansion of the Russian empire. Many of these early traders were descendants of the merchants who fled the city of Novgorod when it was besieged by Muscovite forces loyal to Ivan, Russia's first tsar. Down through the years, the Novgorodians pushed north along the Lena River to the Arctic, and then spread eastward, by sea, to the mouth of the Yana, the Indigirka, and the Kolyma Rivers.

As early as the 1650s, the Russian appetite for stories about voyages across the Eastern Sea was whetted by rumors in Moscow about a group of Russian mariners that sailed from the mouth of the Lena River on the Arctic coast and were reportedly swept off course, across the Pacific, in 1648. Russians were certainly established permanently on the Pacific that year — the Russian explorer Ivan Moskitin had reached the Sea of Okhotsk in 1639, and the establishment of a fur-trade post at Okhotsk in 1648 marks the establishment of the first European settlement in the North Pacific. But the rumors about a Russian Pacific crossing had nothing to do with the wretched little outpost at Okhotsk. The rumors had their basis in what was almost certainly a fact, but by the 1700s, whatever facts were involved in the story had become swept up in the maelstrom of a legend that proved as enduring as the myth of the Northwest Passage and its fabled portal on North America's Pacific coast.

In the chartrooms and libraries of all the world's great powers, most of the North Pacific remained a big blank spot, from Kamchatka all the way around to the mouth of the Columbia River, until well into the 18th century. By the mid-1700s, the Spanish had reached only as far as Northern California, and the Russians were just beginning their first official efforts at cartography. For a time, Portuguese mariners were in the thrall of a legendary island known as Rica de Oro y de Plata (Land Rich in Gold and Silver) that was said to exist in the North Pacific somewhere between North America and Japan. After some halfhearted 16th-century attempts at locating it, the Portuguese seem to have forgotten about Rica de Oro y de Plata. The Dutch version of the myth was Kompagnieland, and the Russian version of it was Gamaland. The myth that drew British, Spanish, and French ships to the North Pacific was the Northwest Passage, but the Russians displayed little interest in that particular folly, preferring instead to become obsessed by a myth of their own that had nothing to do with the Northwest Passage or Gamaland/ Kompagnieland. It was a lost colony of Novgorodians that tormented Russian explorers, and like the Northwest Passage myth, the Russian lost colony legend held serious economic and political implications. If it were true, Russia's claims against other imperial powers in the North Pacific would be strengthened immeasurably.

In 1725, the tsar Peter the Great, anxious to learn whether his reign extended as far as the New World, dispatched an expedition to the Pacific under the command of Vitus Bering, a Danish officer in the Russian navy. The expedition was under orders to build one or two decked vessels on the Pacific coast and sail to the north to determine where the west coast of North America began. In 1728, Bering sailed from Kamchatka on the *Gavril*, and although he made it through the strait that later bore his name, he could not claim to have seen the North American coast. Technically, his exploration was a failure. But during that first expedition, one of Bering's lieutenants, Captain Martin Spanberg, reported rumors circulating among the people of Kamchatka about a group of Russians who were said to have established a settlement on the far side of the Pacific during the previous century. In these local traditions, the descendants of the Russians were alleged to be thriving, somewhere across the sea.

The second Kamchatka expedition was a much bigger deal. Empress Anna, Peter's successor, provided Bering with several thousand soldiers and servants, along with a staff of academics, to accomplish a series of monumental tasks set out by the Russian Academy of Sciences and the Russian admiralty. The project, which began in 1731, was intended to introduce agriculture to Kamchatka, build shipyards, and establish schools, foundries, and mines. Bering was also told to build ships on the coast and to chart the entire coast of the North Pacific, from Japan to California.

One focus of the second Kamchatka expedition was to determine whether a sea route to the Pacific was possible from Russia's Arctic ports. While looking into that question, expedition officials came upon three detailed reports that appeared to demonstrate a Russian presence on the North American coast by the mid-1600s.

Scouring the archives of the offices of the governor of Yakutsk in 1737, G. F. Muller, the leader of one of the expedition's Siberian detachments, came upon an account of the 1648 voyage by Simon Dezhnev and a party of fur traders. Dezhnev was reported to have sailed from the mouth of the Kolyma River, on the East Siberian Sea, around "Chukotskiy Nos," the old Russian term for the Chukchi Peninsula, through Bering Strait, and down to Kamchatka. There were seven small sailing vessels in the Dezhnev party, but only three of them arrived in Kamchatka. The second voyage described in the Yakutsk archives was that of the trader Taras Stadukhin, who was said to have successfully retraced Dezhnev's route from the Kolyma River to Kamchatka in the late 1660s. During his journey, Stadukhin noted that local people told stories of bearded men who lived on an island to the east of Russia's Bering Sea coast "who wear long clothes and call the Russians brothers."

Expedition leaders also noted that a third voyage around Chukotskiy

Nos appeared to have been undertaken by the Russian trader Peter Tatarinov in 1710. Like Stadukhin before him, Tatarinov learned from Chukchi villagers about Russians who lived across the sea to the east. In the stories Tatarinov was told, several vessels set sail for Kamchatka from the Kolyma River in the 1670s, but only a few arrived at their destination. The rest were said to have ended up in the "Great Land" to the east, where they settled in with the local people, married, and raised families. But this story is so similar to the story about Dezhnev's fleet that it was regarded as an account of the same event.

In any case, Muller's discovery of records that appeared to confirm the presence of a lost colony of Russians in North America gave everybody a bit of a start.

For one thing, the travels of Dezhnev, Stadukhin, and Tatarinov appeared to demonstrate that decades before Bering's first Kamchatka expedition, local Russian mariners were already well aware that Asia and North America were separated by water — which was precisely what Bering had been assigned to discover. It was a bit like having Alexander Mackenzie arrive on the Pacific coast in 1793, believing himself to be the first white man to cross North America, only to find parties of Englishmen sitting down to tea on the beach.

For another thing, the Yakutsk archives lent credence to a story that if shown to be true could bolster Russia's imperial status in the courts of Europe.

Muller was reasonably skeptical about whether the Yakutsk archives contained any "proof" that Russian mariners had reached the North American coast. He was convinced that the early voyages around the Chukchi Cape had taken place, but he noted that some of the references to bearded men in robes who lived on islands to the east may well have referred to the Ainu people of the Kurile Islands, that archipelago that sweeps between Hokkaido and Kamchatka. But Muller pointed out that Chukchi people possessed wooden cups, similar in design to Russian cups, that they said they had obtained in trade from the east, and that these cups originated from the same bearded men. Muller concluded that the existence of these people was quite likely and that they were the descendants of Russian mariners who had settled in North America after their ships became separated from Dezhnev's fleet.

There had also been at least one serious attempt to get to the bottom of the lost-colony rumors. In 1728, thirty-two Russians left the Gulf of Anadyr by boat, hoping to reach the other side. Their vessel came to grief on the Chukchi coast, and the surviving Russians walked back to Anadyrsk. For the following two winters, Afanasii Mel'nikov, one of the unsuccessful Anadyr mariners, tried to persuade Chukchi people to take him across the frozen Bering Strait on their sleds, but the Chukchi refused, apparently because they enjoyed their monopoly in trade relations with Alaskan native people and didn't want Russians cutting in on the action.

It wasn't until 1741 that the history of seafaring in the North Pacific allows a definite, unquestionable high-seas crossing from one side of the ocean to the other. In June of that year, Bering, at the command of the *Saint Peter*, left Avancha Bay, south of Petropavlovsk, and headed southeast. Bering and his crew were accompanied by Alexei Chirikov and his crew aboard the *Saint Paul*. Only two weeks into the voyage, after reaching a mid-Pacific latitude of 46 degrees, the two ships became separated from one another. On July 15, Chirikov sighted land, at the Alexander Archipelago, at roughly 55 degrees. The next day, about 500 nautical miles to the northwest, the naturalist Georg Steller, aboard the *Saint Peter*, sighted Mount Saint Elias, and two days later Bering made landfall at Kayak Island, just off the Alaska coast.

For all its accomplishments, the second Kamchatka expedition fell far short of its initial cartographic objectives, and it had its tragedies.

On July 18, 1741, at the northern edge of the Alexander Archipelago, Chirikov sent several crewmen ashore to conduct a reconnaissance and make contact with the local people. Navigator Avram Dementev and ten heavily armed men were sent off in a small boat from the anchored ship, equipped with a variety of presents, including a copper kettle, an iron kettle, two hundred trade beads, some Chinese tobacco, and some fabrics, rattles, needles, and ten one-ruble coins. Chirikov waited anxiously for their return. He ended up waiting for five full days, with no sign of Dementev or his companions. On July 23, boatswain Sidor Savelev, a carpenter, a ship's caulker, and a sailor were sent off to find the shore party, hoping that Dementev's vessel had been stove in on the rocks or that some similar minor misfortune had befallen them. Chirikov waited two more days, without sign of Dementev, Savalev, or the others. Finally, a crestfallen Chirikov weighed anchor and set sail.

Over the next few weeks, the *Saint Peter* and the *Saint Paul* shadowed one another, each making landfall at several islands between the Gulf of Alaska and the islands of the Aleutian archipelago nearest to the Kamchatka coast. Chirikov returned to Avancha Bay on October 9, 1741; Bering never did make it back. On November 28, the *Saint Peter* foundered on the rocks on the island that came to bear Bering's name, about 300 nautical miles off the Kamchatka coast. Bering died on December 8, and the rest of his crew, after spending a bleak winter on the island, managed to construct a sailboat from the wreck of the *Saint Peter* and arrived at Avancha Bay on August 26, 1742.

Perhaps the most important consequence of the second Kamchatka expedition was that it set off a dramatic expansion of the Russian fur trade, which quickly extended throughout the Aleutian Islands to the Alaskan mainland. But the matter of the lost Russian colony was far from settled. Long after Bering and Chirikov sketched their first tentative charts of the Northwest Coast, prisoners taken during the periodic Russian-Chukchi conflicts provided several descriptive accounts of Russian settlers in North America, and as the years passed, stories about bearded Russians across the sea were told and retold from Anadyrsk to Petropavlovsk. The legend of Russians in America was transferred from the aboriginal oral tradition to the oral traditions of the Russian fur trade culture in Kamchatka, occasionally erupting in a local sensation.

In 1762, a report from officials at the Port of Okhotsk, hundreds of sea miles south of the Chukchi Cape, detailed an interrogation of Russian fur traders who insisted that on two islands off the North American mainland, there were bearded people who were like Russians in every way. They were said to live in Russian-type log buildings, and while the old men of the settlement were bearded, the young men were not. And on the mainland itself, there were also "bearded people like the Russians."

In 1765, the Cossack officer Nikolai Daurkin, in Anadyrsk, had compiled a detailed map of the imaginary landscape of Russian America. Fluent in the Chukchi language, Daurkin believed his map to be fairly accurate. It showed a fort, sheltered among trees 3 meters (10 feet) in circumference, on the right bank of a river, the Kheuveren, which flowed from the Alaskan hinterland into the Bering Sea. The Kheuveren was said to flow through a valley of birch, pine, cedar, fir, and spruce, suggesting that the location of the Russian settlement would have to be at least as far south as Norton Sound, which is about halfway between Alaska's north slope and the Alaska Peninsula. Despite his enthusiasm, or perhaps in part because of it — he'd spent a year among the Chukchi, absent without leave, listening to stories about the fabled Russian settlement — Daurkin failed in his attempts to convince Russian authorities to mount another expedition in search of their long lost countrymen.

It wasn't until after the alarms caused by the arrival of Captain James Cook's ships in the Bering Sea, in 1778, that Russian imperial authorities renewed their interest in the fabled colony. After English ships showed up in waters the Russians thought of as their own, the Cossack officer Ivan Kobelev was dispatched to the Chukchi Cape to get to the bottom of all the stories once and for all. He demanded that the Chukchis take him across the strait, if not to the settlement, then at least to some closer sources of the rumors about it. Unlike his predecessors, Kobelev managed to win at least a modicum of cooperation from the Chukchis, who took him to Igellin and Imaglin Islands. Kaiguniu Momakhunin, the chief of the Igellin people, who was himself born on the North American side of the Bering Strait, confirmed the stories that Daurkin had collected, and Momakhunin even had a name for the Russian fort, or *ostrog*, on the Kheuveren River — it was called Kymgovei. There, bearded men were said to speak Russian, read and write, and worship icons.

Another Chukchi, Ekhipka Opukhin, said he had a friend on another island who brought a letter from Kymgovei, written on a small board. The letter was intended to be sent along to Anadyrsk, asking for iron, but Opukhin's friend did not take the letter. Opukhin said that the Russians were known to have a large building at their fort where they prayed, and Opukhin then made the sign of the cross after the Russian Orthodox fashion. Kobelev pleaded with the Chukchis to take him to Kymgovei, but they refused.

But like Daurkin before him, Kobelev became obsessed, and a decade after his first bold attempts, Kobelev and Daurkin teamed up in their efforts to find Kymgovei. The legend had been making the rounds back in Moscow again following the appearance of "Zinov'ev's Account," which was a 1789 report by Russia's Spanish ambassador, S. S. Zinov'ev, about a report filed by a Spanish expedition to the Northwest that allegedly contained evidence of a Russian presence in North America as far south as the 49th parallel. So, in the summer of 1791, Kobelev and Daurkin were busy organizing an expedition to the North American mainland. They got as far as the mouth of a river they believed to be the fabled Kheuveren, in Norton Sound. But autumn was coming on, and they were forced to return.

Kobelev and Daurkin were probably as close as anyone would ever come to proving or disproving the existence of Kymgovei, although attempts would continue for more than a century. Rumors, hints, legends, and fragments of legends continued to feed off one another, until it became impossible to tell whether another fifth-hand or sixth-hand report of an encounter with the residents of the fabled settlement was a "new" rumor or simply an old one, retold with some added twist. Overland expeditions undertaken by the Russian American Company went in search of it, to no avail. All they brought back were more rumors, and more fourth-hand and fifth-hand accounts of meetings with strange people believed to be the descendants of the Russians — bearded men who wore shirts and black skin boots, traveled on skis, carried copper-barreled guns, and spoke a language nobody could understand.

One story, related to Russian American Company officials by an Uglakhmiut elder, was about a group of white people who, rather than arriving from the west, had come from the north, and had gone to live on an island, where they lived in stone and wooden houses with copper roofs. Other stories, from native people along the Kuskokwim River, explained that the European goods they were found to possess did not come from white people who lived across the water to the west, but from the east, a summer and winter's travel distant. These were almost certainly references to Hudson's Bay Company posts in the Canadian interior.

And so the story went, with the legend flaring up every now and again, sometimes for the most dubious of reasons, and sometimes in association with some rumored encounter with Chirikov's ill-fated crewmen. Stories about the 15 lost seamen from the *Saint Paul* persisted during the days of Spanish, British, and American exploration of North America's west coast, as far south as the mouth of the Columbia River. In 1774, crew members of the *Santiago*, with Juan Pérez in command, were trading with a flotilla of native people in the same general vicinity as Chirikov's ill-fated visit and noticed what appeared to be either a bayonet or the fragment of a sword in a canoe. The fact that the local natives were described as "fair skinned" also led to speculation that Chirikov's men had settled in and married local women. The exact location of Chirikov's visit also became a matter of some importance, since it would establish the northern extent, in international law, of the Spanish claims to North America's west coast.

But the English and the Spanish were busy chasing shadows of their own making.

For two centuries, the Northwest Passage had eluded seafarers who probed the icy seas of the North Atlantic. William Baffin, Henry Hudson, John Davis, and Martin Frobisher all searched for it in vain. But it wouldn't have been a passage through the New World at all unless it reached the Pacific, so, somewhere on the Northwest Coast its Pacific portal must lie, and by the 16th century, Britain was offering a reward of £20,000 to any mariner who could find it. The Englishman Michael Lok was convinced he knew just where it was. In 1596, Lok returned to England from Venice with the news that he possessed intelligence gleaned from a certain Greek who went by the name Apostolos Valerianos and also by the name Juan de Fuca. Valerianos claimed to be a seasoned mariner who had spent forty years in the service of the Spanish. Valerianos is reported to have confided in Lok that in 1592 Spain had sent him off into the North Pacific to locate the Northwest Passage's Pacific outlet, which he said he did, at a point on the North American coast between 47 and 48 degrees latitude. Valerianos also claimed to have sailed through the Northwest Passage, passing lands rich in gold and silver, and after twenty days found himself back in the North Atlantic again.

The Northwest Passage was already a well-established myth in Spanish imperial circles by the time Lok caused his excitements in England, but the Spanish believed its Pacific portal lay much farther north. The role Valerianos played for the English was played in Spain by two men.

In 1588, a certain Lorenzo Ferrer Maldonado had written a fanciful account that placed the mouth of the passage behind some coastal mountains, around 60 degrees, in the vicinity of Kayak Island in the Gulf of Alaska, which Vitus Bering had visited in 1741. The other character was Bartholomew de Fonte, who allegedly discovered another route from the Pacific to the Atlantic at a latitude of 53 degrees, or roughly halfway down the Queen Charlotte Islands.

Maldonado's claims were taken most seriously, but getting to his version of the Northwest Passage meant navigating a waterway Maldonado said was the Strait of Anian, first described by the Italian wanderer Marco Polo. Maldonado claimed to have entered the Northwest Passage from the Atlantic and then sailed to the Strait of Anian, which led to the Pacific.

Finding the Strait of Anian was the primary objective assigned to the frigate *Santiago,* commanded by Juan Pérez Hernández, in 1774. The *Santiago*'s voyage was the first serious attempt to find the Strait of Anian.

Although he never went ashore, Pérez is the first European known to have visited what is now British Columbia, although other Spaniards sailed north from Mexico before him. In 1542, Juan Rodriguez Cabrillo sailed northward to the vicinity of present-day San Diego, California, and throughout the 16th century there were several encounters between Spaniards and California's coastal peoples, especially the Chumash, who greeted Spanish ships in their oceangoing planked canoes. But the Spanish had little interest in exploring to the north, especially after 1587, when Pedro de Unamuno put ashore at Morro Bay and a battle ensued with local villagers, leaving one Spaniard dead. After the Morro Bay incident, the viceroy of New Spain issued orders that any Manila galleon making landfall on the coast north of Mexico was not to allow crewmen to go inland and was prohibited from taking any reprisals against local people who resisted their presence.

In 1595 — almost two centuries before Pérez — there was a halfhearted reconnaissance inspired by the Northwest Passage myth. In that year, the galleon *San Augustin,* commanded by a Portuguese seaman, Sebastian

Rodriguez Cermeno, skiffed along the California coast until the ship was wrecked near present-day Drake's Bay. After a brief and unpleasant stay among the Miwoks, the crew made their return south in a smaller vessel outfitted for inshore inspections. Spanish vessels were commonly seen off the California coast, but they were usually galleons on their way to or from Manila. Spanish ships may have come to grief on the Northwest Coast in the years before Pérez, but there is little evidence that such shipwrecks occurred. Pollen analysis of a collection of huge pieces of beeswax found on the Oregon coast, of the type found in cargo manifests during the age of the Manila galleons, has dated the beeswax to the early 17th century. Fort Vancouver journals also record the presence of an elderly "Spanish Indian" named Soto, a high-ranking member of local tribal society, which has prompted some historians to speculate that Soto was a survivor of the wreck of the *San Francisco Xavier,* commanded by Santiago Zabalburu, which failed to arrive in Mexico after leaving Manila in 1705. It wasn't until 1769 that the Spanish made any concerted effort to colonize the California coast. The move was partly prompted by Russian expansion in the North Pacific, and partly due to the evangelical zeal of the missionary Junipero Serra.

But it wasn't a defensive move against the Russians or the zealotry of its priests that brought Spanish mariners into the North Pacific. It was the Strait of Anian, and in 1774, Juan Pérez Hernández set sail from San Blas, Mexico. He reached a point just north of the Queen Charlotte Islands and found himself surrounded for a time by Haida canoes off Graham Island's northwest tip. He anchored briefly at Friendly Cove, on Vancouver Island's west coast, but his crew was ill, making it impossible to go ashore to conduct a formal act of possession. Pérez returned to San Blas in August, after seven months at sea, with most of the *Santiago*'s crew incapacitated by scurvy.

In 1775, Pérez was headed back north again, this time as the *Santiago*'s pilot, under the command of Don Bruno Heceta. Accompanying the *Santiago* was a small schooner, the *Sonora,* skippered by the Peruvian-born Juan Francisco de la Bodega y Quadra. Again, the Spanish had been sent in search of the Strait of Anian. On July 12, the two ships anchored near a village just south of Cape Flattery, at the northwestern tip of Washington State. The ships were greeted by people in canoes, and the villagers seemed friendly enough, but when seven of the *Sonora's* crew were sent ashore for fresh water, hundreds of armed men burst from the trees. All seven Spaniards were killed.

From there, the ships turned north again, but they became separated, and with a crew writhing in scurvy's agony, the *Santiago* turned south. Before it reached San Blas, Pérez was among the dead. Quadra continued north on the *Sonora*, reaching 58 degrees, and after an act of possession in the name of the Spanish king was performed on an island in the Alexander Archipelago, Quadra turned south, keeping a weary eye out for the Strait of Anian. The wretched crew of the *Sonora* continued their southward limp until they finally arrived at San Blas, all sick with scurvy.

After these first Spanish attempts, the next European who arrived looking for the Northwest Passage was the English Captain James Cook, who is perhaps the most important figure in the history of maritime exploration.

A grocer's assistant and the son of a Scottish laborer, Cook began his naval career at the age of 18, when he signed on as an apprentice seaman on ships carrying coal from Newcastle to London. At 27, he volunteered with the Royal Navy, and by the time he was 30 he had been promoted to the rank of ship's master. In Britain's Seven Years' War with France, Cook saw action on the French coast and participated in the siege of Fort Louisbourg at the mouth of the St. Lawrence River; he was trained in cartography and hydrographic surveying aboard the *Pembroke*. Cook's skills were tested during the British siege of Quebec City, and his charts of Newfoundland's coast were still in use more than a century later.

Cook's first major expedition, which began in 1769, was an unprecedented three-year exploration in which he and a staff of scientists were to chart the length and breadth of the South Pacific as well as carry out secret instructions to find a fabled continent that was believed to lie somewhere to the south of New Zealand. Cook's second voyage, which began in 1772, was to continue the search for the southern continent by circumnavigating the globe in southerly waters. On that journey, Cook and his crew were at sea for 122 consecutive days, longer than any ship had been known to be at sea before, and he became the first mariner to cross the Antarctic Circle and come home to tell about it. Cook's contributions to science were staggering, amounting to an 18th-century equivalent of the United States's first moon landing in 1969. One of the greatest contributions Cook made was to the health of high-seas mariners, who routinely died of scurvy and other diseases during long voyages. By supplying his crew with a peculiar diet of sauerkraut and fruit juice, as well as berries and greens wherever they could be found, Cook lost only one sailor during his epic second voyage.

But there remained the unresolved question of the Northwest Passage, and clearly, if anyone was capable of finding it, it was Cook. Cook's third and last voyage began from Plymouth, England, July 12, 1776. The *Resolution* and the *Discovery* were floating scientific laboratories, and the crews included surgeons, naturalists, cartographers, botanists, astronomers, artists, and hydrographers. The expedition was a crowning achievement of the Age of Enlightenment, and its purposes were so universally regarded as beneficial to humanity that despite the U.S. War of Independence — which began eight days before Cook's ships set sail — the American navy was under strict order to give Cook a wide berth. Cook's instructions were to head south, round the Cape of Good Hope, chart the sub-Antarctic waters of the Pacific, keep an eye out for any islands Britain could claim, cruise the South Pacific for a few thousand miles, go north to Hawaii, and then head northeast to the Strait of Anian. If Cook found the Northwest Passage, he was under instructions to sail through it to the Arctic Ocean, meet up with Richard Pickersgill — who had been sent to Baffin Bay just in case the Atlantic entrance to the Northwest Passage could be found there — and sail home in triumph.

On March 7, 1778, Cook sighted the Oregon coast, becoming the first Englishman to have visited North America's east and west coasts since Sir Francis Drake had sailed along the Pacific coast as far north as California two centuries earlier. On March 29, Cook arrived at Nootka Sound, on Vancouver Island's west coast, marking the first moment in history in which Europeans are known to have set foot in what would later become British Columbia.

By May 10, Cook's ships sailed within sight of Mount Saint Elias, which Vitus Bering had seen in 1741. For days, tensions ran high aboard the *Resolution* and the *Discovery*. The Russian charts Cook was relying on were wildly imprecise, and the coast was veering west, at precisely the latitude of Maldonado's Strait of Anian — and at precisely the spot where Russian charts showed a passage to the Sea of the North, as the Bering Sea was then known. The days passed, the ships' officers engaged one another in lengthy debates about the hundreds of people they were encountering in canoes and kayaks, and now and then, through the fog, the islands would give way. From the ships' forward decks, there were occasional glimpses of what might be a passage through what for all intents appeared to be a continent, despite Russian charts that showed the Island of Alashka at that spot. It took more than a month of close navigation, and not a few tense moments along the jagged coast, before Cook's ships finally found their way around the Alaskan peninsula into the Bering Sea.

It took another three months of cartographic work and an almost steady stream of encounters with local people, including a handful of Russians, before the *Resolution* and the *Discovery* were swept through the Bering Strait. As the Alaskan coastline was seen to veer to the northeast, an excited optimism returned among the officers and crew of both ships. James King, second lieutenant aboard the *Resolution*, noted in his diary: "All our Sanguine hopes begin to revive & we already begin to compute the distance of our Situation from the known parts of Baffin Bay." But after a few hours, a strange white light was seen in the distance. As the ships approached it, a solid wall of ice was soon found to stretch from horizon to horizon, and the ships fell into a gloomy routine of creeping through thick fog along an endless cliff face of ice, guided only by the dreary and monotonous groaning of walruses at the edge of the ice floes. Their journey was over, at least until a resumption of efforts the following summer, and it wasn't until Cook announced that the ships were returning to Hawaii that the crews' spirits lifted.

Cook never returned to the Bering Sea. Following the ships' return to Hawaii, there occurred a bizarre sequence of events that utterly baffled the ships' officers and crew and has puzzled anthropologists and historians ever since. During several years of seafaring, Cook and several of the officers and crew aboard both ships had become well acquainted with certain Polynesian customs and were well known to many leading figures in Hawaiian society. But they were not prepared for what was to greet them when they arrived at Kealakekua Bay on January 17, 1779. The ships were surrounded by about 1500 canoes, and several hundred more people were swimming in the waves around them. The ships' decks were swarmed by singers and dancers, causing both ships to come close to capsizing. King reckoned that their welcoming party numbered about 10,000 people. In the days that followed, Cook was treated in a way that appeared to border on worship, and he found himself playing the central role in at least two elaborate rituals. All the evidence seemed to suggest that the Hawaiians had come to regard Cook as the reincarnation of the great god Lono, which makes it that much more perplexing that on the morning of February 14, 1779, in a dispute over the apparent theft of a boat, a mob set upon Cook and killed him, along with four of the *Resolution*'s crew.

In the summer of 1779, the expedition returned to the Bering Sea, where the ships continued the cartography and hydrographic research from the previous year. Another attempt was made to navigate the waters beyond the Bering Strait, but it was clear that the Northwest Passage could not be there, where the sea was a terrifying expanse of ice and snow. After Cook's expedition, it seemed certain that there could be no entrance to any sea route to the Atlantic, anywhere on North America's west coast. But ships kept coming to look for it anyway. Spain mounted several more attempts, most notably that of Alejandro Malaspina.

Malaspina was an Italian-born intellectual and an Enlightenment scholar whose studies at the Clementine College in Rome led him to a life of inquiry. Before his arrival on the Northwest Coast, Malaspina had conducted expeditions of discovery throughout the South Seas, from South America to the Philippines, and it was only by chance that he was assigned to investigate the possibilities presented by Maldonado's purported 16th-century passage from the Atlantic to the Pacific. When Malaspina arrived at Acapulco in March 1790, he was on his way to the Hawaiian Islands, intending to proceed from there to Nootka and then on to Kamchatka. But upon his arrival in Mexico he found royal orders waiting for him, directing him to proceed to the Northwest Coast. The orders were issued following a presentation by mapmaker Phillippe Buache de Neuville to the Academy of Science in Paris the previous November. Buache de Neuville's presentation had revived academic interest in the writings of Lorenzo Ferrer Maldonado, and Malaspina was instructed to proceed to the purported latitude of the Strait of Anian.

Like Cook's expedition, Malaspina's efforts made use of the latest technologies, and his officers included several scientists and artists. Malaspina's two ships, the *Descubierta* and *Atrevida*, were in the hands of crewmen handpicked from the Cadiz Naval Academy. Among Malaspina's scientists was the Bohemian naturalist Tadeo Haenke, whose talents allowed him to serve as ethnologist, botanist, geologist, zoologist, and even musician.

Hopes were high. On June 26, 1791, the ships drew near a bay that British Captain George Dixon had given the name Port Mulgrave several years earlier. Near the northern tip of the present-day Alaska panhandle, Port Mulgrave and the islands and the mountains all around it appeared just as the landscape near the Strait of Anian was described by Maldonado more than two centuries before. Tomás de Suría, the artist aboard Malaspina's *Descubierta*, wrote these words in his journal entry for June 26: "Great was the joy of the commander and of all the officers because they believed, and with some foundation, that this might be the so much desired and sought-for strait, which would form a passage from the North Sea of Europe and which has caused so much trouble to all the nations in various expeditions which they have made for simply this end, and for the discovery of which a great reward has been offered."

Malaspina's expedition spent several weeks exploring the coastline between the Alexander Archipelago and Kodiak Island, a staggering sweep of country that curves around the top of the Gulf of Alaska. The expedition's scientists took voluminous notes recording their impressions of the language, customs, economies, beliefs, clothing, and architecture of the Tlingit, Eyak, and Chugachigmiut peoples. They collected hundreds of specimens, carried out astronomical observations and established precise charts of the coast. Needless to say, they found no Strait of Anian. At least the expedition didn't end in the sort of tragedy that befell Cook, although things did not end so pleasantly for Malaspina. On his return to Spain, he was commissioned to complete a report on what policies Spain should pursue in order to become a nation state shaped by the best ideals of the Enlightenment. Malaspina's report included the recommendation that the Spanish king remove all his ministers and replace them with forward-thinking people. For this audacity, Spain's governing council locked Malaspina away in the prison fortress of San Anton, where he languished for eight years.

Malaspina's 1791 expedition did not lay the myth of the Northwest Passage completely to rest. There was still the uncharted waterway to the east of Nootka Sound, the portal to which was Juan de Fuca Strait, so named in 1787 when its entrance was sighted by Charles Barkley. Juan de Fuca Strait was the one waterway of any significance to the Northwest Passage myth that had been overlooked by Cook's expedition. When he passed the entrance to the strait in 1778, Cook's journal records this entry, for March 20 of that year: "It is in the very latitude we were now in where geographers have placed the pretended Strait of Juan de Fuca, but we saw nothing like it, nor is there the least probability that any such thing existed."

But to both England and Spain, that "least probability" was still an annoying bit of unfinished business. To bring a final end to the legend, by proof or disproof, Spanish and English mariners on the Northwest Coast in 1792 were both carrying instructions to conduct a reconnaissance of Juan de Fuca Strait and its adjoining waters. At the time, the British and the Spanish were engaged in a diplomatic standoff over which nation enjoyed sovereignty in the Northwest Coast. The flashpoint in the dispute was Nootka Sound, which had been sighted by the Spanish in 1774, formally possessed by the British in 1778, then occupied by the Spanish and the English, and then seized by the Spanish. Captain George Vancouver, who had served under Cook, was in command of a British expedition sent to Nootka Sound in 1792 to take it back for the British Crown.

Not intending to make fools of themselves over a dot on the ground that neither the British nor the Spanish kings could locate on a map, the

British and the Spanish mariners turned to other business. After a chance encounter in Juan de Fuca Strait, mariners from the two opposing imperial powers regarded each other cautiously as their ships ended up in the same bay, deep within the strait. At anchor were the British ships *Chatham,* with Lieutenant Robert Broughton in command, and the corvette *Discovery,* which carried Captain George Vancouver, the expedition leader. The approaching Spanish vessels were two small ships, known as goletas. The *Sutil* was commanded by Don Dionisio Alcala-Galiano, accompanied by the *Mexicana,* commanded by his junior officer, Don Cayetano Valdés. The date of the encounter, for the Spanish mariners, was June 13, 1792. But the British had sailed from the Atlantic via the Cape of Good Hope, and across the Pacific, so without benefit of an international date line in the 1790s, the British believed it was June 14, 1792. The British believed they were in a body of water they called the Gulf of Georgia. The Spanish believed they were in a body of water they called the Canal de Floridablanca. But all the evidence suggests that both the British and the Spanish believed that the Strait of Anian and the Northwest Passage were rubbish.

The mariners exchanged pleasantries and mumbled about the folly of their respective assignments. Broughton broached the idea of cooperating on their common purpose. The Spanish agreed. The British ships would take the easterly portion of the Gulf of Georgia/Floridablanca, and the Spanish would take the western side. They would meet back at Nootka, exchange notes and charts, and everybody would be happy. And so it ended. On August 27, the *Discovery* and the *Chatham* arrived back at Nootka, after rounding what was then proved to be an island, via Cape Scott. The *Sutil* and the *Mexicana* arrived four days later. The following year, Alexander Mackenzie completed his journey from Canada to the Pacific coast, encountering no broad transcontinental canal along the way, and the length and breadth of the North Pacific were finally known.

But there remains one last voyage across the Pacific that bears mention. It involves a dugout canoe of the type that carried Swaneset into the Pacific on his mythical voyage to the land of the salmon people. It was being carved from a huge cedar at about the same time that George

Vancouver was making his way out of the terrifying rapids that separate Vancouver Island from the British Columbia mainland.

In April, 1901, a young *Vancouver Sun* reporter, Norman Kenny Luxton, came upon the canoe at anchor in a small cove on northern Vancouver Island. From his conversations with the canoe's owner, Luxton determined that the canoe was more than a century old. He bought the canoe to fulfil his side of a bargain that he'd struck in a Vancouver beer parlor with a disreputable character by the name of John Voss, a Danish sailor. Luxton had grown up on the prairies. Voss had spent much of his life at sea. Both of them started talking about the seaworthiness and general impressiveness of the west coast's cedar dugout canoes. They hatched something of a plan. One thing led to another, and on May 20, 1901, in the canoe they had christened the *Tillikum*, Luxton and Voss pushed off the rocks at Oak Bay, near Victoria, British Columbia, and pointed the bow of the canoe in the general direction of Tahiti.

The *Tillikum* was slightly more than 10 meters (32 feet) in length, and almost 2 meters (6½ feet) across at the beam. In the seven weeks between the day Luxton bought the canoe and the day it embarked on its voyage into the Pacific, Voss and Luxton had fitted the *Tillikum* with three masts, added a cabin, fashioned a set of close-hauled sails, laid in more than 150 kilograms (330 pounds) of ballast, and took on what they hoped would be enough food and water for a few months beyond the sight of land.

On September 2, 1901, fourteen weeks after leaving Victoria, the *Tillikum* arrived at Penrhyn Island, in the Cook Islands of the South Pacific. On October 17, the *Tillikum* reached Suva, Fiji, where Luxton decided to pack it in. The voyage had been hard on him, and it didn't help that Voss was prone to paranoid rages, one of which got so out of hand that Luxton aimed a .22 calibre long-barreled Stevens pistol at Voss with the thought of putting him out of his misery. Luxton eventually made it back to Canada by steamship, but Voss continued in the *Tillikum*, rounding Cape Horn, eventually making it as far as England.

For twenty years, the *Tillikum* lay rotting on a mudflat on the Thames River outside London. Thanks to the interventions of the Vancouver Island Publicity Bureau during the 1920s, the *Tillikum* was shipped back to Victoria, where the Thermopylae Club and the B.C. Historical Society restored it. In 1940, the canoe was put on display at Victoria's Thunderbird Park, and in 1965, the *Tillikum* became a permanent exhibit of the Maritime Museum of British Columbia in Victoria.

Muskets, Manchu Nobles, and Machines

*I have seen many fascinating things here, have performed
an out-of-the-ordinary work, have conversed with many and learned to
know people who came to this isolated place from Norway, Sweden, Russia,
Scotland, Ireland, England, Japan, China, and other distant places . . .
of great leviathans whose homes are under the sea,
of men whose homes are nowhere.*

— *Lewis L. Robbins, Rose Harbour Whaling Station, 1937, quoted in
Robert Lloyd,* On the Northwest — Commercial Whaling
in the Pacific Northwest

IN THE STORIES NORTH AMERICANS tell themselves about the history of
the North Pacific, the rise of the Industrial Age is often recounted as a
triumphalist saga in which white men set about the business of exploiting natural resources that had gone largely untapped until the arrival of
Europeans. Asians are often mere bit players in this saga, sometimes
confined to roles as "recent immigrants" to North America who were
economically insignificant until perhaps sometime after the British
turned Hong Kong back to the Chinese government in the late 20th
century. "Indians" disappear very early in conventional histories. Sometimes they disappear because they fall victim to evil forces. Sometimes
they disappear because their contributions to history aren't considered
important enough to notice. But almost always, they disappear, and

what's left is usually a story of a few Indians, quickly followed by some Spaniards, then Captain Cook, Alexander Mackenzie, Simon Fraser, and Lewis and Clark. Then too many sea otters get killed, the salmon canneries arrive, railroad lines are blasted through the mountains, sawmills start churning out timber, and finally, there is the world as we have come to know it.

But to set that story aside, or to look farther offshore, is to encounter people who are not supposed to be there, doing things they're not supposed to be doing. There are Nuu-chah-nulth people sailing their own schooners in the Sea of Japan and in the waters around Sakhalin Island, there are seal hunters from the Aleutian Islands raising cattle in California, and there are fleets of little boats roving the ocean in between. One finds whale ships chasing humpback whales in the warm waters of the Strait of Georgia, Hawaiian villages in what is now suburban Vancouver, and Russian-Alaskan "creoles" attending to their studies at the medical college in Saint Petersburg. Chinese shipbuilders are busy on the west coast of Vancouver Island several years before George Vancouver shows up, and Russian saints live out their lives in meditation on lonely Alaskan islands. Generations before the British and the Americans divided North America's Northwest Coast between them in the 1840s, the North Pacific was a very cosmopolitan place, involving myriad relationships between peoples from both sides of the Pacific, as well as the Atlantic.

These cosmopolitan and multicultural traditions, as raw edged as they often were, thrived during the maritime fur trade era, through the history of the North Pacific whaling industry and through the rise and fall of the fur seal industry, and formed the basis of the cultural demography of the Northwest Coast throughout the industrial revolution. Ten years after British Columbia had entered Confederation, "white" people were still only a minority in the province. The 1881 *Report of the Fourth Census of Canada* shows that British Columbia was home to a mere 47,000 people that year. Of these, 25,661 people are identified as "Indian." The settler populations included English (7297), Chinese and Japanese (4350), Scottish (3892), Irish (3172), French (916), and a variety of other ethnic categories, including Scandinavian, Jewish, "various," and "not given." Racism is part of the story, but only a part. In the history of race relations in the North Pacific, bigotry and discrimination were not bit players, but there are other traditions in that history as well. And those traditions go back a long way.

On a sunny day in 1792, George Vancouver, his Spanish counterpart Bodega y Quadra, and Chief Maquinna of the Nuu-chah-nulth took a break from the dreary deliberations involved in the Nootka Sound negotations. The journal of Archibald Menzies, the surgeon aboard Vancouver's ship, describes how the European officers and ships' crew members gathered at Tahsis, where they were entertained by Nuu-chah-nulth performers "in imitation of various characters of different Countries, some represented Europeans armed with Muskets & Bayonets, others were dressed as Chinese & others as Sandwich Islanders." The English and Spanish entertained the Nuu-chah-nulth with a performance of fifes and drums, and Vancouver's crew performed various jigs and reels "to the no small entertainment of the Natives."

Even before George Vancouver's time, Hawaiians were making routine visits to the west coast of Vancouver Island, and in the following years, many Hawaiians settled down all along the Northwest Coast. English gentlemen were strolling the streets of Macao, Kamchadals from Russia's Pacific coast were peering through the specimen collections at the museum in New Archangel — the Russian colonial town that later became Sitka, Alaska — and dozens of ships were making regular journeys across the Pacific. All this had nothing to do with any saga involving industrialists pushing relentlessly westward until they finally breached the Rocky Mountains and established their dominions on the Pacific. It was a story with a center of gravity far out in the North Pacific, and it began with the eccentric tastes of China's Manchu ruling class. The Manchu nobles wanted sea otter fur for capes, for hats, and for trimming the hems and sleeves of their robes. In this way the North Pacific's first transoceanic industry was born.

Almost immediately after Alexei Chirikov arrived back at Avancha Bay aboard the *Saint Peter* in 1741, Russian fur traders, known as *promyshlenniki*, headed east in ships. The Aleutians were quickly subdued — infectious diseases took their usual tragic toll, as did cannon shells and musket fire. By 1762 — sixteen years before Captain James Cook floated by, looking for the Northwest Passage — the Russian entrepreneurs S. G. Glotov and S. T. Ponomarev had already spent several years in the fur business in the Aleutian Islands and were familiar with the Fox Islands — the islands in the Aleutian chain closest to the Alaska peninsula. They were also aware of the Alaskan mainland coast, but they thought it was part of a big island. Cook noted that Russians seemed to be everywhere, on all the major islands between Unalaska and Kamchatka, as well as the Kurile Islands. There were probably 500 Russians and Kamchadals throughout the Aleutians by the time of Cook's voyage. Ten years after Cook, the Spanish explorer Esteban José Martinez reached Alaskan waters only to find that more than 400 Russians were already there, between the Kenai Peninsula and Unalaska Island, settled in at least eight establishments. By 1799, when the Russian American Company was established, the industrialization of the North Pacific was already well under way.

In a charter that provided trade monopolies similar to those granted to the Hudson's Bay Company and the East India Company, the Russian American Company was granted exclusive trading rights from the Kurile Islands to the Alexander Archipelago. Company officials were entitled to expand their dominion by exploring to the north and south and by establishing new settlements wherever other imperial powers had not already established claims. For a time, it was rough going. A Russian stronghold at Yakutat Bay was attacked and burned in 1805, and Tlingit warriors, armed with English muskets, attacked the Russian fort Arkhistratig Mikhail (Archangel Michael), at Sitka. It took years before the outpost was reestablished as New Archangel, the Russian American Company's North American headquarters. But the Russians managed to do it, without the help of Hawaii's high chief, Kemehameha, who offered to send warriors to assist the Russians in case they ran into further troubles with the Tlingits.

There was much that distinguished Russia's commercial ventures in the North Pacific from John Jacob Astor's efforts on the Columbia, the Hudson's Bay Company's operations, and the Northwest Company's. The difference lay partly in the enormous distances between Russia's

Pacific fur trade operations and Russia's commercial centers. The dis-tances between most North American trading posts and their head-quarters in Montreal or London paled in comparison with the travels the Russians had to make, as Russian naval officer Lavrentiy Alekseyevich Zagoskin quickly learned. The journey from Saint Petersburg to New Archangel took Zagoskin from December 30, 1839, to April 30, 1840. He described the journey this way: "As things actually are, one must sit in a carriage for 6,300 versts [a "verst" is roughly equivalent to a kilometer], sail 2,400 versts on a river, travel 1,400 versts on horseback or with rein-deer or dogs, and then . . . one must sail 80 degrees of longitude, or 4,080 versts, across the Eastern Ocean, in all a journey of over 14,000 versts. Certainly, one has an excuse to be weary."

Another thing that distinguished the Russian enterprise in the North Pacific was the influence of the Russian Orthodox Church, which was interested in saving souls, as might be expected, but was also concerned that a just and honorable relationship prevail between the Russian im-perial power and the aboriginal societies within the Russian American Company's spheres of influence. The first Russian Orthodox monks in North America were eight clerics from the Valaam and Konevista monasteries on the Russian-Finnish border. They arrived at Kodiak Island in 1794, but six years later, the mission was a shambles. The monks had complained about the Russian American Company's treat-ment of Alaskan natives; five monks had been placed under house arrest for their protests, and the other three monks, who brought their com-plaints to Russia, died in a shipwreck on their return journey to Kodiak Island. The Russian Orthodox Church eventually succeeded in exerting a civilizing influence on the Russian American Company, and converts to Orthodoxy continued in native communities long after the United States acquired Alaska in 1867. The Orthodox faith was "indigenized" by Tlingits, Aleuts, and other tribal societies, which found ways to inte-grate aspects of Orthodoxy with long standing beliefs and rituals.

Justifiably, the Alaskan mission is remembered fondly throughout the Russian Orthodox Church, which canonized three saints from the period. Saint Herman of Alaska lived as a recluse on Spruce Island for a decade and is credited with several miracles. The evangelist John Veniaminov, who built schools for Aleuts and translated the gospel according to Saint Matthew into the Aleut language, went on to become the Metropolitan of Moscow, one of the highest offices in the Orthodox clergy. Veniaminov was eventually canonized as Saint Innocent, Enlightener of the Aleuts and Apostle to America and Siberia. Jacob Netsvetov, a "creole" of Russian and Aleut ancestry who was educated at the Irkutsk seminary, spent most of his life among the Yupik people and the Yukon River tribes. Knighted by Tsar Nicholas I, Netsvetov was canonized in 1994, becoming Saint Jacob, Enlightener of the People of Alaska.

With the isolation of "Russian America" from supply sources and Russian centers of commerce, and with a more civilized approach to the business of the fur trade encouraged by the influence of Orthodox monks, the Russian American Company attempted to establish a colonial infrastructure throughout its North American possessions. In many ways, the Russian American Company was more "democratic" than the Hudson's Bay Company, its counterpart in the North American interior. Relations between Russian company officers and aboriginal hunters were also far more stable than those that developed in the gold rush atmosphere that prevailed during the period of the sea otter trade elsewhere along the Northwest Coast, which was dominated by individual seafaring entrepreneurs from Britain and the United States.

South of the Russian operations, ships put into villages and engaged in trade for furs, usually directly with village chiefs who were perfectly capable of driving hard bargains. Although the Russians bought furs from tribal groups and individual hunters who maintained their independence, as was generally the case with the militarily powerful Tlingits, the Russian American Company did at least as much business by engaging hunters on long-term contracts that set out fixed rates for pelts. The company's hunters were mostly Aleuts, Kodiak Islanders, Chugach Eskimos, Kamchadals from Kamchatka, Kurile Islanders, and "creoles" — the mixed-blood descendants of Russian *promyshlenniki* and aboriginal women. The Russians even attempted crude forms of conservation and harvest management by closing certain areas to hunting for up to two years, prohibiting the harvest of female fur seals and sea otters, and banning firearms from the hunt in various locations.

In its first quarter-century, the Russian American Company's operations in the North Pacific harvested a staggering 1.2 million sea otters, 73,000 fur seals, 41,000 foxes, 35,000 beavers, 15,000 river otters, and 17,000 sables. The company also carried on a brisk trade in walrus tusks (which required the slaughter of tens of thousands of walruses), lynx pelts, bear skins, and other furs. The sea otter pelts went to Irkutsk by sea, then overland to the Chinese market city of Khiakhta near the Russia-China border. Fur seal pelts went to Saint Petersburg, Shanghai, and New York, although some were sent along to Kiakhta to trade for Chinese tea. Beaver pelts went to Kiakhta and Shanghai, fox pelts to Kiakhta, walrus tusks and bear skins to Saint Petersburg, and so on. During the California gold rush of the 1850s, the Russians exported more than 8000 tonnes of ice to California's parched miners.

Although their primary theatre of operations included the coastlines and islands from just north of the Haida territories on the Queen Charlotte Islands to the southern Kurile Islands a few sea miles north of Japan, the Russians had established themselves as far south as California by the early 1800s. In November 1811, the company officer I. A. Kushkov was sent south in the schooner *Chirikov*, accompanied by forty Aleuts in baidarkas, to establish an agricultural colony. By the 1850s, the Russians' Fort Ross operations, located on the coast north of San Francisco Bay, included several farms, a shipyard, and a flour mill. The colony's livestock included 1345 cows, 355 bulls, 940 horses, and 300 sheep, tended mostly by Kodiak Islanders. The company's most southerly permanent base on the North American coast was a sea-lion-hunting station on the Farallon Islands off San Francisco Bay, staffed mainly by Aleut hunters.

All told, before Alaska was sold to the United States in 1867, the Russian American Company maintained thirty-two settlements around the North Pacific, from Japan to California. But New Archangel was its crowning achievement. A stroll through the streets of New Archangel in 1861 would take a visitor past a dizzying assemblage of enterprises, including three sawmills, a copper and iron smelter, a water mill, a flour mill, a navigational-instrument shop, a forge, a laundry, a metal workshop, a cooperage, a tannery, and a brassworks. There were dozens of houses; small farms; a college for the education of clerks, navigators, and crafstmen; a boys' school; a girls' school; a Russian Orthodox seminary; the Russian Orthodox Cathedral of Saint Michael; a museum; and a library containing 1200 titles in Russian, French, English, German, Latin, and other languages.

The mercantile culture that developed around the North Pacific during the days of the Russian American Company completely contradicts widely held assumptions about the exploitation of aboriginal peoples by European powers during the early post-contact period. Oppression and barbarism were commonplace during the first few years of the Russian fur trade, but North Pacific maritime peoples actively embraced opportunities that trade presented, and aboriginal peoples from both sides of the North Pacific were active participants in what was, in effect, a new, North Pacific culture — a proletarian, syncretic, cosmopolitan culture.

In the entire history of the Russian American Company, there are very few incidents of the stereotype in which timid, tawny-skinned children of the forest run away from big bad white men. Instead, there are standing Tlingit armies and polite Russian *promyshlenniki* going about their business taking care not to give the hereditary chiefs offense. There are white men who are completely indistinguishable from Tlingit commoners: As early as 1794, Captain George Vancouver noticed that the white Russians on the Alaskan coast had "adopted entirely their [aboriginal] food and clothing, and in outward appearance there is very little difference from the indigenous natives." Meanwhile, there are Aleuts who are easily distinguishable from everybody else because of their enthusiasm for frock coats, waistcoats, and neckties. Although European diseases eventually proved too much of a risk for aboriginal people, as early as 1805 "creoles" from Alaska and the Aleutian Islands were attending school in Saint Petersburg, enrolled at the Kronstadt Navigation College, the Saint Petersburg Medical-Surgical Academy, and other colleges, and by the 1820s, books were being published in the Aleut language.

It may be that the Russian history of the North Pacific has been largely ignored by North Americans because, like so much of the North Pacific's history, it doesn't neatly fit with certain preconceived ideas about the way history is supposed to work or the way "Indians" are supposed to behave. Historian Lydia Black, from the University of Alaska at Fairbanks, says a simplistic "white and non-white" model has been misapplied to the history of the Russian Pacific, with all the stereotypes of both natives and Russians that such approaches normally involve. The Russians generally did not interfere with tribal laws or institutions and made no attempt to impose judicial powers upon Alaska's peoples. Some historians have observed that the Russian presence in North America has been forgotten at least partly because the American purchase of Alaska was followed by attempts to purge the territory of "foreign" and "un-American" influences. Those attempts neatly coincided with the zeal of Protestant missionaries, who tried in vain to stamp out Orthodoxy along with Alaska's tribal belief systems. The long period of the Cold War didn't help to shed light on Russian traditions in North America, either, but a brilliant work, written by the Russian historian Svetlana Fedorova and translated into English in 1973, shows just how deeply North Pacific peoples were involved in the North Pacific's Russian enterprise.

Despite the presence of thirty-two Russian American Company settlements around the top of the North Pacific, Fedorova found that there were rarely more than 600 "white" Russians involved in company activities at any time. An 1860 census of the population of the Russian Pacific reads a lot like British Columbia's 1881 census — except that the white people are an even smaller minority. By 1860, there were 529 Russian men and 66 Russian women associated with the Russian American Company, most of them situated in New Archangel. In that same year, 1896 "creoles" were associated with the company, along with 7649 Aleuts, Kenais, Kuskokwim Indians, Kurile Islanders, Aglemiuts, Chugach Eskimos, and others.

By conventional mercantile standards, the Russian American Company was a failure. Over such vast distances, it was impossible to maintain a profitable enterprise, certainly not in comparison with monopolies such as the Hudson's Bay Company or the East India Company. Meanwhile, Russia's imperial pretensions in North America were destined to be outflanked by the British and the Americans, whose advantages included strongholds throughout the North American continent. And the Russian American Company, with its schools, churches, and cumbersome trade practices, couldn't match the low-cost, high-profit operations of British and American fur traders, whose ships had started showing up on the west coast of Vancouver Island almost as soon as the news of Captain Cook's death in Hawaii reached England. That news was relayed to England, incidentally, courtesy of the Russian governor of Kamchatka, who received the officers of Cook's expedition in 1779, presented them with several cows, 180 kilograms (400 pounds) of tobacco, and a variety of other trifling gifts, such as figs, butter, and honey, and agreed to send Cook's journals and the maps of his discoveries back across Siberia to Europe and England.

From the Columbia River to the Alexander Archipelago, all those coastal societies that had not participated in the sea otter trade with the Russians greeted the opportunity with enthusiasm as soon as the first British trading ships began arriving at various coastal villages in the 1780s. At the very first landfall by Europeans on what was to become British Columbia's coast — Cook's visit to Friendly Cove in 1778 — it was obvious that the Pacific coast's aboriginal peoples were not going to conform to anybody's romantic notions that they had no sense of land ownership or were gullible unfortunates ripe for the picking by unscrupulous entrepreneurs.

If any such notions were held by John Webber, an artist with Cook's expedition, he was disabused of them during his visit to the village of Yuquot, where he intended to sketch some of the houses. Webber was especially impressed by a gigantic house post decorated with carvings of animal figures, but shortly after he sat down to begin sketching, a young man of the house covered the post with a cedar mat and refused to allow Webber to continue until he'd been given a brass button from Webber's coat. Webber complied and was allowed to sketch for a few more minutes before the young man covered the house post with the cedar mat again. Webber gave him another button and the mat came down. A few minutes later the mat went back up, and so it went until Webber had no more buttons, at which point the young man took the mat down and allowed Webber to finish his sketch.

Cook himself got a taste of this sort of thing when he sent a shore party to a quiet cove to cut some grass for the ships' goats. The party was accosted by a group of local people who demanded payment for the grass. The men from the ship complied, but the matter didn't end there. A ruckus ensued, so Cook went to investigate and found that "a dozen men all laid claim to some part of the grass." It was only after Cook had emptied his pockets of all his baubles that his shore party was allowed to proceed. After his stay among the Nuu-chah-nulth, Cook noted that he had never before encountered any people "who had such notions of everything The Country produced being their exclusive property."

It is true that the sea otter trade produced some fabulous profits during its early years. Sea otter pelts in Canton were practically worth their weight in gold, and it was not uncommon for a coastal trader to purchase sea otter furs on the B.C. coast for bits and pieces of iron or copper. In 1787, George Dixon, aboard the *Queen Charlotte,* obtained 300 sea otter pelts in his first half-hour of trading with the Haida. Within a month, Dixon and his partner, Nathaniel Portlock, were on their way to China with 2552 sea otter furs, worth more than U.S. $50,000, a tidy sum in the 1780s. But by the 1800s, a chisel just wasn't good enough. First, it was six chisels. Then it was six chisels and a blanket. Then it was six chisels, a blanket, a bottle of molasses, and a musket. Just as powerful coastal chiefs monopolized trade and established themselves as middlemen between the ships and other tribes, native traders played one vessel off against the next, holding out for the highest price and engaging in business practices every bit as sharp as those employed by the Yankee traders who had bested them the previous season. Still, the trade continued, and between 1785 and 1825, 330 ships made the trip across the Pacific, between China and the Northwest Coast.

By the 1840s, the commerce that fueled the sea otter trade between the Northwest Coast and China had begun to shift its center of gravity away from coastal aboriginal villages to fur trade posts established on the Pacific by British and American interests from the other side of the continent. The range of commodities expanded, and the material culture of Northwest Coast societies flourished. Access to new markets had ushered in a renaissance in works of monumental art, weaving, and cedar sculpture, and the new trade goods had provided for profitable exchanges through the potlatch system that elevated the rank of the coastal nobility's royal families to unprecedented heights. But ships traversing the North Pacific carried more than just muskets, blankets, iron, molasses, and sea otter furs. They carried people.

Whatever might be said about ancient Chinese mariners, or Chinese seafarers washing up on the coast in dismasted, rudderless junks, it is certain that Chinese shipwrights were hard at work on the B.C. coast in 1788. In June of that year, the Englishman John Meares arrived at Friendly Cove with a gang of Chinese carpenters he had employed to help establish his fur trade base in Nootka Sound. By September, the carpenters — from Macao, which was then a Portuguese redoubt on the Chinese coast — had completed the construction of the first planked sailing vessel ever built on the B.C. coast, the *North West America.* The fate of the Chinese shipwrights has bedeviled historians, and there has been speculation that at least some of the Chinese settled down among the local Nuu-chah-nulth people. But it is almost certain that all of them ended up back in Macao after a confusing series of events set off by the Spanish seizure of Meares's possessions at Friendly Cove. The fate of the ship they built, the *North West America,* is also a bit confusing. After Meares left Friendly Cove for Canton in 1789, the Spanish commander Esteban José Martinez took possession of the *North West America* after the ship had given only brief service as a coastal fur trader. The Spanish christened her the *Santa Gertrudis la Magna* and put her into service with the Spanish navy. Three years later, rechristened as the *Santa Saturnina,* the ship was under the command of José Maria Narvaez, one of the first explorers to reconnoitre the Strait of Georgia.

From the outset of the coastal sea otter trade, Hawaii was a favored port of call, and Hawaiians were among the first outsiders to set foot on North America's North Pacific coast. Young Hawaiian men, mindful of their own people's history as great seafarers, were anxious to sign on with the impressive new kinds of deep-sea vessels that were arriving, in increasing numbers, in the coves and bays outside their villages. The first Hawaiian to make it as far as North America's west coast appears to have been "Winee," a young woman who signed on as the personal servant of Frances Barkley, wife of Captain Charles Barkley, who arrived on the B.C. coast in 1787. Later that same year, a Hawaiian chieftain, "Tianna," arrived on the west coast of Vancouver Island with the fur trader John Meares. But by the first decade of the 1800s, Hawaiians were routinely serving as deckhands on ships putting in on the Northwest Coast. And Hawaiians were among the employees of the first fur trade posts established on the coast.

By 1812, 38 Hawaiians were building John Jacob Astor's Pacific Fur Company post on the Columbia River. In 1847, Hawaiians comprised 10 percent of the population of San Francisco, and by the 1850s, Hawaiians comprised about a tenth of the non-native population of Vancouver Island. By the end of the 1850s, Hawaiians were regular crewmen aboard whaling ships hunting in the Bering Sea, and Hawaiians could be found in Kamchatka, in Canton, and all along the Northwest Coast. Known in fur trade parlance as Kanakas, Hawaiians were among the workers who built Fort Langley, on the Fraser River, in the 1820s. In 1846, more than half the work force at Fort Vancouver and the nearby Cowlitz farm were Hawaiians. By the 1840s, more than 300 Hawaiians were employed by the Hudson's Bay Company, working as laborers at practically every fur trade post in North America west of the Rocky Mountains. There were Hawaiians at the mouth of the Columbia River and Hawaiians at Fort Stikine, adjacent to the Alaska panhandle.

Most of the fur trade Hawaiians had signed on for three years' service, after which the Hudson's Bay Company was obliged by agreement with Hawaii's governor Kekuanoao to return them to Hawaii. But as often as not, the Hawaiians decided to stay on in North America. There were once Hawaiian settlements in the Gulf Islands, at Vancouver's Coal Harbour, at Newcastle Island in Nanaimo Harbour, and on the Fraser River at Derby, near Fort Langley. They worked as stevedores, fishermen, and sawmill workers, and their memory is recorded in such place-names as Kanaka Bluffs, Kanaka Bar, and Kanaka Road. Most of the Kanakas eventually blended into aboriginal and white society. Even though Hawaiians comprised between a third and two-thirds of the work force at most Hudson's Bay Company posts west of the Rocky Mountains, they have been all but ignored by conventional histories. In Peter C. Newman's otherwise delightful 1987 history of the Hudson's

Bay Company, *The Company of Adventurers*, the role played by Hawaiians doesn't even rate a mention.

The North Pacific's industrial history is generally held to have begun with the sea otter trade, but industrial whaling followed immediately after sea otter furs first began causing a sensation in Canton. And although the sea otter trade resulted in the first documented wide-scale extirpation of any species on North America's Pacific coast, a variety of whale species were also hunted to the brink of extinction, throughout the North Pacific, during the same period.

The importance of whale oil to the industrial revolution cannot be overstated. Without it, the machines wouldn't work, and enormous amounts of whale oil were used in factories every year. In 1851, a single cotton mill in Lowell, Massachussetts, required 25,635 liters (6772 gallons) of sperm whale oil — an amount requiring the slaughter of three sperm whales — just to keep running. Because of the value of whale oil, the Nootka Convention of 1790, which settled the dispute between Spain and Britain over sovereignty on the Northwest Coast, contained a provision that guaranteed British whale ships access to Spanish waters. Also, like sea otter fur, which was so desired by the Manchu nobility and the Russian ruling classes, whale products were coveted by the garment industry. Baleen — the sievelike "teeth" of plankton-feeding cetaceans — provided the raw material necessary for the production of hoop skirts, tight-waisted corsets, shirt collars, and so on.

For thousands of years, people had been setting out in boats to harpoon whales throughout the North Pacific. Coastal fishing communities from around the Sea of Japan to the Chukchi Cape engaged in whaling, as did Bering Sea Eskimos and Aleuts. Long before the time of X:als and Wiigyet and Coyote, the ancestors of the Haida, the Tlingit, the Tsimhsian, the Kwagewlth, the Nuu-chah-nulth, the Coast Salish, and other peoples were engaged in whaling. The archeological record shows that marine-mammal hunting was a key component of maritime economies before the time of the great salmon runs and the towering cedar forests. Despite their diversity and distinctiveness, there are striking affinities among the whale cults of North Pacific peoples, suggesting that an orientation toward marine-mammal hunting is as old as the

story of North Pacific itself. Various ritual elements of the whale cult —
individual ownership of whaling songs, special amulets hidden away
between hunts, the observance of certain taboos, the ceremonial treat-
ment of certain parts of the whale, and so on — are found replicated in
one way or another among peoples as widely separated as the Quileute
of the Washington coast, the Nuu-chah-nulth of the B.C. coast, the
Kodiak and Prince of Wales Islanders of Alaska, and the Chukchi and
Koryak of Russia's Pacific coast.

The Makah of Cape Flattery and the Nuu-chah-nulth of the west
coast of Vancouver Island are often described as the only peoples south
of Alaska engaged in intensive whaling by the time of European contact, but the story is a lot more complicated than that. The Haida of
Ninstints almost certainly mounted annual whaling expeditions, and
even the peoples of the "inside" waters of the Strait of Georgia and
Puget Sound appear to have engaged in occasional whaling. The straits
peoples were certainly whaling in the early 1800s, at least in response to
the trade opportunities presented by the arrival of the Hudson's Bay
Company traders. Hudson's Bay records of the time show that whale oil
was traded from the Saanich and the Cowichans of southern Vancouver
Island. It may be that this valuable commodity was processed from the
remains of whales they hunted in the Strait of Georgia, or from whales
that occasionally washed up on their beaches, or from trade with the
Makah or Nuu-chah-nulth whaling communities on Vancouver Island's
outer coast. Two Salish peoples — the Klallam of Juan de Fuca Strait
and the Quinault of the Washington coast — are known to have engaged in whaling before the period of the Hudson's Bay Company, but
only a few men of these tribes chose to engage in the risky business of
hunting giant sea mammals from oceangoing canoes.

The first European explorers in the North Pacific noted great abundances of whales along the coast of Asia, in the Aleutian Islands, and
along the west coast of North America. But independent British whalers
were initially prevented from exploiting these opportunities by the
monopoly granted to the East India Company between the equator and
the Russian possessions to the north. In 1791, a fleet of British ships left
London for the Northwest Coast to hunt whales, and if possible, to

establish a whaling station in the vicinity of Nootka Sound. This was the Butterworth squadron, a fleet of three ships that arrived at Nootka Sound in 1792 while George Vancouver was there to settle the final terms of the Nootka Convention with the Spanish. For reasons that have left historians scratching their heads, Vancouver fails to mention the whaling ships in his otherwise meticulous account of his time at Nootka Sound. Vancouver's apparent oversight has led to speculation that he deliberately looked the other way to avoid the embarrassment of acknowledging British ships violating British law. But because the East India Company did not engage in whaling, accommodations were soon made to allow whalers to get around the company's monopoly.

William Brown, the captain who led the Butterworth squadron, reported that prospects weren't great on the Northwest Grounds. American traders lured there for sea otters found that carrying whale oil from the Northwest to China was unprofitable. The Chinese didn't really need whale oil; they had few factories and plenty of vegetable oil besides, and they paid a lot more for sea otter fur. Still, the manifest of the fleet's flagship, the *Butterworth*, returned to London in 1795 with 17,500 seal skins and 85 tonnes of whale oil — an amount equivalent to the oil from about ten average-sized right whales — all procured from "No. West America." But from its beginnings in the early 1800s, the whaling industry on the Northwest Grounds, which extended roughly from the seas off Vancouver Island's west coast to the waters adjacent to the Queen Charlotte Islands, was largely the preserve of French and Yankee captains. Almost all the whale ships of the early days were stout, round-bottomed, three-masted square riggers out of ports such as Nantucket, Mystic, New Bedford, Providence, Wiscasset, and Sag Harbor.

Yankee whalers were hunting sperm whales off the Japanese coast in the first decade of the 19th century, and by the 1830s the "Japan Grounds" comprised the most important whaling area in the Pacific. But it wasn't long before the Northwest Grounds were being intensely hunted. Although blue whales, sperm whales, fin whales, and humpbacks were taken, the whalers' preferred quarry was the right whale, so called because right whales produced more oil than other whales, they were baleen whales, and they didn't sink when they were killed. The North

Pacific's right whales were much larger than any the Yankee whalers had seen. At least 100 ships were hunting the Northwest Grounds by 1843, reporting at-sea processing of almost 150,000 barrels of oil, and by 1845, when more than 260 ships hunted in the Northwest Grounds, right whales were showing signs of depletion. By 1846, almost 300 whale ships were on the Northwest Grounds, which by then were largely barren of right whales, and by the 1890s, right whales on the Northwest Grounds were considered commercially extinct.

The North Pacific's gray whales, meanwhile, underwent massive declines in the latter half of the 19th century. A gray whale population that once migrated up and down North America's Atlantic coast had already been hunted into extinction by the 17th century, so it was a welcome sight that greeted two American whaling captains who decided to reconnoiter the Gulf of California for whales in 1845. The whalers found gray whales by the hundreds in each of the coves and bays along Baja California's gulf coast. Within weeks, they had taken 32 whales, and they knew they had discovered something important. What they didn't know was that they had found the calving grounds of the North Pacific gray whales' vast eastern herds, which traversed thousands of sea miles every year along an ancient migratory path that took them to the Bering Sea and back. Every year, at least 20,000 gray whales returned to the Gulf of California. By 1875, almost all the gray whales were gone. They were slaughtered on the calving grounds and harried from shore stations all along the California coast. By the end of the 19th century, fewer than 2000 gray whales remained.

One of the difficulties in sorting out the effects of industrial whaling on various cetacean species is the lack of reliable information about specific populations of whales before the advent of high-seas whale hunting. "Catch data" from the industry's early period consist of estimates of the kill based largely on the number of oil barrels recorded in the holds of whaling ships when they returned to port. Such imprecision persisted well into the age of "regulated" whaling, when a "blue whale unit" remained the measurement for determining quotas between whaling nations as late as the 1970s. A blue whale unit was the equivalent of 1 blue whale, 6 sei whales, 2½ humpback whales, or any such combination that amounted to the same in weight. A similarly preposterous unit of measurement was still in use in the 1990s in the "sockeye equivalent" that determined shares of salmon between Canada and the United States under the Pacific Salmon Treaty.

Historian Daniel Francis reckons that more than two million whales were slaughtered throughout the world between the 1920s and the 1970s. But industrial whaling, even during its early years, may have caused even more damage to cetacean populations than those numbers suggest. Many whale populations were clearly wiped out in their entirety, but it is impossible to determine how many of the North Pacific's specific and distinct whale populations, or subspecies of whales, were hunted into extinction. One population that appears to have met this fate was the humpback whale of the Strait of Georgia.

Of all the whales in the world's oceans, the humpback whale is probably best known for its "song," a feature of its vocalization repertoire. Called humpback because of the humplike ridge along its back, it is one of the world's largest whales, known to reach up to 18 meters (60 feet) from its barnacle-encrusted snout to its graceful flukes. The plankton-feeding humpback often weighs more than 27 tonnes, which is twice the size of the largest killer whale.

Humpback whales were seasonal visitors to the Strait of Georgia, occasionally straying into the warmer waters of the strait during their annual coastal migrations. In Alaska, researchers have recorded the same individuals returning to specific inlets and bays every year. In the 19th century, some humpbacks apparently developed the habit, over succeeding generations, of turning east at Cape Flattery to spend some months in the Strait of Georgia. But among the strait's humpback whales there was also a year-round population that exhibited small-scale migratory patterns not unlike those of the strait's resident killer whale community. Before industrial whaling came to the Strait of Georgia, humpbacks were plentiful from the summer to the dead of winter.

There were two reasons the Strait of Georgia's humpback whales were spared assault during the early decades of industrial whaling. The first is that large whaling ships avoided the treacherous inside waters. The second reason involves the trade monopoly enjoyed by the Hudson's Bay

Company. Sir George Simpson, a governor of the Hudson's Bay Company, proposed that the Hudson's Bay Company get into the whaling business in Juan de Fuca Strait and the Strait of Georgia, because of the "very numerous" whales in those waters. An 1842 visit to Lahaina on Maui, in the Hawaiian Islands — a bustling stopover port for whalers who had recently discovered the whale-rich North Pacific grounds — had stirred Simpson's imagination, and he proposed that several whaling stations be established on the B.C. coast. Simpson also suggested a refit of the Hudson's Bay Company steam paddlewheeler, the *Beaver,* to hunt whales when the ship wasn't doing duty in patrols and freighting. But the last thing the Hudson's Bay Company wanted was to attract the attention of more Yankee whalers and traders to the B.C. coast. The Americans had already pushed the Crown's sovereignty north of the 49th parallel, and Sir James Douglas, the chief Hudson's Bay Company factor and governor of the Colony of Vancouver Island, expressed alarm that Simpson would propose an endeavor that would attract American ships to Vancouver Island's inside waters and "endanger the security of our trade."

So, the Hudson's Bay Company rejected Simpson's suggestions, and the Strait of Georgia remained free of commercial whaling ships until a scrappy French whaler, Jean Baptiste Morin, arrived at Fort Victoria aboard his whale ship the *General Teste,* on August 30, 1847. Governor Douglas didn't go out of his way to make Morin feel welcome. Besides, Morin had been involved in a nasty diplomatic rumpus in Hawaii, where he protested a $500 fine for failing to abide by British port-clearance rules and was still demanding compensation for his trouble even after the fine was reduced to $25. After buying some provisions and lounging around Fort Victoria for a few days, Morin and his crew headed up Haro Strait and turned north, to the chagrin of the governor. Morin left the sheltered waters of the Strait of Georgia in January 1848 and appears to have killed only one whale, off Texada Island, sometime in the fall of 1847. The whale reportedly sank and was lost.

As the years passed, however, American whaling ships were becoming a frequent sight around the mouth of Juan de Fuca Strait. Victoria merchants had long dreamed that their port would become a base for a high-seas whaling industry under the Union Jack, so it caused a sensation when Victoria businessman James Dawson recruited three Americans whalers in the 1860s and bought a small schooner called the *Kate*. In 1868, the *Kate*, fitted with explosive-head harpoon lances, killed eight whales, probably humpbacks, in Saanich Inlet. Before winter set in, several more whales were taken from Saanich Inlet, and Dawson sold 100 barrels of humpback oil at the Dickson, Campbell and Company wharf in Victoria. That same summer, the whaler Thomas Roys set up his own business in Victoria and spent the next two years in the strait, in Howe Sound, and farther up the coast, shooting at whales, missing whales, losing dead whales that ended up in the hands of "the savages," and losing money. Dawson, meanwhile, set up operations at Whaletown, on Cortes Island, and by July of 1869 his whalers had taken five whales, producing an average of eighty barrels each. Dawson then established another shore station, Whaling Station Bay, on Hornby Island. But Dawson's fortunes were short-lived, and his operations were over by the mid-1870s.

There were various attempts at whaling in the Strait of Georgia over the years, including a 1904 effort by the Gulf of Georgia Fish and Curing Company, which applied to the federal government for permission to kill whales with a surge of electric current, by means of an electrical device in place of the standard explosive head. But the strait's humpbacks managed to survive, and they became the star attraction of one of the world's first "whale-watching" businesses, run by the family of J. A. Cates, manager of Vancouver's Terminal Steamship Company. The Cates family ran tourists in a passenger vessel from Vancouver to Howe Sound and back. Cates was an outspoken opponent of the activities of the Pacific Whaling Company, which began its operations in the Strait of Georgia in 1907. The Pacific Whaling Company brought Norwegian whaling technology to the North Pacific, and the company had two major operations on Vancouver Island's west coast, at Kyuquot and Sechart. After the company secured a federally sanctioned whaling monopoly in the Strait of Georgia, the company ship, the *Orion*, began its operations during the winter of 1907, taking more than forty humpback whales in a few weeks. A year later, the strait's humpbacks were gone.

Thomas Roys, meanwhile, left a far greater mark on the history of whaling than his money-losing venture in the Strait of Georgia. Roys invented a bazookalike weapon that fired rockets at whales and revolutionized the industry. Roys also skippered the first whaling ship into Bering Strait, opening the Pacific's "Arctic Grounds" to industrial whaling. In 1848, the owners of the *Superior* hired Roys to engage in a brief cruise of whale hunting in the North Atlantic, but Roys proceeded around Cape Horn into the Pacific and kept on going until he was skirting the edge of the sea ice on Alaska's north slope. When the *Superior* put in at Honolulu on its homeward leg, filled with whale oil, word of the Bering Sea's rich whaling grounds quickly spread. The following season, the *Superior* was north of the Aleutians again, this time accompanied by at least 50 other whaling ships. By 1852, 220 whaling ships were hunting north of the Aleutians, and some companies had established shore stations on both the Alaskan and Chukchi coasts. The Bering Sea proved so profitable for whaling firms that the first steam-driven whaling ship to hunt whales in the Bering Straits, the *Mary and Ellen,* returned from its maiden voyage with a cargo worth $100,000, which not only covered the vessel's outlandish construction costs but turned a handy profit to her owners, besides.

As on the Northwest Grounds, right whales were the preferred catch in Bering Strait, and right whales were soon decimated there. The Arctic Grounds were also home to bowhead whales, and by the close of the 19th century, Bering Strait's bowhead population had declined by two-thirds to an estimated 10,000 whales.

It wasn't until the 1890s that the Russians and the Japanese entered the high-seas whaling industry. Russian whaling began with Count Keyserling's Pacific Whaling Company, which was running two chaser ships off Sakhalin Island and throughout the Sea of Okhotsk in the mid-1890s, using a floating factory ship to can whale meat and to process whale oil and baleen. By the first decade of the 20th century, after a modest beginning with the *Choshu Maru* in 1899, a dozen Japanese companies with twenty-eight modern vessels were in operation on the Japan Grounds, relying mainly on Norwegian captains and gunners. Korea also made some ambitious efforts in the Sea of Japan and the Sea of Okhotsk. But by this time, whales were becoming scarce on the Japan

Grounds, and whaling captains were reporting depleted populations throughout the North Pacific — on the Kodiak Grounds in the Gulf of Alaska, in Bering Strait, in the Gulf of Anadyr, and in the Sea of Okhotsk. The industry's strategy was to turn increasingly to the establishment of shore stations supplied by fast steel-hulled, steam-powered, and deisel-powered vessels. At sea, whaling ships were capable of handling mainly whale oil and baleen. At shore stations, the entire whale could be processed, with bones and intestines going to fertilizer and whale meat going into cans, and all species of whales, not just right whales, sperm whales, gray whales, or bowheads, were worth the effort.

By the 1920s, whaling stations began to pop up all along North America's west coast. Prominent among them were the Pacific Whaling Company operations at Sechart and Kyoquot, and soon Rose Harbour and Naden Harbour on the Queen Charlotte Islands were industrial whaling centers. Like the North Pacific's whaling ships, which typically relied on Norwegian, American, Hawaiian, and Japanese crew members — and like the B.C. coast's salmon canneries — whaling stations were cosmopolitan places. Japanese and Chinese workers joined with Newfoundlanders, Finns, and native people, but the whaling stations often relied overwhelmingly on Asian labor; at Rose Harbour in the 1930s, the work force consisted of five white men and sixty-three Japanese and Chinese workers. British Columbia's last whaling station was at Coal Harbour, on Vancouver Island's northwest coast, which closed in 1967.

On the Asian side of the North Pacific, local whaling continued throughout the 19th century much as it always had. Japanese whalers had been hunting whales from ships since the 16th century, but both Japan and Russia were at a disadvantage in the new high-seas industry. Most of the productive whaling grounds had been depleted by the time Japanese and Russian ships arrived on the scene. In later years, the Japanese-Russian war further forestalled the two countries' whaling industries, as did World War II, which also put the North American and European whaling fleets into dry dock, or into service for coastal patrols. During the 1940s, on the Pacific coast, skilled Japanese workers were shipped off to internment camps, and the huge Japanese whale-meat market was closed to the Allied powers. Russia and Japan remained minor players in industrial whaling in the North Pacific until the 1960s. By then, while Japan was focusing on the Antarctic grounds, Russian factory ships were taking up to 18,000 whales every year from the North Pacific, mainly from the Northwest Grounds and the Kodiak Grounds, just beyond the Canadian and American territorial limits. During the 1960s, Russian whalers eliminated the last large herds of sperm whales off North America's Pacific coast.

After sea otters and whales came the first encounter between salmon and the industrial revolution, which occurred at what is now the foot of K Street, in Sacramento, California, in 1864. It was there and then that the first salmon cannery in North America was established, by the firm of Hapgood, Hume and Company. Andrew Hapgood and the Hume brothers managed to pack and sell 2000 cases of salmon that year. Within three years, the Humes had moved to the Columbia River, and in 1867, at Eagle Cliff, Washington, the company packed 4000 cases of 48 one-pound cans. Within 30 years of the industry's modest beginnings on the Sacramento River, it had expanded to a point, in the words of R. D. Hume, that "there was not a stream putting into the ocean along the Oregon and California coast ... that has not one or more canneries located on its banks." And Hume wasn't counting all the canneries on the Fraser and the Columbia. It was not long before Hume's words could have applied, without much exaggeration, to the whole coast, from the Columbia River to southeast Alaska.

The first attempt at canning salmon in British Columbia, which followed shortly after the last brutal sweep of smallpox along the coast in the 1860s, is generally credited to Alexander Loggie and Company's "very primitive affair" at Annieville, on the Fraser River, in 1870. Around the same time, Captain Edward Stamp was engaged in canning at Sapperton, just upriver from New Westminster. By 1874, a year in which Loggie produced 6500 cases of canned salmon along with 1000 barrels of salted salmon, he had been joined by several more operations on the Fraser that met or exceeded his production in canned salmon, salted salmon, and pickled salmon.

By the dawn of the 20th century, there were more than a hundred canneries in operation on the coast between the Fraser River and the

Nass River, and the Union Steamships line had more than twenty regular ports of call. In the mere 100 or so sea miles between the northern tip of Vancouver Island and Bella Bella, there were once twenty-three thriving cannery towns. This is in the heart of a section of the coast known to coastal old-timers as The Jungles, but by the end of the 20th century, The Jungles had come to be known to younger people, mainly environmentalists, as the supposedly pristine and untouched Great Bear Rainforest.

The coast's first canneries were generally owned or managed by individual industrialists or consolidated companies situated in places such as New Westminster and Victoria. The canneries depended upon contracts for capital and for distribution with banks, transportation firms, and marketers in New England, eastern Canada, and Great Britain. In standard histories, the industrial development of the Pacific coast is generally told as the story of this managerial class, made up almost exclusively of white males, most of them English, English-Canadian, or Anglo-American. The stories of the "cannery men" figure prominently in the conventional histories of North America's industrial development. And so they should. But the industrialization of the salmon fisheries of the Northwest Coast also unfolds as a chapter in the long story of coastal peoples from both sides of the North Pacific.

The cannery culture arose along the B.C. coast from the ruins of ancient fishing villages from Musqueam to Gingolx, but its economy was not based upon the local production, accumulation, and distribution of wealth. It was based upon commodity production and export to markets throughout the British Empire. Still, although smallpox and other epidemic diseases had reduced the coast's tribal societies in numbers and in power, aboriginal peoples were active participants in the strange world rising up around them. They served the cannery economy as harvesters, pieceworkers, and wage laborers, as did Chinese and Japanese fishermen and laborers. They all played out their parts in the industrial revolution, in patterns of rigid segregation repeated at one cannery after another from the Fraser estuary to the mouth of the Nass.

Typically, native, European, and Japanese fishermen caught the salmon, built boats, and mended nets; native women gutted and cleaned the fish; Chinese men cut the fish into can-sized chunks; native women stuffed the pieces into cans and weighed the cans; Chinese men soldered, cooked, sealed, and tested the cans, labeled the cans, and packed them into cases. Although the contribution made by European laborers, fishermen, managers, and investors should not be discounted, without aboriginal and Asian fishermen and workers, the coast's canneries could not have operated.

The first Japanese fisherman in B.C. waters is believed to have been Manzo Nagano, a sailor, who went to work fishing for the Fraser River canneries in 1877. Within a few years, Nagano was joined by a dozen more young men from Japan, and by the 1890s a full-fledged Japanese community had established itself in Steveston, at the mouth of the Fraser River. Most of the early Japanese at Steveston came from the small Japanese fishing village of Mio, in the prefecture of Wakayama, which lost its offshore fishing rights to a neighboring prefecture in the 1880s, leaving seventy small-boat fishermen to face destitution. Many of those fishermen ended up fishing for the canneries that were popping up all over the B.C. coast. More than 150,000 Japanese laborers passed through Hawaii during the 1800s, often remaining for years in the Hawaiian Islands, where they worked as indentured laborers. Many of these laborers ended up in Canada, the United States, and South America, and by the turn of the 20th century, almost all the coast's canneries employed their complement of indentured Japanese fishermen.

Most coastal cannery towns also had a China House, a barn-like dormitory that housed Chinese workers, and almost all the Chinese cannery workers were from the Chinese coastal province of Guangdong, particularly from the Canton delta. Like the Haida, Nuu-chah-nuulth, and Tsimshian towns on the North American side of the Pacific, the villages along Guangdong's coast had become dependent upon foreign trade goods by the 1870s. Canton's economy had been disrupted by the oversupply of goods off European traders' ships, and one of the few economic opportunities available to the city's jobless was emigration. Many of the first Chinese cannery workers were veterans of the Fraser River gold rush of 1858 who had come to North America under long-term contracts with brokers and labor agents to whom they remained indentured for years. The canneries' "China bosses" supplied cheap labor in the form of single Chinese males, many of whom had worked for Hawaiian plantation owners and American railroad companies before finding themselves in the salmon canneries. By 1900, there were 6000 Chinese immigrants working in the B.C. salmon canneries.

There was racial tension in the cannery culture, and it wasn't confined to conflicts between whites and nonwhites. Japanese labor contractors sometimes underbid Chinese labor contractors, and many north coast tribal fishermen resented the intrusion of Japanese fishermen, especially in the chum salmon fisheries. But there were many things that participants in the cannery culture shared, despite their ancestry. Chinese, Japanese, and aboriginal people were paid less than white workers, and they were denied the vote in British Columbia until the late 1940s. And one thing that the Chinese, Japanese, aboriginal, and white cannery workers shared was their own unique language, usually known as the Chinook jargon, after the Chinook peoples of the Columbia River, where it was first noted by language scholars during the fur trade era of the early 1800s.

Strictly speaking, a jargon is a specialized or technical terminology, and Chinook was more than that. It is probably best understood as a "creole," a composite of two or more languages. Chinook was composed of words from several coastal aboriginal languages from which the heavy guttural sounds had been excised, along with other sounds that Europeans found difficult to enunciate. Similarly, English and French terms were grafted onto the linguistic trunk of aboriginal terms, but with f's and r's removed because many native people had difficulty with those sounds. In 1935, the historian Edward Harper Thomas estimated that 100,000 people spoke Chinook daily during the late 1800s. Hundreds of books were written in Chinook, and for several years, British Columbia had its own Chinook newspaper, *Kamloops Wawa*. Chinook was vital during the fur trade period and eminently useful west of the Rockies, where more than thirty aboriginal languages were spoken between the Columbia River and the Nass River. Cannery managers were often required to be fluent in Chinook, which became the lingua franca of the cannery culture.

After its engagement with salmon, the industrial revolution quickly pulled the North Pacific's fur seals into its orbit, utilizing fur seal skins in the manufacture of everything from boots to carriage canopies.

From their rookeries in the Kurile Islands, the Pribilof and the Commander Islands of the Bering Sea, and Robben Reef in the Sea of Okhotsk, fur seals once roamed the North Pacific in the millions. Fur seals make ancient, annual journeys that begin and end at rookeries that seeth in roiling masses of life, sex, birth, and death. In this way, the great fur seal herds of the pre-industrial period were more like the bison of the North American plains than the nonmigratory harbor seals of North America's west coast. The Pribilof herds journeyed in a broadly sweeping arc traversing 7000 sea miles, extending well below the 40th parallel, along the California coast, up the British Columbia coast, around the Gulf of Alaska, and back to the Pribilofs. The pre-industrial population of the Pribilof herds is estimated to have been as much as three million animals. During that time, a bluff on Saint George's Island, one of the Pribilofs, commanded a view of the greatest single aggregation of mammals on the planet.

For thousands of years, fur seals made significant contributions to the maritime economies of coastal peoples from Hokkaido to Oregon. They were intensively hunted by the Ainu, the Chukchi, the Aleuts, the Haida, the Tsimshian, the Nuu-chah-nulth, and the Makah. The first industrial harvests began in the late 1700s, with the arrival of Russian ships in the Bering Sea and the Aleutian Islands. South of the Russian possessions in Alaska, however, the only significant commercial fur seal harvest before the 1870s was a joint venture established in 1803 between Boston-based traders and Aleut hunters from the Russian American Company. Centered on the Farallon Islands off San Francisco Bay and the Channel Islands off Santa Barbara, the enterprise concluded in 1812.

Apart from some minor trade in seal skins facilitated by the Hudson's Bay Company, there wasn't much commerce in fur seals until the 1870s, when William Spring, the Russian-born son of a Scottish engineer, established fur seal posts at Neah Bay, Ucluelet, Hesquiat, Dodger Cove, Friendly Cove, and other villages on the west coast of Vancouver Island. Buying fur seal skins from Makah and Nuu-chah-nulth hunters for resale to the Hudson's Bay Company, Spring and his associates had acquired about a dozen small schooners for the trade, taking hunters to sea to hunt fur seals from canoes.

At its zenith, the industrial fur seal harvest took two basic forms. The first, pioneered by the Russian American Company and adopted by the Alaskan American Company after 1867, was the gruesome but historically sustainable method of slaughtering animals directly on the rookeries. The second form of harvest was the pelagic seal hunt, waged on the high seas by schooners from San Francisco, Puget Sound, Victoria, and Yokohama. When fur seals were encountered at sea, hunters set out from the schooners in canoes and longboats to pursue the animals with harpoons, rifles, and shotguns. Only one in seven seals — some estimates suggest one in ten — was recovered from the sea after being shot. As early as the 1880s, Victoria's schooners were returning home with up to 50,000 skins, suggesting an annual kill of at least 350,000 fur seals.

The pelagic seal hunt provoked the first great international controversy about the overharvesting of the world's marine mammals. Unlike the Pacific driftnetting controversy of the late 20th century, however, Asian fleets weren't the problem in the seal hunt. Canada was the villain of the piece, and the repeated failure of diplomatic efforts at regulating the hunt poisoned relations between Canada and Britain and inflamed tensions between Canada and the United States. The North Pacific became an international powderkeg, eventually pitting Russians, Japanese, and Americans against Canadians and the British, and editorialists in England, Canada, and the United States routinely speculated about whether the matter would lead to a shooting war.

By the 1880s, Canadian and American sealing schooners extended their reach beyond the west coast of Vancouver Island to the Fairweather Grounds between the Queen Charlotte Islands and the Alaska Peninsula. Relying largely on experienced native seal hunters from Northwest Coast villages, the schooners sailed as far as the Pribilof Grounds, the Kurile Islands, and the Sea of Japan. Makah, Nuu-chah-nulth, and Japanese hunters were joined by American vagabonds from San Francisco and down-at-heels English remittance men from the Yokahama Club.

When the Pribilof Island rookeries were transferred to American control in 1867, the islands' new landlords entirely abandoned Russian conservation measures, which included a ban on the slaughter of nursing females and strict harvest limits. The Russian/Aleut operations on the Pribilofs had usually produced about 10,000 skins every year, with a peak of 30,000 a year during the final years of the Russian American Company's tenure. But in its first year on the Pribilofs, the Alaska Commercial Company slaughtered 240,000 fur seals. There were more than 85,000 walruses on the Pribilofs when the Americans arrived in 1867. Seven years later, the Pribilofs' walrus herds were gone.

By the first decade of the 20th century, scores of American and Canadian schooners were involved in fur sealing, and a lawless gold rush mood prevailed in the fleet. The sealing schooners made a habit of raiding sea lion rookeries, and before the end of the 19th century, the waters around the Kuriles had been scoured of sea otters, walruses, and fur seals. From a single voyage to the Bering Sea in 1881, the Victoria schooner *Cathcart* filled its holds to the hatches with sea otter furs, fur seal skins, and 2300 kilograms (5000 pounds) of walrus tusks. Rookery raiding was commonplace. The practice spread from the Pribilofs to rookeries in Russian and Japanese waters, often involving pitched gun battles and the arrest and imprisonment of schooners' crews. After dozens of Nuu-chah-nulth seal hunters found themselves marooned in Petropavlovsk and Sitka, arrested by Russian and American authorities for rookery raiding, Northwest Coast native people became increasingly unwilling to offer themselves for foolhardy adventures on the far side of the Pacific.

Several native communities refused to work for the Victoria and San Francisco schooner captains and instead sought their own independent access to the fur seal herds. By the end of the 19th century, the small Nuu-chah-nulth community of Ditidaht on Vancouver Island boasted three schooners, owned and operated by Charlie Chipps, Jimmie Nyetom, and Jim Nawassum. Usually, native-owned schooners were bought directly from shipyards or were outfitted from schooners engaged in other trades, but Heiltsuk fisherman Fred Carpenter built his own schooner at Bella Bella, with local labor, at a cost of $4000. The Makah chief, Maquinna Jongie Claplanhoo, owned three sealing schooners, one of at least twelve owned by Makah skippers. Makah sealer Chestoqua Peterson owned the 42-ton *Columbia,* along with his own trading post.

As more and more Canadian and American vessels raided their rookeries, the Russian and Japanese governments sought different solutions. Although Russians engaged in some high-seas hunting after 1867, their main effort was to continue their rookery harvests. Japan attempted to protect its fur seals rookeries just as diligently and initially banned its citizens from serving on foreign schooners. But Japan later decided to enter the schooner trade itself, offering generous subsidies to Japanese fishermen to hunt fur seals at sea, on both sides of the North Pacific. By the first decade of the 20th century, about forty Japanese sealing schooners were making regular visits to the Northwest Coast, just outside the U.S. and Canadian 3-mile limit.

Meanwhile, the United States adopted several responses to overharvesting and lawlessness in the industry. A U.S. investigation in 1897 concluded that more than a million Pribilof seals had been slaughtered during the preceding four-year period, not counting the number that drowned and sank after being shot. The study also reckoned that at least 100,000 nursing pups on the rookeries had starved to death during this period, after losing their mothers to the schooner fleet. The Alaska Commercial Company's rookery harvest on the Pribilofs was scaled back dramatically, but the United States quickly realized that conservation measures on the rookeries would be fruitless as long as American and Canadian sealing schooners continued their high-seas hunts. Faced with this dilemma, the United States declared the Bering Sea off limits to commercial fur seal hunting, a unilateral action that defied several conventions in international maritime law, not the least of which was the generally applied 3-mile limit of a coastal nation's sovereign authority. There was also the unprecedented declaration of national sovereignty over a species of *farae naturae* beyond the U.S. borders, and the U.S. also ended up contradicting its own firmly held policies in such matters. The United States had opposed similar conservation measures attempted by the Russian government only a few years before (and the United States would contradict itself again a century later in negotiations for a renewed Canada-U.S. salmon treaty, arguing that the ocean was a pasture for salmon, trumping international legal principles vesting property rights to salmon in the nation of the salmon's origin).

In hindsight, the Americans clearly were right, at least in what they were attempting, if not in the way they attempted it. But when U.S. revenue cutters began arresting schooners' officers and crews and seizing both Canadian and American ships in the Bering Sea, the political fallout was spectacular. Sea captains and traders from San Francisco and Victoria took equal umbrage at the notion that a government could assert jurisdiction over commerce on the high seas. But the seizure of Victoria schooners by U.S. government vessels touched a nerve in Canada, not just because of Canada's long-standing resentment of American bullying, but also because Canada's external affairs jurisdiction was still controlled by Britain at the time.

In the first few years of the 20th century, several Canadian vessels were apprehended in the Bering Sea. American spies skulked around the Victoria waterfront; terse diplomatic notes went back and forth between London and Washington; the pages of Canadian newspapers filled with gripping tales of plucky Canadian schooner skippers who outwitted American revenue cutters. Elaborate compensation packages were put together to ease the Victoria fleet's bad feelings, international arbitration panels were convened, and diplomatic intrigue took its usual course. The fur seal slaughter continued, however, with Japanese schooners playing a larger role as the years passed. A breakthrough was reached when the governments of Russia, Japan, and the United States agreed to cooperate on conservation and enforcement measures, but it wasn't until 1911 that Canada came on board.

The result was a treaty that banned all high-seas harvests of fur seals and sea otters in the North Pacific. The Ainu, the Aleuts, and Northwest Coast communities could continue their small-boat hunts, but otherwise fur seal harvests were confined to the rookeries. Canada and Japan were guaranteed a financial share of any U.S. rookery harvest of the Pribilof herds. Canada and the United States were guaranteed a similar share of the profits from Japanese harvests on Japanese rookeries. Canada and Japan would also share in the profits from any harvests from Russian rookeries.

But the importance of the 1911 treaty went beyond the regulation of the North Pacific's fur seal hunts or the protection it offered sea otters.

The 1911 fur seal treaty marked the beginning of humanity's attempts to fully *know* the North Pacific. The treaty foreshadowed every subsequent attempt to contain an industrial maelstrom that had pulled salmon and sea otters and whales and fur seals into its maw and just kept moving across the horizon. The treaty laid the groundwork for every international effort devoted to comprehending the dynamics of the North Pacific. Those efforts were under way at the close of the 20th century with a particular intensity of purpose, because at the storm front of technology's hurricane, fleets of Asian driftnet ships were at work, and so were American trawlers, setting nets in the Bering Sea that were big enough to hold a dozen 747s.

Salmon Domains, Trophic Highways, and Bute Wax Episodes

Because nature represents both ideas in human heads
and an actual world of plants and animals, changes in the natural world
have shaped such meanings, even as changes in meaning have
brought changes in the natural world. The conversation
is a long and complicated one.

— *Richard White, "Discovering Nature in North America,"*
The Journal of American History

THE ALEUTIAN ISLAND OF Adak bursts from the North Pacific about halfway between Kamchatka and the northern tip of Vancouver Island. When it's sunny, Adak is brilliant green, but it's usually shrouded in thick fog or whipped by such furious winds that the rain falls sideways. It's a U.S. Armed Forces outpost that came alive during World War II, when Japanese armies threatened to fan out across the Aleutians, and it remained a busy place during the more outrageous days of the Cold War. But by the 1990s, the talk around the tables at the Eagle's Nest bar wasn't about Russian submarines. It was about Asian pirate driftnet ships, and over the blare of you-done-me-wrong country songs on the jukebox, we swapped stories and compared notes. The American score was the highest.

Cradling a beer, Brett Schnyder, a special agent with the U.S.

National Marine Fisheries Service, tallied his count for the week: twenty driftnet pirates. The U.S. Coast Guard C-130 patrol plane he was aboard got close enough to see salmon on the decks of several of them, salmon in their nets, and dolphins in their nets, too. Our count of pirate driftnetters had been eight, all of them fishing well north of the 15-degree isotherm, a wavy imaginary line that moves up and down the middle of the North Pacific during the year and generally marks the southern temperature limit of salmon's high-seas range. Officially, the northern boundary of the mid-Pacific squid grounds had been set at the latitude of 42 degrees north, because the 15-degree isotherm barely dips below that. Ships fishing with longline gear and hydraulic squid-jigging arrays were permitted below 42 degrees. We'd found our pirates drift-netting, clearly fishing for salmon, about 40 sea miles above the line. But Schnyder bested us there, too. One of the ships his patrol came across was 120 sea miles north of the line.

Finding pirate driftnet ships in the North Pacific was harder than I thought it would be. As a ride-along with the Crew Six, 407 Squadron of the Canadian Forces' Maritime Pacific Command, I soon realized that the 777,000 square kilometers (300,000 square miles) of ocean we were assigned to patrol was a pretty big place. It takes luck to find a poacher out there, even from the vantage point offered by a CP-140 Aurora, and even though it's an aircraft designed for antisubmarine war-fare that can pick up a tin can in the water on its supersensitive radar from a distance of 15 sea miles.

When one is flying at 3600 meters (12,000 feet), with two of the four engines shut down to conserve fuel, the hours turn into days. The bore-dom of the triangular routine, from Comox to Adak to Honolulu and back again, was broken only when a suspicious-looking blip showed up on the screens in the eerie half-light of the Aurora's technical compart-ment. The Aurora's surveillance equipment could quickly distinguish a pirate driftnetter from a freighter or a tanker, and when that happened, the drill was to fall from the sky at 260 knots and open the bomb bay to drop a bathythermograph buoy into the ocean beside the ship to take the sea's temperature. That way we could determine which side of the 15-degree isotherm the ship was fishing on. Pulling up at an altitude of about 60 meters (200 feet), we'd set off a series of blinding flashes from a bulb on the plane's belly that clicked in unison with the shutter of the Aurora's nose-mounted camera. Looking at the high-resolution photographs the camera produced, you could almost make out the terrified looks on the faces in the ships' wheelhouse windows.

The pirates had cause to be terrified because getting caught from the air usually meant their fishing days were over. Throughout the 1990s, driftnet pirates were being chased back and forth across the North Pacific, usually ending up in the clutches of a U.S. Coast Guard vessel or a Russian naval ship. A joint Canadian-U.S.-Russian effort was in effect by the late 1980s, aimed at keeping driftnetters out of salmon waters. By 1991, a United Nations resolution had banned high-seas driftnetting in the Pacific. There was the occasional poacher pushing his luck by steaming north of the squid grounds, and there were the full-time pirates funded by Taipei-based organized crime syndicates that laundered driftnet-caught salmon into world markets. It was a vicious and dangerous cat-and-mouse game, but by the 1990s, the high seas north of 42 degrees were largely empty of driftnetters.

Large-scale high-seas driftnetting had become the marine equivalent of clear-cutting tropical rain forest, and the 1991 UN resolution outlawing the fishery was a rare triumph in the history of international conservation efforts. In the long and grisly history of the North Pacific's industrial fisheries, the ban was a welcome event, following heightened public concern throughout the world about the state of the planet's oceans. The 1991 UN resolution was also a direct descendant of the 1911 fur seal treaty.

But a lot had happened in those intervening eight decades.

After World War I, diesel-powered fishing fleets with increased catching power and improved catch capacity began to move deeper into the North Pacific. American boats from Seattle and Portland began to make regular forays into the Gulf of Alaska and the Bering Sea. Some of those first vessels were fur-sealing schooners that had been converted to codfish schooners. Other boats were longliners, crewed by Scandinavian immigrants, fishing the rich halibut banks.

Meanwhile, after V. I. Lenin's 1922 edict ordering the development of a modern commercial fishing fleet, Soviet vessels were becoming an increasingly frequent sight in the North Pacific. By the early 1930s, more than thirty deep-sea trawlers, bearing the USSR's distinctive red hammer and sickle on their smokestacks, were plying the Sea of Okhotsk, the Russian Pacific, and the Bering Sea.

During the 1930s, Japan had also developed a significant fleet in the North Pacific. Like the Soviet Union and the United States, the Japanese regarded the development of a high-seas fishery as a matter of historic destiny, part of God's plan for the Japanese people. The Japanese industrialist and salmon canner A. K. Takasaki put it this way, in 1937: "In compensation for the scarcity of natural resources in Japan, God has endowed her with a unique gift of excellent fishing talent to take care of her population. Her destiny is therefore to develop that art further and further, and to exploit the fisheries even from the open sea. . . ."

Toward that destiny, Japanese fishermen fairly hurled themselves. By the 1930s, Japanese fishermen were engaged in shore-based salmon fisheries on the Kamchatka coast, governed by lease arrangements with Russian fisheries authorities, and Japan also pursued "mothership" salmon fisheries — the deployment of small fishing vessels from a large ship, like sealing canoes dispatched from schooners — that targeted Kamchatka salmon on the high seas, in agreement with Russia. But after the Kamchatka salmon runs collapsed, the Japanese started moving east, and in 1936, the Tokyo Fishing Institute arrived in Bristol Bay, Alaska, just outside the U.S. 3-mile limit, to test various types of fishing gear. Japanese vessels were already trawling for cod, halibut, and hake in the area, and Japanese companies were also operating floating crab canneries in the Bering Sea. But when they turned their attention to North American salmon, it was like the fur seal wars all over again. Except this time, the bad guys weren't Canadians. The bad guys were Japanese.

The arrival of Japanese driftnet ships off the Alaskan coast, and the reports of massive overfishing of salmon that followed, caused widespread panic in the United States. It wasn't entirely unjustifed. The Japanese government responded calmly, proposing a treaty to regulate high-seas salmon interceptions, but the United States wasn't in the mood for moderation. The Seattle Labor Central Council and the

Association of Pacific Fisheries called for trade sanctions against Japan, and longshoremen threatened to dump Japanese goods off Seattle's docks unless the fishing stopped. The Washington State legislature joined the protest but also supported a fishing treaty with Japan. The Alaska Fishermen's Union demanded that the U.S. government unilaterally declare ownership of all salmon from U.S. rivers on the high seas. Japan's fishing industry responded by declaring the Bering Sea an extension of the Bay of Tokyo. And then bombs fell on Pearl Harbor.

Diplomacy took a holiday during the carnage of World War II, when the North Pacific and the Aleutian Islands became key theaters of operation. But not long after the end of the war, the old arguments about high-seas fishing rights were back on track again. Japanese ships were seen on the fog banks off Kvichak River in Bristol Bay, and Alaskan fishermen reported coming upon the remains of Japanese camps on the beach. A flurry of unilateral statutory measures and international agreements followed.

Most of those agreements were based on the principles articulated in the 1911 fur seal treaty. In 1951, Japanese, American, and Canadian delegates met in Tokyo to establish a fisheries treaty, and the result was the International Convention for the High Seas Fisheries of the North Pacific Ocean. Joint research efforts had begun, with the aim of learning exactly where salmon went in the ocean and which countries caught which fish.

By 1958, most Pacific nation-states had signed the 1958 Convention on the Continental Shelf, but at the same time most coastal states were considering the lead of Peru, Ecuador, and Chile, whose Santiago declaration proposed a jurisdictional extension into the seas of 200 nautical miles. By 1966, the United States — wary of the military and fisheries implications of confining its ambitions to waters outside other countries' 200-mile limits — had extended its own 3-mile limit to only 12 miles. But the United Nations had begun its law-of-the-sea conferences by the late 1950s, and a 200-mile limit was quickly becoming the standard.

International agreements were also beginning to curtail the world's whaling fleets. In 1972, the United Nations Conference on the Human

Environment met in Stockholm and called for a ten-year moratorium on all commercial whaling. The International Whaling Comission rejected the UN proposal, but Canada and the United States declared unilateral closures in 1982, and the whaling commission agreed to begin closures of whaling seasons in 1986. Although the Soviets had invested heavily in whaling, the whaling moratorium didn't put the brakes on their North Pacific fisheries. By the early 1960s, the Soviet Union's fishing fleet was arguably the largest and most modern in the world. Its fleet of high-seas trawlers had grown to more than 200 vessels, and its catch quadrupled between the early 1950s and the late 1960s.

Through the 1960s and 1970s, U.S. federal edict declared Bristol Bay a "natural disaster" three times, and high-seas interception of Bristol Bay sockeye was probably a contributing factor. In 1980, an estimated 900,000 Alaskan chinook salmon ended up in high-seas Japanese driftnets, and the United States finally abandoned its Wild West "freedom of the seas" enthusiasms. By the 1980s, the United States had extended its own marine jurisdiction to 200 miles, and Japanese driftnet interceptions of North American salmon were severely curtailed. Just as sealing schooners were converted to codfish schooners, salmon driftnet ships were converted to squid driftnet ships, and it wasn't until 1991 that the UN finally acted and banned driftnets from the North Pacific.

All these events played themselves out on an ocean that was utterly changed from the days before the Industrial Age.

Right whales that once numbered in the thousands, and drew the first whaling ships to the Northwest Grounds, were all but gone from the entire ocean. By the 1990s, the entire North Pacific right whale population was believed to number fewer than 200 animals. Pacific walruses had fallen from a pre-industrial population of about 250,000 to about 50,000 by the 1950s, but they slowly recovered through the rest of the 20th century. Before the International Whaling Commission acted, about 9000 blue whales were being hunted in the North Pacific every year. By the end of the 20th century, the North Pacific blue whale population was hovering around 1500 animals. Gray whales, however, did recover. From a remnant population of fewer than 2000 at the close of the 19th century, the gray whales that migrated from the Bering Sea to

Mexico had grown in number to their pre-industrial population levels, numbering more than 22,000. Elephant seals, meanwhile, managed to escape extinction only by dumb luck. For thousands of years, elephant seals migrated in the tens of thousands from their rookeries on the coasts of California and Mexico to the Aleutian Islands and back. At the beginning of the 20th century, they were believed to be extinct, but a small herd of less than 1000 had survived, unknown to hunters, on Guadalupe Island off the Mexican coast. A century later, the North Pacific's elephant seals had recovered to a population of more than 120,000 animals.

By the time the 1911 fur seal treaty was signed, fur seals had come perilously close to the fate that had befallen sea cows and spectacled cormorants. The fur seals of the Pribilofs, once believed to number as many as three million, had been reduced to about 120,000 animals, and it took decades for the fur seal populations to rebound. The rapid decline of the North Pacific's sea otters, meanwhile, was similarly slowed by the 1911 treaty. The pre-industrial population of North Pacific sea otters is estimated to have been perhaps 300,000 animals, ranging from the Japanese island of Hokkaido, through the Sea of Okhotsk and the Kurile Islands, along the Kamchatka coast and through the Aleutian chain, and along North America's Pacific coast as far south as Mexico. By the end of the 20th century, sea otters remained only in a few isolated pockets outside Alaskan waters. There were perhaps 9000 along the Russian coast, about 2300 in California waters, and a few hundred between Oregon and the Alaska panhandle. The Alaskan population, by the early 1970s, had revived to an estimated 100,000 animals.

The near-extinction of sea otters produced the first industry-induced "ripple effect" through North Pacific ecosystems. Sea otters feed on sea urchins. Sea urchins feed on kelp. With the sea otters gone and nothing to keep sea urchins in check, vast forests of kelp that once rimmed the Northwest Coast's islands and inlets were denuded, creating "urchin barrens" and resulting in severe disruptions to local ecosystems. But by the 1990s, the trawl fishery for pollock in Alaskan waters, mainly the Bering Sea, was causing what appeared to be a far broader ripple effect throughout the North Pacific. There was nothing localized about it.

A walleye pollock is not an attractive fish. It's not the sort of fish you find displayed nicely in the ice trays of a supermarket's seafoods section. But it's one of the most important sources of food in the North Pacific's ecosystems. It comprises an estimated 60 percent of the entire marine biomass in the Bering Sea, providing food for dozens of marine species. The North Pacific's seabirds and marine mammals are reckoned to consume more than a million tonnes of pollock every year, all by themselves.

Pollock was never an important food source for human beings, showing up as a significant industrial harvest, in trawl landings, only in the 1950s. Pollock isn't generally sold whole or filleted. It's processed into surimi, a generic seafood product marketed in the form of fish sticks and imitation crab. It's hard to make money catching pollock, which has rarely fetched more than an American dime per pound. But in the 1970s, the expansion of high-seas trawl fleets had resulted in staggering increases in the North Pacific pollock catch. Japanese, Soviet, Chinese, Polish, Korean, and American pollock trawlers were becoming a frequent sight in the Aleutian Islands and in the Gulf of Alaska. By the early 1980s, the Bering Sea fisheries comprised more than half of all the fish landed by American fishermen.

During the 1980s, the North Pacific pollock catch had risen to an annual average of six million tonnes. A regulatory agreement between the United States, Russia, Japan, and several other fishing nations had closed the center of the Bering Sea in the 1990s. But by then, the so-called Bering Sea doughnut hole — which lies outside the exclusive economic zones of both Russia and the United States — had been scoured of pollock. Still, pollock trawling was proving a big money-maker in both Russian and American waters. So it continued.

Factory trawlers, mostly from Seattle, had begun fishing Alaskan waters with a vengeance in the early 1980s. Some of the trawlers were 100 meters (300 feet) in length and carried crews of fifty and more, setting nets big enough to devour skyscrapers. They inspired fierce opposition, uniting Greenpeace activists with the likes of conservative Alaskan Republican senator Ted Stevens. But the fishery continued.

While this was going on, the Pribilof Islands' fur seal herds, which had been slowing recovering from the slaughter preceding the 1911 fur seal treaty, started shrinking again. Between the early 1980s and the late 1990s, the fur seal populations declined from about one million animals to about 750,000. The decline in Steller's sea lion populations was far more dramatic, falling from about 250,000 animals in the late 1960s to fewer than 80,000 animals by the middle of the 1990s.

It wasn't until after the Steller's sea lion was placed under the protection of the U.S. Endangered Species Act in 1990 that any measures were taken to curb the pollock fishery. It took another eight years for federal and state fisheries managers to scale back on pollock trawling, closing certain areas and pushing the fleet away from sea lion feeding areas. But even after those changes in fisheries management — changes that were hotly protested by the fishing industry and criticized by conservation groups for being too little, too late — populations of fur seals and sea lions showed no early signs of recovery.

The absurdity of this is not just that nobody could say what kind of impact pollock trawling was having on such a vital link in the Bering Sea food chain. It was not just that pollock trawling persisted, with little restraint, in the absence of this knowledge. It was that the human hand had become involved in practically every living thing, throughout the North Pacific. From California to Kodiak Island, industrial fishing had preceded collapses in populations of rockfish, herring, halibut, sole, flounder, sea urchin, abalone, geoduck, and just about every other species one might care to mention. And the effects of these collapses on ecosystems, whether good or bad, were largely unknown. The most dramatic of all declines in fish populations — at least the best-documented of all these declines — was suffered by salmon.

Salmon are not little-known creatures that live only at the bottom of the sea, and anybody who lived on North America's west coast could see the many ways that the Industrial Age had radically altered salmon abundance. There were clear-cut mountainsides, culverted creeks under suburban roads, and dams on the rivers, and what all this added up to, south of the 49th parallel, is displayed on the walls of the headquarters of the U.S. National Marine Fisheries Service, in Silver Springs, Maryland. When I visited the NMFS headquarters in the summer of 1998, those maps displayed a landscape between Southern California and northern Washington State that was a multicolored quilt of biological trauma wards. Huge swaths of terrain marked seventeen separate "evolutionarily significant units" of five salmon species that were officially registered as patients within the emergency room of the Endangered Species Act. Not quite dead, but almost. From the hills north of Los Angeles to the Canadian border, the maps showed that salmon had already disappeared from more than a third of their former range. By the summer of 1999, nine more sections were added to the NMFS quilt, which brought twenty-six wide-ranging salmon populations under the ministrations of U.S. federal endangered species law. On the NMFS maps, the only white spaces left, from Los Angeles to Vancouver, were those places where salmon runs were already extinct.

Without benefit of federal legislation that requires the collapse of salmon runs to be tracked so efficiently, Canada's Department of Fisheries and Oceans had not developed many comprehensive data about the status of salmon from Canadian rivers. An October 1996 American Fisheries Society review found that assessments were possible for only slightly more than half the roughly 9600 salmon stocks in British Columbia and Yukon. But of those, 624 were found to be at "high risk" of extinction, 78 were at "moderate risk," and 230 were "of special concern." Another 142 were already extinct.

The overall decline of salmon in the North Pacific is difficult to get a handle on. Among those scientists who have tried are Ted Gresh, Jim Lichatowich, and Peter Schoonmaker — the trio we met in the second chapter of this book, where they were trying to sort out the consequences of salmon declines in the terrestrial ecosystems south of the 49th parallel. Lichatowich, Gresh, and Schoonmaker reckon that there existed, at the beginning of the industrial salmon fisheries, a biomass of North American salmon in the Pacific of between 640 million and 991 million kilograms. Their estimate of the total salmon biomass, by the late 1980s, was between 305 million and 606 million kilograms. In the early 1800s, 56 to 65 percent of the salmon arose from Alaskan rivers, 19 to 26 percent were spawned in British Columbia rivers, and 15 to 16 percent came from rivers as far south as Southern California. By the late

1980s, however, between 80 and 90 percent of all the North American salmon in the Pacific came from Alaskan rivers. British Columbia's share was down to between 8 and 17 percent. A mere 1 percent of the North American salmon in the Pacific — or perhaps, in some years, as much as 1.5 percent — were from rivers south of the 49th parallel.

These declines occurred under the auspices of domestic salmon fisheries management regimes in both Canada and the United States — management systems fully sanctioned by science. And these declines also occurred under the ambit of a treaty between Canada and the United States, first concluded in the late 1930s and renewed in 1985. The Pacific Salmon Treaty had failed to accomplish either of its objectives, which were to avoid harvest-share disputes and to control overfishing by the fleets of both countries. Instead, the treaty caused significant strains in relations between Canada and the United States, and even between Canada and the province of British Columbia. The treaty also codified a fisheries management regime that produced disputes between Alaska and the Pacific Northwest states about the protection of salmon runs that Washington, Oregon, and Idaho were attempting to conserve and restore. The treaty was a constitutional instrument that entrenched "mixed-stock" fisheries of the very type that were known to cause extinctions of small salmon runs.

If one reviews the catch estimates assembled by biologists from the Pacific Salmon Commission, by Canada's Department of Fisheries and Oceans, and by the U.S. National Marine Fisheries Service, it becomes immediately evident that there was rarely agreement between the two countries' biologists about how many salmon from each country's rivers were caught by each country's mixed-stock fisheries in any given year. These were not minor quibbles. In 1987, for instance, Canadian fisheries managers estimated that Canadian fishermen caught 904,000 Alaska-bound pink salmon. That same year, Alaskan fisheries managers reckoned that Canadians had actually caught 3.3 million Alaskan pink salmon. In 1987, Alaskans said they caught 342,000 Canadian pink salmon. Canadians said the Alaskans caught more than a million Canadian pink salmon that year. In 1988, Canadian fisheries managers said Canadian fishermen caught 725,000 Washington State coho. U.S.

fisheries managers said that Canadians actually caught 1.34 million Washington State coho that year. In 1990, Canadians said Washington State fishermen caught 229,000 B.C. coho. Americans said the Washington fleet only caught 63,000 B.C. coho that year.

The treaty broke down several times after it was signed in 1985. These breakdowns led to two "fish wars" in the 1990s, which featured overfishing by both countries' fleets, incidents of civil disobedience, and badly damaged relations between the two countries. It had all degenerated into a kind of medieval delirium. Hopeless fish war stratagems were played out as though salmon runs were just enemy flags fluttering over a 15th-century battlefield. Fishing industry warlords dispatched fish boats against one another like catapults, arquebuses, and siege wagons. Canadian gillnet boats took an Alaskan passenger ferry hostage in 1997. The White House had to get involved. In 1998, British Columbia's salmon fishermen threatened to assemble a flotilla to surround American submarines at the Nanoose Bay missile-testing site. B.C. premier Glen Clark accused federal fisheries minister David Anderson of treason, and in one of the Vancouver dailies Mr. Anderson's name appeared with the word Anti-Christ in the same huge headline. All that remained was the burning of sorcerers.

Still, despite the extirpation of whales and sea otters and sea lions, the collapse of so many fish populations, and the extinction of so many salmon runs, the North Pacific, at the beginning of the 21st century, contained the planet's most productive fishing grounds. More than 25 million tonnes of fish were being harvested from the North Pacific annually. Close to 800,000 tonnes of those fish were salmon, from rivers as far afield as Korea and Los Angeles. That's an amount of salmon equal to the weight of the human population of Alaska, British Columbia, Washington, and Oregon combined, every year.

It is not as though North Pacific nation-states learned nothing during the eight decades between the 1911 North Pacific fur seal treaty and the 1991 UN resolution banning high-seas driftnets from the North Pacific. Clearly, much had been learned, and the 1991 UN resolution was at least partly evidence of that. By the end of the century, several international regulatory and scientific bodies had developed a much broader understanding about the way things worked in the North Pacific. Technology played its part in that knowledge — the very technologies that allowed the expansion of the high-seas fishing fleets also provided the means to monitor those fleets. Because fisheries management is necessarily about history — and in no small part about trial and error — the 20th century closed with more than a century's worth of catch statistics, which in themselves comprised a database from which the effects of fishing, trends in abundance of fish, and other necessary information could be gleaned.

By the time of the 1991 UN driftnet ban, dozens of agencies and institutions had made their contributions. These agencies included Canada's Department of Fisheries and Oceans and its Institute of Ocean Sciences, the U.S. National Oceanographic and Aeronautics Administration and the National Marine Fisheries Service, the Japanese National Research Institute for Far Seas Fisheries, the Soviet Academy of Sciences, the Russian Pacific Scientific Research Centre, and the multinational PICES (the North Pacific Marine Science Organization). A variety of academic and semipublic institutions were also at work in the North Pacific, such as the Scripps Institute of Oceanography, the University of Washington, the College of Oceanic and Atmospheric Sciences at the University of Oregon, the University of British Columbia Fisheries Centre, the Alaskan Fisheries Science Center, and so on.

The 20th century began without the most basic understanding, for instance, of where salmon went during their sojourns in the ocean. By the century's end, it was clear that the North Pacific was really several oceans, each of which maintain relationships with each other that differ in intensity and complexity, and which exhibit striking differences in the abundance and distribution of marine species.

As it turns out, North American salmon traverse several of these oceans, known to oceanographers as production domains. The most productive of these domains, and the ones where North American salmon usually spend their time at sea, are the Coastal Upwelling Domain, the Coastal Downwelling Domain, and the Subarctic Domain.

The Coastal Upwelling Domain, situated between Vancouver Island's northern tip and Baja California, is marked by southward-flowing ocean

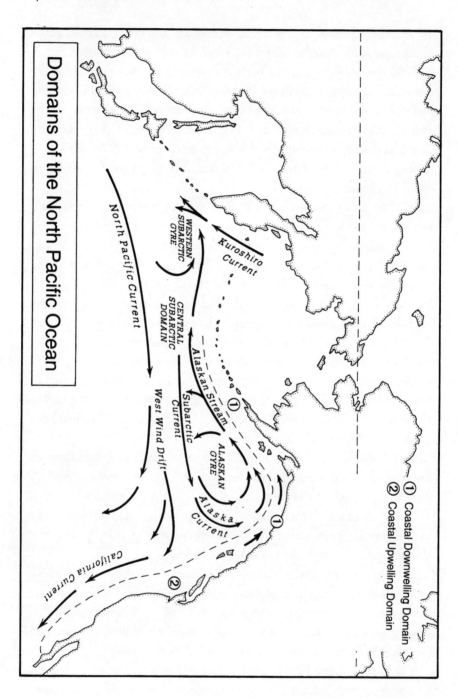

Domains of the North Pacific Ocean

North Pacific Current

West Wind Drift

California Current

WESTERN SUBARCTIC GYRE

CENTRAL SUBARCTIC DOMAIN

Kuroshiro Current

Alaskan Stream

Subarctic Current

ALASKAN GYRE

Alaska Current

① ①

②

① Coastal Downwelling Domain
② Coastal Upwelling Domain

currents that comprise the California Current. Although this is a domain of salmon, the dominant pelagic fish in this ocean are hake, sardines, anchovy, and mackerel.

The Coastal Downwelling Domain extends from Vancouver Island's northern tip to the Alaska Peninsula. In this ocean, the currents flow generally northward, becoming the Alaska Current and the Alaska Coastal Current. Salmon swim here, too, but the main fish species are pollock, cod, halibut, sablefish, herring, and hake.

The Subarctic Domain — a key domain of salmon — traverses the greatest swath of the three. Its eastern gyre is bounded on the south by the North Pacific Current — a narrow superhighway that rarely exceeds 100 sea miles in width — which sweeps across the ocean from Japan. This is the freeway that most of those unfortunate Japanese mariners ended up on, stuck in the middle lanes in dismasted junks. The North Pacific Current eventually loops north to become the Alaska Current, which forms the boundary between the Subarctic Domain and the Coastal Downwelling Domain. The Alaska Current continues north, around the Gulf of Alaska, and turns west to become the Alaska Stream, which follows the southern shore of the Aleutian chain. The Central Subarctic is situated roughly between the Alaska panhandle and the central Aleutians and is dominated by sockeye, chum, and pink salmon.

The Western Subarctic Gyre is a lot more complicated, with three times as much in the way of freeway on-ramps and off-ramps as its eastern counterpart. The Alaska Stream, which makes its way back across the North Pacific, forms the northern boundary of the Western Subarctic Gyre. The East Kamchatka Current, flowing out of the Bering Sea, loops around the western boundary of the western gyre, and the North Pacific Current — which begins here on the Asian side of the ocean — forms the western gyre's southern boundary. But around the perimeter of the western gyre there is also the Kuroshio Current, as well as the Oyashio Current, which brings a lot of extra traffic in the form of warm water, cold water, and entire convoys of species rarely seen on the North American side of the Pacific.

Although it is considered a single faunal province, meaning its animal life is more or less consistent in composition from one end to the other, there are major faunal differences between the North American side and the Asian side of the Subarctic Domain. The differences are sometimes so great that several species will appear in the far west that do not appear at all on the eastern side, and vice versa. And the two "sides" of the Central Subarctic show marked differences in ecological productivity.

There are several oceans again, in the realm of seabirds. Tufted puffins, which can exploit a variety of prey, are fairly evenly distributed across the North Pacific, as are Leach's storm petrels, because they like the high seas, and the rare parakleet auklet can be found almost anywhere in the North Pacific because it will eat almost anything. Cassin's auklets, meanwhile, prefer the B.C. coast, where they find an abundance of zooplankton off the continental shelf. Ancient murrellets also like the shelf's waters for the sand lance. In the Aleutians, common murres are uncommon except on islands with lots of shallow water around them. But it is not just the place that determines what birds are out there; it's the time of year. In the summer, sooty shearwaters and short-tailed shearwaters are practically absent from the North Pacific. They spend the spring south of the equator, but they spend the rest of the year in the North Pacific. And there are a lot of them. Population estimates in the early 1990s proposed a figure of 50 million for the number of these shearwaters in the North Pacific during the summer, autumn, and winter months. Various sorts of shearwaters comprise probably half the total biomass of seabirds in the North Pacific, but they comprise a small minority of the types of species found in North Pacific waters. The Subarctic Domain is especially rich in avian life, with birds such as albatross, pomaraine jaegers, mottled petrels, horned puffins, fulmars, and rhinocerous auklets.

At the century's close, biologists and oceanographers were still only beginning to understand what goes on in the several oceans of the North Pacific and in the relationships between them. At the time of this writing, little was known about the extent to which currents carry influences from one part of the North Pacific to the next, or the factors that cause various North Pacific ecosystems to expand and contract as they do. Little was known about the composition of species within ocean domains or why the mix of species within these domains tends to change over time or what industrial fisheries do to the elaborate mechanics at work within these oceans.

It wasn't until the 1970s, for instance, that science came to realize how the bottom rung of the food chain in the world's oceans — in particular, a specific single-celled form of blue-green algae known as cyanobacteria, among the very smallest of the ocean's smallest phytoplankton species — accounts for perhaps 70 percent of the primary production and maintenance of all life in the oceans. Science should be excused for not having understood this. Except when it "blooms" and changes the color of the sea surface, phytoplankton is invisible to the naked eye. But phytoplankton is where it starts. More precisely, photosynthesis is where it starts — that miraculous process in which inorganic elements combine with sunlight to produce life, something that happens every millisecond of every day in the biomass of phytoplankton. Those microscopic plants live a few hours, sometimes a few days, providing food for zooplankton, which, in turn, provides life for everything else in the ocean, and to an extent, for everything that walks or crawls on the planet.

Although the North Pacific was late in showing itself on the horizons of Western science, by the end of the 20th century, it was becoming, in certain respects, the best-known of the world's oceans. Scientists were naturally drawn to the North Pacific because of its importance as a producer of fish, because of its growing geopolitical importance, and because of heightened public concerns about the state of the planet's key ecosystems. Much had happened during the 20th century that caused the "modern" world to change the way it saw the North Pacific. Science made enormous contributions to those changes.

But scientific knowledge comes slowly. And sometimes it comes in the most peculiar ways, as in the case of Bute Wax, a substance that bursts forth in bizarre fashion every few years from the waters of Bute Inlet, a fjord that cuts into British Columbia's coastal mountains.

Reports of Bute Wax episodes go back to the 1920s. Apart from an account of a jellylike substance erupting from the sea at the mouth of Toba Inlet in 1922, such events appear to be confined to Bute Inlet, which pierces deep into the B.C. coast east of that maze of islands around Euclataw Rapids, about 120 sea miles north of Vancouver. In times of extremely cold weather, a freezing wind will arise from the glacier on top of Mount Waddington, pour out of the Homathko Canyon, and roar down Bute Inlet. This produces a bone-chilling and hair-raising version of a notorious wind known as "a Bute." On several such occasions in the 20th century, rafts of thick, oily goo were seen drifting down the inlet, often forming into large, waxlike spheres as big as basketballs, which were reported washed up on the beaches to a depth of 3 meters (10 feet).

Homesteaders named it Bute Wax, and it appeared in 1922, 1935, 1936, 1950, 1951, 1955, and 1956. It may well have occurred many other times, but as far back as the 1930s, reliable information about Bute Wax was obscured by a sort of local taboo. Fishermen and hand loggers were known to become abstruse and downright evasive about it.

It wasn't until 1957 that Bute Wax made its first appearance in the scientific literature. In June of that year, M. Y. Williams wrote an article for the *Transactions of the Royal Society of Canada* that provided a sketchy description of the phenomenon, along with a chemical analysis of a sample obtained from Frank Lehmann, a prospector who claimed to know a Bute Inlet old-timer who had fifteen 45-gallon drums of the stuff hidden away somewhere. Williams's chemical analsyses were undertaken by Dr. Tikam Jain of Victoria, who found only that Bute Wax contained something similar to the seed pollen of a plant that grows in Nevada and California. This was intriguing, because pine pollen is known to fall thickly on the surface of Bute Inlet.

But the reticence of the Bute Inlet settler community to discuss Bute Wax with the outside world had its roots in the Depression, when local people saw Eldorado in it. It was found to be more flammable than kerosene; it made a dandy machine oil and a perfect solvent. Frank Lehmann, the prospector who provided a sample to Williams for his *Transactions* article, reckoned it could be pumped from the ground like oil from a well. Munday McCrae, an eccentric Irish dowser, had wandered the mountains above Bute Inlet, hoping to find the motherlode. There were apocryphal stories of a map that marked the location of an oil-soaked stump, said to be the source of Bute Wax. There were those who dreamed of becoming tycoons, so some Bute Wax stories were whispered. Some were not told; others were called rumors. Most were half-forgotten by the time the *Vector*, a Canadian Hydrographic Service ship chartered to Environment Canada, and the *Dolphin*, a Scripps Institute of Oceanography research vessel, slipped into Bute Inlet in 1971.

It was Williams's 1957 article that brought the *Vector* and the *Dolphin* to Bute Inlet. The Scripps Institute and Environment Canada had obtained some Bute Wax of their own somehow, and their analysis had found that almost 50 percent of it was composed of a type of lipid, a fatlike substance common in marine animals from tiny amphipods to squids and whales. The lipid could also be manufactured — it's a primary ingredient of bubble gum. While in Bute Inlet, the two vessels dragged small-mesh trawl nets, like huge nylon stockings, through the waters of the inlet. Most of the creatures hauled up by the *Vector* and the *Dolphin* were copepods, mainly of a type known as *Calanus plumchrus*. When you look at a dead *Calanus plumchrus* under a microscope, you can see that its little body is almost half lipid. In a 1979 article in the *Journal of the Fisheries Research Board of Canada*, scientists R. F. Lee and Judd Nevenzel summed up the Bute Inlet study: "We conclude that the origin of Bute Inlet wax is a copepod lipid, mainly from *C. plumchrus*."

This might not seem like a staggeringly important contribution to science. But at the time, it was important. By the time the Lee and Nevenzel paper appeared in the *Journal*, it had only been about thirty years since scientists had recognized the importance of zooplankton in the North Pacific. Much of the early research on zooplankton in the North Pacific was done by Russians, such as the scientist K. V. Belkemishev, who was busy analyzing zooplankton such as *Calanus plumchrus* in the late 1940s and early 1950s in the Bering Sea. Belkemishev was one of the first scientists to show that copepod grazing was a significant factor in the abundance of phytoplankton and small zooplankton (because copepods eat so much of the stuff), primarily copepods of the type that ended up as Bute Wax, the key conduit between phytoplankon, the source of life in the sea, and every creature that swam in the North Pacific.

International efforts to understand zooplankton and the role those little creatures play in the North Pacific followed quickly upon the Russian research in the Bering Sea. Zooplankton research is tedious work. It consists mainly of pulling tiny-meshed trawl nets — the meshes are usually between .2 millimeters and .35 millimeters wide — with net mouths only .35 meters (1 foot) wide — through the surface layers of the ocean. Every couple of hours or so, you haul the catch aboard, note the time and date and other conditions under which the little creatures were caught, and then spend hours in front of a microscope looking at what the net brought up. American and Canadian scientists were undertaking such research on the high seas by the 1950s, and Canada began to make annual research contributions from Ocean Station Papa, an anchored facility about 1500 sea miles off the B.C. coast, in the 1980s. Hokkaido University researchers began annual, Pacific-wide zooplankton studies in 1980.

It may be dreary work, but it has allowed a picture of the North Pacific to emerge that is far more complex and elaborate than any scientist had imagined before the 20th century.

Zooplankton abundance varies widely across the North Pacific, and the mechanics affecting its distribution are not well undertood. Zooplankton is usually divided into three types — macrozooplankton, mesozooplankton, and microzooplankton (microscopic, smaller, and ridiculously small) — but size is not just about different types of creature but also about the age of the creature, because older ones are bigger than younger ones. For some zooplankton species, abundance is higher in the summer than in the winter. Throughout much of the North Pacific, zooplankton appears to consist mainly of copepods, such as Bute Wax. Zooplankton is eaten by everything from other zooplankton to planktivorous fish such as salmon, saury, and pomfret to seabirds and whales. One patch of ocean may have ten times as much zooplankton as another place only a mere sea mile distant, and total zooplankton abundance tends to be higher on the continental shelves than offshore. Although the key domain of Pacific salmon — the subarctic Pacific — is generally considered a "single faunal province" of zooplankton, research in the 1980s began to show that on the North American side of the subarctic

Pacific, the dominant species was a copepod of the Bute Wax type, whereas on the far side the dominant species was *Neocalinus cristatus,* another type of copepod. Along the southern perimeter of salmon's domain, meanwhile, the dominant zooplankton was *Calanus pacificus.*

This information might not seem all that important. But it is, because it may at least shed some light on why the average annual harvest of fish from the Asian side of the subarctic Pacific — mainly the Oyashio region, off Japan's northeast coasts — is three times as high, and sometimes five times as high, as the harvest on the North American side of the North Pacific.

What causes these differences in fish abundance was continuing to perplex biologists and oceanographers at the close of the 20th century, but Akira Taniguchi of Japan's Tohuko University reckoned he might have at least part of the answer. It goes something like this.

Zooplankton abundance is at least partly a function of phytoplankton abundance, and phytoplankton abundance is largely a function of the abundance of iron and nitrate particles, which are swept from continental shelves into the North Pacific and are also sometimes scattered on the ocean surface in dust carried on the wind from places as far away as the Gobi desert in Central Asia. The greater productivity of the western portion of the subarctic Pacific may also be, at least in part, a consequence of the volcanic activity on the Kamchatka Peninsula, Taniguchi says.

Sometimes an increasing presence of iron in the North Pacific, either because of volcanoes, winds from Asia, or storms that produce higher-than-average upwellings along coastlines, can cause dramatic effects. An example is the effect on the stock size of Japanese sardines in the Oyashio region, which climbed from 40 million tonnes to 70 million tonnes during the 1980s. This boom in sardine abundance didn't increase the total biomass of fish in the Kuroshio and Oyashio areas, however — the total biomass appeared to remain fairly stable, but the mix of species changed, giving sardines an edge. Also, odd as it sounds, an increase in the abundance of planktivorous fish can cause a growth in the size of the zooplankton biomass: Intensified predation depletes zooplankton abundance, which eases the zooplankton's grazing pressure on phytoplankton, which causes rapid rises in phytoplankton productivity, which sets off a bottom-to-the-top chain reaction that enhances an ecosystem's total productivity. Observing these things, Taniguchi is one of those scientists who see possible benefits in the artificial manipulation of the broad-scale ecosystems of the North Pacific by means such as iron enrichment. Says Taniguchi: "It would be, right or wrong, one of the practical subjects in the future to increase food from the sea for the world human population."

Right or wrong, such considerations arise when science begins to comprehend some of the dynamics involved in the several oceans that comprise the North Pacific. And there are other oceans out there that occur in a different sort of dimension, and they have come to the attention of science in ways every bit as unexpected as the eruptions of gelatinous basketballs from the depths of remote B.C. inlets.

In 1942, during the early days of World War II's Pacific theater, scientists with the "division of war research" at the University of California were busy trying to develop better sonar and echolocation technology for the pursuit of Japanese submarines. During this research, a wholly new ocean appeared to science as a series of strange blips and blotches on depth-sounder screens. Dubbed the "deep scattering layer," the phenomenon was researched by G. H. Tucker at the U.S. Navy Electronics Laboratory in San Diego, California; he found that sometimes there appeared to be two anomalous "scattering" layers, deep beneath the surface of Pacific, and the strange sound-scattering phenomena changed their depths from day to night. It wasn't until the 1950s that the deep scattering layer was found to be caused by sound waves reverberating off the swim bladders of enormous swarms of fish, mainly from the family of fish known as myctophids. The upper layer, it turned out, was caused by extremely dense concentrations of zooplankton, mainly euphausiids.

It was in this way that a wholly new ocean revealed itself to science. The scattering layers first observed in 1942 in the North Pacific — and eventually discovered to exist in varying forms in all the world's oceans — were forms of sea life, in almost unimaginable abundance, engaged in a daily migration from the mesopelagic deeps of the North Pacific to the surface mixing layer, often within 200 meters (650 feet) of the sea surface.

Whales had been familiar with this ocean for millions of years. Dolphins, porpoises, elephant seals, and northern fur seals regularly harvested it, and so did salmon and seabirds — murres, puffins, and auklets descended to it, as did short-tailed shearwaters, sooty shearwaters, and thick-billed murres. Trawlers had now and then skimmed the surface of this ocean, but it was only halfway through the 20th century that science became aware of it. And it wasn't until the late 1970s that scientists discovered a single, diffuse "sound scattering" in the North Pacific, lying at depths of between 275 and 375 meters (between 900 and 1200 feet). Another layer was found that rose to within 100 meters (300 feet) of the sea surface. The deep layer would rise to join the upper layer at night, sinking again just before dawn.

Within this new ocean, meanwhile, there are also several oceans. In the subarctic Pacific, the "mesopelagic" ocean is now known to be frequented by 196 species of fishes. Of those, 38 are believed to be common to both of the major gyres of the subarctic — the eastern and western — with 13 species unique to the eastern gyre and 48 species unique to the western gyre. Among the common fish are squids and lightfishes and grenadiers and deep-sea smelts, strange jawless fishes that are little changed since the Jurassic period, lampreys, pollock, and the deep-sea daggertooth. Salmon are frequent visitors to this ocean, as the slash-marks on homeward-migrating salmon, caused by the fangs of the deep-sea daggertooth, clearly attest — in some years, one in every ten sockeye returning to B.C. waters bears the distinctive battle scars of encounters with a daggertooth.

Within the mesopelagic ocean, the most abundant species belong to the family Mychtophidae. The most ecologically important of these appears to be the myctophid known as *Stenobrachus leucopsarus*. This creature is otherwise known as the northern lanternfish because of the little light-producing organs — the "lanterns" — that appear all over its body. Lanternfish migrate every night from depths of 7000 meters (23,000 feet) to the surface layers, sometimes just a few meters below the ocean surface. They are believed to live to an age of 12 years and have been known to reach lengths of 130 millimeters (5 inches).

The total biomass of the midwater fish of the North Pacific is still a subject most scientists, in the 1990s, preferred to leave to idle conjecture.

In 1991, Russian scientists were prepared to offer a ballpark estimate of 12 million tonnes of midwater fish species in Russian Pacific waters. Scientists with the Canada's Pacific Biological Station, meanwhile, developed an estimate of the abundance of a single species within the midwater fish community. They focused on the northern lanternfish and estimated that the North Pacific holds some 75 million tonnes of that one species. By way of perspective, that is three times the amount of fish that was being taken from the North Pacific at the close of the 20th century by all fisheries combined.

The reason lanternfish are so ecologically important is that they are planktivorous — they feed on the zooplankton that feed on the phytoplankton that arise from photosynthesis, where it all starts — and the lanternfish then form a crucial food source for other small midwater species, pollock, salmon, dolphins, and whales. During research conducted in the 1980s, scientists were finding lanternfish in the stomachs of whales, albacore, and bluefin tuna. Off the Oregon and Washington coasts, 15 percent of the stomach contents of chinook were commonly found to be lanternfish. In the Sea of Okhotsk, Russian scientists estimated that the daily consumption of lanternfish by pollock and salmon amounted to 1500 tonnes. Other fish that rely on lanternfish throughout the North Pacific include spiny dogfish, Kamchatka flounder, perch, rockfish, skate, sculpin, sablefish, and sleeper sharks.

Along with the North Pacific Current, which carries seabirds and whales and salmon across the top of the North Pacific, and the California Current, which brings fur seals to and from their feeding grounds along North America's west coast, the study of midwater fish at the mesopelagic layer revealed another freeway in the North Pacific. This one was a superhighway, carrying enormous volumes of traffic in two directions. It carried nutrients from the surface layers to the realm of grenadiers and deep-sea daggerteeth at depths of up to 7000 meters (23,000 feet). It also carried nutrients back up again, every 24 hours, into the realm of rhinoceros auklets and sea lions and dolphins. It is also a nutrient transit system connecting phytoplankton to zooplankton, and lanternfish to northern fur seals, which sometimes rely on myctophids such as lanternfish for 90 percent of their diets. Myctophids are also a primary prey of squid, which comprise up to 90 percent of the diets of northern right whale dolphins and Dall's porpoises.

At the beginning of the 21st century, so much more remained to be understood about the energy transfers that occurred between one realm of the North Pacific and another. So little was understood about the relationships between the North Pacific's different trophic levels — the niche that various species occupy in the food chain — and the impact of large-scale industrial fisheries on these relationships. But it was beyond question that a consequence of the scientific research that followed the 1911 Pacific fur seal treaty was that it was impossible to look out at the North Pacific and see the same ocean. It was a different ocean. It was many oceans. It was not the ocean that it was when Swaneset set out in his canoe for the land of the salmon people. It was not the same ocean that drew the Chinese mariner Hsu Fu to the Land of the Immortals. It was not the same ocean that James Cook sailed across.

It had changed.

It is not an easy thing to assess the consequences of such changes in the way human beings have come to see the North Pacific. But Judith Williams, an artist who works with canvas, tarpaulin, fiberglass bug-screen, and archival records, has certain personal insights into what happens when paradigmatic blinkers fall away.

Williams's insights involve Bute Wax, the subject of such whispering and rumor making among the local people around Bute Inlet. Years after the scientists R. F. Lee and Judd Nevenzel resolved the mystery of Bute Wax, the substance was still a mystery to Bute Inlet people. It remained a mystery to Williams, who had been intrigued by Bute Wax for several years, as late as 1997, even though she taught art courses at the University of British Columbia only a short walk from the university Fisheries Centre, where the true nature of Bute Wax had been well known since 1979.

Williams had imagined Bute Wax as a magical paint base of some kind. She allowed herself to speculate that regardless of whether it came from a stump or from a trickle in a fissure of rock in the mountains above Bute Inlet, it may have occasionally provided a fixative for the ochre the Homalco people used, for centuries, to paint Bute Inlet pictographs. In 1997, Williams finally came into possession of a small amount of Bute Wax in a jar. She got it from the daughter of a long-dead logger and trapper who homesteaded in Bute Inlet in the 1920s. Williams regarded the substance as beautiful, golden, opaque, thick, exotic, deep, rich, and delightful, "like some cross between honey and caramel." She wanted it analyzed. So she made a ten-minute walk from her studio and presented the jar at the Fisheries Centre, learning straight away that Bute Wax had actually been known to science for some time. Scientists and artists don't usually talk to each other. Bute Inlet people often choose to talk to no one at all, if it suits them, about The Wax. And science, at the best of times, is often little better than a sort of occult knowledge, reserved for a privileged caste.

But Williams was not disheartened by what science had discovered about Bute Wax, even though there was something sad about the story science had to tell about it: A cold wind roars down from Mount Waddington, a great tumult overwhelms Bute Inlet, billions of copepods die, their lipid shells congeal and erupt on the sea surface in something oily and waxy, and that's the stuff that's been there, all along, in the jar the dead logger's daughter gave Judith Williams.

Williams's insight is that information is not knowledge, and truth cannot diminish beauty, and what science has revealed about Bute Wax might also be said about what science, since the Pacific fur seal treaty of 1911, has revealed about the North Pacific.

"The more layers of information you add, the more you obscure its pure presence," Williams observed. "You can't destroy its mystery."

SEVEN

The Necessary Mysteries of the North Pacific

We will always be, I think, the children of our surroundings,
unable to see the world through anyone's eyes but our own,
always filled with biases, assumptions, passions and commitments.
It is not clear to me why we would want things otherwise.

— *Donald Worster, "History as Natural History:*
An Essay on Theory and Method," Pacific Historical Review

THE FIRST TELEPHONE CALL came from a logging company at Beaver Cove, a dot on the map of northern Vancouver Island. A handyman at TimberWest's log-sorting yard called the local offices of the Department of Fisheries and Oceans in nearby Port Hardy to report what appeared to be a "fish kill," likely the result of a fuel spill of some kind. There were tiny fish strewn along the beach. It was the winter of 1998.

Fisheries officer Cam Blacklock went out to Beaver Cove to have a look. What he found were pilchards, *Sardinops sagax*, otherwise known as Pacific sardines, covering the shore. Every step Blacklock took, he found a dead fish. When he peered into the shallows, he could see more dead pilchards beneath the surface of the water. Farther around the cove, the fish blanketed the shoreline. There were tonnes of dead pilchards. They were everywhere, and in the days that followed, Blacklock's telephone rang off the hook. Reports of dead pilchards came in from Knight Inlet, Hardy Bay, Gilford Island, Broughton Island, and almost every bay and cove within 50 sea miles of Port Hardy.

All winter, an ecological pandemonium played itself out throughout Johnstone Strait, among that maze of islands and rapids between northern Vancouver Island and the British Columbia mainland. Huge drifts of dead pilchards provided impromptu banquets for herds of seals and sea lions. Raucous clouds of seagulls followed pods of killer whales and schools of chinook and coho salmon, all roving about the strait, feasting on great rafts of dead and dying pilchards. Laboratory tests showed that the fish had succumbed to viral hemorrhagic septicemia, or VHS. Like the common cold in humans, the virus erupts during times of stress or fatigue. Although VHS is not generally infectious, it is deadly. Fisheries pathologists reckon the pilchard die-off was triggered by one of those rapid cold-water events that routinely occur on the B.C. coast, of the sort that results in Bute Wax, when freezing winter winds pour down from glacier-topped mountains and churn up the waters of narrow inlets. But what was peculiar about the pilchard die-off was that the pilchards were there at all.

Pilchards had never been known in any abundance in the waters between Vancouver Island and the B.C. mainland, and pilchards had vanished entirely from the B.C. coast in the late 1940s. Then, in the late 1980s, hake trawlers off the west coast of Vancouver Island started reporting the occasional pilchard in their nets. By 1997, biologists with the federal Fisheries and Oceans department estimated that the waters off Vancouver Island were seething with about 60,000 tonnes of pilchards — roughly 250 million fish. In the fall of 1998, huge schools of pilchards began making their way around the northern tip of Vancouver Island and down into the maze of Johnstone Strait, and millions of them died over the winter in places like Beaver Cove.

Fisheries scientists had always been at a loss to explain why pilchards left the B.C. coast in the 1950s. But fisheries scientists, at least the really honest ones, are often at a loss for explanations. When the pilchards vanished in the 1950s, almost everybody chalked it up to overfishing. And that's where the matter sat. But when pilchards started showing up on the B.C. coast again, the event captured the attention of biologists, oceanographers, and climatologists from as far away as Russia and Japan. The return of the pilchards seemed part of a pattern of strange events unfolding in the North Pacific.

By the middle of the 1990s, salmon runs were failing to appear on several B.C. rivers. One river on the coast might be chock-full of pink salmon, but the next river would be barren of coho salmon. Russian catches also began to falter, and salmon in Japan were getting smaller. In 1998, Alaska governor Tony Knowles declared western Alaska a disaster area after the salmon runs failed for the second year in a row. Off the California coast, where rare, short-beaked dolphins numbered perhaps 15,000 in the 1970s, the sea was writhing in something on the order of 400,000 short-beaked dolphins. There were other strange things occurring in the ocean, from Hokkaido to San Francisco.

In the late 1980s, oolichans were returning to the Fraser River every year in the billions, as well as to the Columbia River, where they're known as Columbia River smelts, and to Kingcome Inlet, where they're known as *t'lina*. Biologists know them as *Thaleichthys pacificus*, a member of the Osmeridae family. They are a mysterious little fish. They're notoriously oily, and their fat was prized by coastal tribes that rendered oil from the fish to produce a highly valued trade commodity known as oolichan grease. The grease was used as a sort of a condiment for all the dried foods that people relied on during the winter. Every year on the Fraser, the oolichans' return was accompanied by clouds of seagulls, a riot of mergansers and western grebes, and herds of California sea lions, huge bachelor bulls that made the trip all the way from San Francisco Bay just for a feast of the fish. The oolichans' return signaled winter's end, and from the moment the first rafts of gulls started forming in the Fraser's lower reaches, everybody knew that spring had come and summer was on its way. That is the way I remember it, and I remember going to sleep at night to the sound of sea lions barking out in Annacis Channel and the faint and comforting smell of fish coming through my open window. But by the end of the 1990s, oolichan populations had crashed all along the coast. In some rivers, they failed to show up at all. They also started turning up in rivers where they'd never been seen before.

And on it went.

Something had changed, and it was abrupt and dramatic, and Gordon McFarlane sat at the edge of his desk at the Pacific Biological Station, a federal research facility housed in a concrete-block sort of building overlooking Departure Bay in Nanaimo, and took at stab at explaining it. "It's like Canada's Pacific coast has shifted and floated south, down to where the coast of Oregon should be," he said. "The whole ecosystem has changed."

Whatever was at work, it appeared to be reordering the ecological structures of the North Pacific. A growing number of scientists from Canada, the United States, Russia, and Japan were starting to use the term "regime" when they talked about it. The idea of climate regimes had been around for a while, so the concept of ocean regimes seemed like a reasonable way of comprehending what they had begun to see in the North Pacific. You could use the term "ocean regime" to describe a period of persistent trends in various kinds of data — fish abundance, the mix of marine species, the survival rates of marine organisms, climate, and weather patterns. And when regimes changed, you could use the term "regime shift" to describe the event.

This was an important idea. It was wholly contrary to the idea of a steady state in nature, of complete balance and equilibrium in broad-scale ecosystems, which was an assumption as old as Aristotle. Cicero argued for it as evidence for God's wisdom and benevolence. Plotinus relied on it to reconcile the coexistence of good and evil. Carolus Linnaeus had tried to define it, and Charles Darwin tried to make it fit with his ideas about natural selection. Whatever its philosophical merits, it was a fundamental assumption that lay behind a range of scientific hypotheses, and it had led fisheries scientists to construct theories that took for granted the presence of an endlessly bountiful, unchanging ocean. In 1992, when he looked back on more than a century of fisheries collapses, Gary Sharp, a biologist with the National Oceanographic and Aeronautics Administration in Monterey, California, declared: "The lack of success of most modern fisheries management is partially due to an underlying myth of population stability." What was troubling to Sharp was that even in the early 1990s, most of the mathematical models for population biology and global climate research were still based on an unquestioned assumption of long-term equilibrium in nature. It was a fundamental orthodoxy of Western science. And it was wrong.

By the end of the 1990s, however, fisheries scientists from throughout the Pacific Rim who gathered at a Vancouver conference hosted by the North Pacific Anadromous Fish Commission were no longer prepared to accept such assumptions. After the scientists considered the significance of recent findings in the study of ocean "regimes," the conference organizers summed up the proceedings this way:

> There was a recognition that environmental conditions need to be explicitly accounted for in our assessment and management of fish stocks. This concept is not new and has been alluded to in the process of explaining away large discrepancies encountered with traditional fisheries models. What is new is the relative importance given to the environment and ecosystem changes. The effects of climate change on fish production are now being given nearly equal consideration to the competing hypothesis that fish production is governed solely by an intrinsic stock-recruitment relationship and fishing. . . . Such fundamental changes in approach will require time and, above all, education, both within and outside the scientific community.

The idea of ocean regimes, and of regime shifts, challenged fundamental assumptions in fisheries science that were based on notions as ancient as Aristotle, Cicero, and Plotinus. Generations of salmon biologists had been taught to believe that what happened in the ocean didn't really count, and that what limited salmon abundance, for instance, was only the number of spawners and the availability and quality of spawning habitat. By the late 20th century, it was obvious that things were not working that way, and in fact, they never had worked that way.

By the 1990s, a lot of the excitement about the idea that "regimes" determine the productivity and abundance of species in the North Pacific's ecosystems was coming from the Pacific Biological Station. That was partly because of scientists like Gordon McFarlane, but it was also because Dick Beamish also worked at the station. Beamish had been granted membership in the Order of Canada because of his pioneering work on the regime concept. Beamish is generally credited as being the first scientist to identify and document the effects of acid rain in North America. He'd been appointed the station's director, but after he started finding startling synchronicities in the boom-and-bust patterns of several North Pacific fisheries, he decided to get back into the laboratory. The research he was producing was causing old orthodoxies about limits on fish abundance, and about the way oceans worked, to collapse.

Those orthodoxies had begun falling years before, and one of the reasons for that was the work of another scientist at the Pacific Biological Station, one who wrote Haiku poetry as well as Sherlock Holmes mysteries and who had authored a Russian-English dictionary of scientific terms; he also did such a good job teaching himself to play the bass viol that he ended up in the Nanaimo Symphony Orchestra. By 1998, Bill Ricker was a frail man in a buttoned-down cardigan sitting behind a desk stacked with books and papers in a small ground-floor office. He was ninety. He didn't exactly command a striking presence, but the *W. E. Ricker*, a fisheries research vessel, was named after him, and so were about eighty species of stoneflies. Ricker's name was well known in Vladivostok, Ottawa, Monterey, Tokyo, Bergen, and Rome. It was upon Ricker's own slide rule that population dynamics formulas were developed that fisheries managers around the planet had come to rely upon, and down through the decades governments have turned to him for advice on conservation measures to protect herring, fur seals, halibut, and whales.

When I met him, he looked the part. The archdruid of modern fisheries science was wearing a white shirt, a brown tie, a brown cardigan, brown trousers, brown socks, and brown shoes. He was sitting quietly, thinking. When he stood up to adjust the Buddy Holly glasses on the bridge of his nose, he was only slightly stooped. There was no room for the two of us to stand. "Yes, yes," he said. "Please. Sit. A chair. Here. Is this all right?"

Officially, Bill Ricker had retired more than a quarter of century before, but he did some of his most important work long after his retirement, and most days he'd still come down to his office at the biological station. He lived only a few blocks up the hill, so he didn't have to walk far. I notice an old IBM Selectric typewriter on a small, slide-away table. "Oh yes, electric," he says, acknowledging one of his few concessions to modern technology. Ricker, who still had no use for computers, fondly remembered the day he got his first automatic adding machine back in the 1930s. The biggest changes have been the little things, he said. He opened a drawer in his desk and pulled from it, almost with reverence, a pocket calculator. He didn't use a slide rule anymore, and hardly anybody, he pointed out, took the train anymore. He remembered that when he began his work with the Fisheries Research Board of Canada, staff had to get special permission to travel to and from Ottawa by airplane. "Nowadays, you have to get special permission to go by train," he said, and added, a bit wistfully, "I did so many of my computations on trains."

One of Ricker's most important computations resulted in what has come to be called the Ricker Curve, which fisheries managers now use the world over to assess population dynamics in a variety of aquatic species. It was revolutionary in its time, which was the 1950s, because most people back then figured that the only thing that really limited the number of fish entering a particular fish population was the number of spawners in its parent generation. So to predict, say, salmon abundance, you deducted what people caught and then drew a straight line on a graph, heading off at an angle from its x-y axes: The more spawners, the more fish come home. Ricker was among a generation of scientists who ventured the opinion that life was a bit more complicated than that.

In the early 1950s, Ricker came across some obscure papers written by a Russian scientist, Theodore Baranov, whose findings in 1916 seemed to confirm what a lot of North American scientists in the 1950s suspected. Baranov was decades ahead of his time. His work was unknown in North America, so Ricker learned Russian and translated Baranov's papers. The result was a formula Ricker set out in a scientific paper of his own: $R = a\,S\,exp(-bS)$. To make a long story short, the immediate meaning of Ricker's formula was that the way people were imagining the impacts of fisheries upon fish abundance, which involved that straight line on a graph, heading off at an angle, was wrong. It's not a straight line. It's curved, and the slope it forms is the number of juveniles that will replenish the population. The line is curved because that number is determined not just by the number of spawners but by a whole bunch of things, like competition between individual fish for available food and the relationship between the mortality rate of juveniles and the size of the parent generation. The thing is, it works, and it can be made to work with just about any fish species.

Ricker's Curve opened roads that went in a variety of directions. One popular direction led to justifications for the notion of managing fisheries to "maximum sustained yield," which was generally calamitous. But the Ricker Curve also introduced new ways of seeing what happens with living things and ways to take notice of the intricacies of inter-species relationships, the functioning of ecosystems, the finite nature of things as big as oceans, and the dizzying complexities of population dynamics. And when scientists like Dick Beamish started looking at the North Pacific this way, a different ocean began to appear on the horizon. It's not necessarily an ocean that has been ruinously and irreversibly overfished. It's a complicated place, with a complicated ecology, and its history is a story marked by several chapters that scientists like Beamish chose to call regimes, although some Russian scientists like to call them epochs.

The way the North Pacific tells its story has also been called the Pacific Decadal Oscillation, because the North Pacific appears to take several decades to read each chapter of its story. Because the story is unfolding, and science has only recently begun to hear it, little is understood about the story's meaning. What appears certain, however, is that when one chapter ends and a new one begins, it happens quickly. When one chapter ends and a new one begins, everything in the ecosystem responds, from plankton to whales and everything in between. That's what regime shifts are.

Looking back on a century's worth of fish-catch statistics, trends in broad-scale weather systems, studies of sea surface salinity, and the results of all that dreary work of peering through the lenses of microscopes at various kinds of plankton, scientists like Beamish could say certain things, with some confidence, about the history of regimes in the North Pacific. At least four such regimes appear to have defined the 20th century. One regime prevailed between about 1900 and 1924, another between 1925 and 1946, another between 1947 and 1976, and another began in 1977 and may or may not have ended sometime around

1990. Looking at the North Pacific this way reveals that not only are there are several oceans out there in spatial terms, both vertically and horizontally, which expand and contract and change from year to year, but several other oceans also emerge, last for decades, and then fade away, becoming replaced by successors.

The regime that began in 1977 was marked by a substantial recovery in salmon populations — at least among the more northerly salmon runs, and especially sockeye, pink, and chum — after a long period of lousy salmon seasons. That long period of poor salmon abundance in northern waters appears to have begun in 1947, which was also about the time that pilchards vanished from British Columbia's coast.

The regime idea has not been without controversy, and some of the strange events in the Pacific, particularly in the 1990s, might be more properly attributed to global warming, which has been under way for some time. The 20th century was the warmest century in a thousand years, and the 1990s was the warmest decade of the 20th century. The upper atmosphere was cooling rapidly at the same time that the earth's surface was getting warmer. Droughts and El Niño events were becoming more frequent the world over. El Niño is a climate phenomenon that arises in the equatorial Pacific and influences weather patterns around the world. El Niño events cause the southerly portions of the North Pacific to warm, resulting in poor conditions for salmon survival at sea. It is not clear how the Pacific Decadal Oscillation is related to El Niño, which took an especially harsh toll on southerly populations of salmon in 1957, 1983, and 1997.

When scientists looked out at the North Pacific in the 1990s, it was often unclear how much of what was happening in the ocean was part of El Niño's story and how much was some other story. The increased loading of greenhouse gases in the atmosphere, caused mainly by the burning of fossil fuels, was at least partly responsible for the global warming trend. Other long-term trends in the North Pacific — such as a decline in surface-water salinity, which occurred over vast areas of the North Pacific in the late 1900s — were also at work, which could not be readily explained by El Niño, the Pacific Decadal Oscillation, or the concept of ocean regimes.

There are also several reasons why people might prefer not to accept the idea of regimes, which is an idea that implies that the North Pacific's fisheries history is an ongoing narrative in which human beings aren't always the central characters. In Alaska, a reluctance to accept the regime concept is related to a cultural consensus that Alaskan successes in salmon fisheries management are a credit to Alaskans' own sensible practices following the end of federal fisheries management, which came when statehood was established in the 1950s (maximum-sustained-yield fisheries are entrenched in Alaska's constitution). In Japan, where the major salmon fisheries depend almost wholly upon high-technology hatchery complexes, it has been almost inconceivable that poorly understood ocean dynamics, and not just human ingenuity, should be credited with years of good salmon catches. In Canada, bad years in the fisheries are always regarded as the fault of the Department of Fisheries and Oceans, or the Indians, and good years are usually attributed to some policy shift or management initiative that the industry had been telling the government to get on with from the beginning. In California and Oregon, where El Niño has brief but dramatic effects on salmon, it is possible to match the years that hatchery managers were especially boastful about their successes and the years that they were especially critical of commercial fishermen for poor salmon returns with the years that El Niño effects were absent and the years that its effects were singularly ferocious, respectively.

There is always good cause to be skeptical about any theory that downplays the effect of human activity, such as plain old overfishing, bad fisheries management, or fisheries management decisions that fail to anticipate the ripple effects of large-scale fisheries throughout entire ecosystems. Sometimes those effects are almost impossible to predict. Although it should have been fairly obvious that the phenomenal growth of the Bering Sea pollock fishery would likely affect populations of Steller's sea lions, the pollock fishery's effect on sea otter populations in western Alaska, which began a rapid decline in the 1980s, was not so easy to anticipate. Sea lions feed on pollock, and killer whales prey on sea lions, but when sea lion populations crashed, killer whales started hunting sea otters. Biologists with the U.S. Geological Survey didn't confirm this until 1991.

Daniel Pauly, a fisheries scientist at the University of British Columbia, is skeptical about anything that unnecessarily shifts attention away from the effects of overfishing. Pauly has spent much of his career examining the insidious structural changes in ocean ecosystems that overfishing produces. Pauly says he is troubled by the idea that human beings are still bit players on the grand stage of ecosystem dynamics — it's too seductive, and it could easily become an excuse for a slackening of diligence in restraining fisheries. Pauly's concerns arise from his own findings that the planet's fishing fleets have been steadily working their way down the food chain in the oceans — as one species is overfished, the fleets move down to the next species in the food chain. By analyzing fish-catch statistics assembled by the United Nations' Food and Agriculture Organization, Pauly established that a clear downward trend is occurring in the trophic level of the fish harvested by the world's fishing fleets.

In the North Pacific, despite the phenomenal resurgence in the catch of certain salmon species after 1977, and despite the phenomenal growth of the Bering Sea pollock fishery (salmon and pollock are relatively high in the food chain), the trophic level of the all-species catch from the North Pacific actually dropped after the 1970s. Pauly says it is unreasonable to believe that apparent shifts in regimes in the North Pacific, at least since the 1970s, are completely unrelated to fishing. Even if a "steady state" existed in the ecology of the North Pacific — a proposition Pauly doesn't support — heavy fishing of low trophic-level fish would have caused disruptions in that ecology.

The regime concept also carries an implied rebuke to deeply entrenched, highly popular government policies. Canada and the United States have spent billions of dollars on salmon hatchery programs, artificial spawning channels, fish ladders, and lake-fertilization programs, all to maintain or boost salmon catches. Fisheries managers are predictably reluctant to conclude that their efforts may not be all that relevant when compared with the "natural" regulation of fish populations that occurs as a result of complex dynamics at work in the ocean. They are often even less prepared to admit that a diversity of wild salmon populations, spread out over a broad area, would be better suited to cope with fluctuations and shifts in ocean conditions than are genetically uniform hatchery salmon.

But the evidence for ocean regimes, and for shifts in those regimes, is too overwhelming to ignore.

The evidence started to emerge in 1991, when a U.S. oceanographer, Curt Ebbesmeyer, published a study of climate variables that identified an abrupt change that had occurred in North Pacific weather systems around 1977. Beamish reviewed Ebbesmeyer's data, and in 1993, he and a DFO colleague, Daniel Bouillon, published a groundbreaking study that made a persuasive case for the occurrence of broad-scale ecological regimes in the North Pacific. The study concluded that regimes had shifted at least twice during the 20th century. Beamish and Bouillon compared the peaks and valleys of salmon catches throughout the North Pacific with fluctuations over the years in the intensity of a powerful winter-weather system known as the Aleutian Low. The similarity in trends was astonishing — the two sets of data appeared as almost exactly the same wavy line on a graph, with the year 1900 at one end and the year 1985 at the other. The line rises in the mid-1920s, dips down at the year 1947, and begins a dramatic incline at the year 1977.

Two years later, Beamish and Bouillon added more detail to the regime shift picture by comparing the trends they identified in 1993 with estimates of the abundance of a dozen other marine species over the years. Some data, such as catch statistics for halibut, go back as far as 1927. For zooplankton, reliable data go back only to 1965, when measurements began at Ocean Station Papa, a research facility 1500 sea miles off the B.C. coast. Still, the same sort of landscape appeared — a valley becomes a flat plain around 1947, and the base of a cliff rises out of the valley at around 1977.

For almost two decades prior to the 1940s, nearly every year was a "good year" for salmon fishermen throughout the North Pacific. From the Columbia River, along the British Columbia coast, and all the way to Russia's Pacific coastal villages, just about every fishing season was better than the one before. Throughout the North Pacific, annual salmon catches rose to almost a million tonnes. By the late 1930s, there were more than sixty salmon canneries in operation along the B.C.

coast, from Ladner, on the Fraser River, to Gingolx, on the Nass. These were good years for sardine fishermen from California to Japan, too, with catches rising almost every year. On the west coast of Vancouver Island, the inlets were ringing with the clamor of pilchard canneries and reduction plants. By the late 1930s, the B.C. pilchard fishery ranked second in volume among Canada's fisheries, outpaced only by North Atlantic cod. The pilchards that supplied British Columbia's plants were from that same huge North Pacific sardine stock that provided the basis for the California fisheries during the glory days of John Steinbeck's "Cannery Row," when twenty-four canneries clanked and whirred along Ocean View Avenue in Monterey.

By 1940, salmon and sardine catches were rapidly declining. Every season, it seemed, was worse than the one before. Catches continued to decline until the harvest bottomed out around 1947 and stayed that way, more or less, for thirty years. Overfishing and habitat loss were generally cited as the culprits behind salmon declines. Little science was needed to support that hypothesis, but in the 1940s scientists still believed that the North Pacific was so vast that there was no way the salmon abundance might be limited by the carrying capacity of the ocean. As for the disappearance of pilchards, fisheries scientists concluded that overfishing was at least partly at fault. But old-timers in the native communities on the west coast of Vancouver Island explained that pilchards had come and gone before, long before the advent of industrial fisheries. It wasn't until about 1977 that Pacific salmon catches started picking up again. Every year, catches of sockeye, pink, and chum salmon continued to rise, as in the 1930s and 1940s, until they reached an historic high of about a million tonnes in 1989. Japanese and California sardine catches rose to heights not seen since the days of Cannery Row.

Throughout the 1990s, scientists from government agencies and research facilities around the North Pacific added more statistical data to the picture, contributing more detailed contours to what is essentially the same terrain. Their research had produced unprecedented agreements for information sharing and cooperation between scientists with the Department of Fisheries and Oceans, the U.S. National Oceanographic and Aeronautics Administration, the Russian Federal Institute of Fisheries and Oceanography, and Japan's National Institute of Far Seas Fisheries.

The Russians have been especially open to the idea that broad-scale environmental conditions can affect fish populations. For decades, Russian scientists have been trying to anticipate long-term weather patterns, predict the movement of sea ice in Russia's Arctic sea lanes, and forecast salmon abundance. It was at a 1991 symposium in Vladivostok that Beamish first presented his comparison between the all-nations salmon catch and the Aleutian Low weather system — findings that he and Bouillion were to publish two years later in Canada. The Russians thought Beamish made eminent sense.

But the Russians can get carried away with their propensity to predict things. At a 1998 symposium of scientists in Vancouver, Russian scientist Leonid Klyashtorin caused a stir when he presented a comparison of the all-nations harvests of salmon, as well as the catches of sardines off California and Japan, with a variety of other trends. In each data set, the trends are almost exactly the same and follow the same lines on a graph. Starting from the 1920s, each line bottoms out around the late 1940s, begins a rapid incline in the late 1970s, and begins what appears to be a decline in the late 1980s. It was the same landscape portrait Beamish and Bouillon had painted in 1993, except this time the picture was supported by trends in air temperatures at the sea surface, atmospheric circulation, and so on. So far, so good. But Klyashtorin concluded that Pacific salmon catches peaked in the 1990s and should be expected to decline for at least the following twenty years. "There is good reason to believe that future changes in climate and salmon stocks will follow the same dynamics that took place in the last climatic phase in the 1940s–50s," Klyashtorin concluded.

Most scientists wince at attempts to predict how long a particular chapter in the North Pacific's story will take to unfold. A better course, according to some Japanese scientists, is to try to look at what has happened in previous chapters and to see whether it's possible to reconstruct the form the story has taken in the past. At the Tokai Regional Fisheries Research Laboratory in Tokyo, research scientist Keicho Kondo identified six "prosperous periods," each lasting about seventy years, in the sardine fisheries of Chibo prefecture on the island of Honshu. If sardine catches are a reliable indicator of ocean regimes throughout the Pacific — and the distinct pattern in sardine fisheries is that they appear to rise and fall more or less simultaneously throughout the ocean — Kondo's research may provide outlines to the chapters of the story unfolding in the North Pacific going back to the late 1500s.

Meanwhile, in 1992, U.S. scientists completed an analysis of sediment samples at the bottom of Santa Barbara Channel, on the California coast, which left a fingerprint of sardine and anchovy abundances going back more than 1700 years. The scientists then matched the peaks and valleys that appeared on their sardine/anchovy abundance graphs with the peaks and valleys on a graph showing fluctuations in the tree-ring widths of coastal bristlecone pine trees going back 1700 years. The sardine, anchovy, and pine tree data showed what was more or less a single, wavy line. Not only was there a clear link between weather patterns and fish abundance, but the important thing was that the wavy line oscillated up and down in declines and inclines every seventy years or so.

The history of sardine abundances in the Santa Barbara Channel also matched the history of Japanese sardine abundances that Keicho Kondo found in the six "prosperous periods" enjoyed by the fishermen of Chibo Prefecture between the late 1500s and the late 1900s. Among other things, the Santa Barbara data and the Chibo data appear to suggest that sardines respond synchronously, or at least with a remarkable degree of uniformity, right across the North Pacific. You could say that sardines, everywhere in the North Pacific, are dancing to the same music. But not all species are dancing to the sardines' tune. It could be said that there are regimes within regimes. The Pacific Decadal Oscillation, for instance, seems to dance to a rhythm that's faster than whatever it is the sardines are dancing to. Or maybe it's all the same music and the sardines are just hitting every second beat.

The consensus among oceanographers is that El Niño appears to work independently of the Pacific Decadal Oscillation, and the Pacific Decadal Oscillation does not always exhibit internal consistency. The regime shift that occurred in 1977, for instance, appears to have had certain opposite effects upon two key domains of Pacific salmon — the

Subarctic Pacific and the Coastal Upwelling Domains. In the Subarctic Pacific, which is such an important pasture for North American chum, pink, and sockeye salmon, summer zooplankton biomass doubled after 1977. But in the Coastal Upwelling Domain, which is important to so many southerly coho and chinook salmon runs, zooplankton biomass declined by as much as 70 percent.

What's going on out there isn't just a matter of a big pendulum swinging back and forth every two or three decades. Years of good salmon fishing aren't necessarily followed by years of bad salmon fishing. It's complicated, and a century's worth of catch statistics is just a brief moment in time for the North Pacific. It's like reading a single faded and crumbling onionskin page from an early draft of Wagner's *Tannhäuser*, in a dimly lit room. You might make out the French horns, the gloomy cellos, some cascading violins, or an upheaval of brass and woodwinds. You might not recognize it as Wagner's work. You might not be able to make much of his barely legible penmanship. You would be forgiven for not being able to say anything about where the music was going to go next.

One of the most striking contributions to this complicated sheet music comes from the Earth Rotational Velocity Index, which measures minute fluctuations in the length of the day. Since the 1600s, astronomical observations have measured minute fluctuations in the time it takes for the earth to rotate on its axis. The velocity of the earth's rotation is generally declining at a rate of 1.4 milliseconds a century, but fluctuations occur because the earth's core, the planet's landmass, the oceans, and the atmosphere do not turn at exactly the same speed. Since 1958, when the development of the atomic clock established standard calculations, it has become easier to track fluctuations in the speed of the earth's rotation. When Beamish started looking at trends in the length of the day, especially trends after 1958, he noticed that just before 1977, when northerly salmon and sardine catches began to rebound across the North Pacific, the length of the day started decreasing. Then he noticed that the fluctuations in the length of the day since the 1600s correspond with the "prosperous periods" among Chibo fishermen since the 1600s.

In the late 1980s, something else happened out there in the ocean, between Oregon and Alaska. The post-1977 years of intense Aleutian Lows changed to years of average Aleutian Lows. The winter coastal sea surface began to get colder. The westerly and southwesterly wind and current patterns began to slack off. Everything else seemed to just start wobbling. Through the 1990s, Alaskan sockeye and Fraser River sockeye — which, if anything, usually show opposing trends in abundance — both started exhibiting extremes in abundance. In the 1990s, Alaska had some of its best sockeye seasons and some of its worst sockeye seasons ever. Fraser sockeye returns in 1993 were higher than any on record, but in 1998 and 1999, Fraser sockeye stock sizes shrank to their lowest level since record keeping began. Throughout their range, south of Alaska, coho salmon, which had fared so badly after 1977, began to almost drop off the charts entirely. The marine survival rates (the rate at which smolts survive to adulthood) of southerly coho salmon populations, which had been as high as 12 percent in the 1970s, began a long decline. During the 1990s, those declines changed from a downhill slide to a sheer drop over a cliff, with marine survival rates falling to less than 1 percent. Throughout the B.C. coast, coho were becoming museum pieces. Across Burrard Inlet from Vancouver, on the Seymour River, coho spawners fell from 14,000 in the early 1980s to fewer than 500 in 1996. Up the Fraser River, in the bunchgrass country of the Thompson River watershed, six coho stocks were reported extinct in 1996. In the north, two of the hardest-hit coho runs were those that arise from the Babine River and from the Upper Bulkley River, both tributaries of the Skeena River, which enters the Pacific at Prince Rupert. From 10,000 Babine spawners in the 1960s, only 500 coho were making it home to spawn in the 1990s, and on the Upper Bulkley, coho spawners dropped from about 7000 in the 1970s to fewer than 700 in 1997.

But while this was going on, a series of anomalies began to show up in the spawning behavior, recruitment rates — the rate at which juveniles are recruited into the adult population — and distribution of hake, herring, and several groundfish species throughout much of the Northwest Coast. By the early 1990s, all those fish species appeared to benefit handsomely from whatever it was that was harming coho salmon.

If these were signs that a new regime had emerged in the North

Pacific sometime in the late 1980s, the signs suggested it would be a regime characterized by extremes — by significant spikes on every strange index oceanographers had managed to assemble about the North Pacific. And if it was a new regime, it began around 1987, a year in which the planet began to slow its rotation, ever so slightly, allowing the length of the day to increase.

After a while, when science offers explanations about why the fishing is bad or good by describing the ways in which the earth moves through the very firmament, it all becomes a bit like metaphysics. But at least the story isn't one in which the sun dances in the heavens, frogs rain from the sky, the moon turns blood-red, and the world comes to an end. At the beginning of the 21st century, the world wasn't coming to an end. Mythologies were.

It is without controversy that aboriginal fisheries management systems were guided and informed by mythology. Xa:ls taught the people of the Fraser Canyon how to fish salmon and what to fish with. Coyote did the same for the people of the Thompson and the Columbia. Up and down the Pacific coast, nations, tribes, communities, and families cited the authority of their myths to account for their rights to certain fishing grounds. The myth of Swaneset explained the origins of the relationship between salmon and people. The myth also set out the content of an elaborate "first salmon" ceremony, which included an obligation to return the bones of the season's first salmon to the river to ensure the renewal of an ancient relationship and the survival of the people.

It is less common to consider the ways mythology informed and guided industrial fisheries management regimes, which were held to differ from their aboriginal antecedents partly because of their foundation upon reason and science. But as we have seen, science is not uninformed by myth.

It was an enduring belief in fabled waterways that brought science to the North Pacific in the first place. Deep religious convictions lay behind the system of taxonomical classification devised by Carolus Linnaeus, and the zealotry of hatchery managers was fuelled in no small part by Livingstone Stone's religious epiphanies. Through the 20th century, rights of access to the North Pacific's fisheries resources were asserted by

North American governments by the authority that came from solemn rituals formalizing sovereignty that invoked God and the divine right of kings. Japan saw its high-seas fisheries as part of God's plan for the Japanese people, and a faith in science, progress, and technology overshadowed practically every major decision made by fisheries management agencies with jurisdiction over North Pacific marine species. Industrial fisheries were managed with the explicit objective of securing a "maximum sustained yield" of the North Pacific's marine resources — an objective founded upon a mythical ocean of boundless pasturage. At the heart of it all was something the American environmental historian Joseph E. Taylor III has called a system of beliefs that "combined theology and technology into a righteous cause."

At the beginning of the 21st century, what was ending was the idea of the North Pacific as unknowable and too vast to be moved by the hand of humanity. Humanity's effects on the North Pacific could be found from the smallest to the largest creatures in the ocean. There was mounting evidence that pollution, greenhouse gases, and perhaps an increase in the intensity of ultraviolet light were affecting the photosynthesis of phytoplankton, and the North Pacific's whales, though no longer the target of industrial whalers, were showing disturbing signs of toxin contamination. Gray whales and porpoises were being contaminated by lethal polychlorinated biphenyls (PCBs), and by 1996, British Columbia's southern resident killer whales were among the most contaminated cetaceans on the planet.

What was also ending was the old, industrial, volume-based salmon fishery, at least south of Alaska, because there was no future in floating around in boats and going broke so that some integrated food conglomerate could stuff all the fish into cans. During the very years that salmon catches in the North Pacific were as high as they had ever been, much of the fishing economy of North America's west coast was collapsing in ruins. There were still salmon trollers on the California coast, and there was the occasional commercial fishery for Columbia-bound salmon in Oregon, and in most years there were a few openings for gillnetters and seiners from Puget Sound ports in Washington. But the fleets existed only in remnants. On the B.C. coast, the salmon fleet had shrunk from more than 7000 mostly rickety inshore boats in the 1960s to fewer than 3000 efficient vessels that could take all the catch in only a few days. There were once more than 100 major fish-processing plants on the B.C. coast. By the end of the 20th century, there were a half-dozen, situated in Prince Rupert and the Lower Mainland.

Adjusted for inflation, the price salmon fishermen from Japan to California could command for their fish had fallen, by the end of the 1990s, to a third of the price they could command in the 1980s. The value of wild salmon had dropped below one-half of 1 percent of British Columbia's gross provincial product. The laws of supply and demand didn't even work anymore. These absurd market distortions had resulted mainly because of the rise of salmon farming, which had gone from nothing, in the late 1970s, to production volumes that eclipsed wild salmon production twenty years later.

Salmon farming — breeding salmon from brood stock, and raising them in pens — occurs almost exclusively in Scandinavia, Ireland and Scotland, eastern Canada, British Columbia, and Chile. Salmon farming is practically without precedent in the history of agriculture. At no other time in history have people raised carnivores exclusively for food stock. It remains a controversial industry, even though salmon farmers had done much, by the late 1990s, to improve their practices: the majority of salmon farmers in the Pacific were raising only Atlantic salmon, which can't interbreed with and thus reduce the genetic integrity of Pacific salmon; salmon farmers were developing methods to reduce diseases that could be transferred from farmed salmon to Pacific salmon; and salmon farmers were taking pains to ensure that farmed fish didn't escape into the wild. But salmon aquaculture was still widely regarded, not undeservedly, as something of a rogue industry. For all its attractiveness as an alternative to unsustainable salmon-fishing practices, it is also an industry that requires 3 tonnes of low-trophic-level fish from the oceans to feed enough farmed salmon to produce a single tonne of product. Banned in Alaska, kept at 1980s levels in Washington State, and alternatively tolerated and encouraged in British Columbia, salmon farming grew by leaps and bounds in the late 20th century. It was not uncommon to find farmed salmon for sale in great abundance and at low prices in west coast towns, while a short walk away, salmon fishermen sat in boats listing in disrepair.

But there was still a future for fishermen who marketed their own fish and paid attention to quality and handled their fish carefully. There were growing niche markets for wild salmon, and the future for fishermen would probably mean adding more value to fewer fish. And so long as there was the justifiable hope that conditions in the salmon realms of the North Pacific would improve, and so long as there was still freshwater habitat remaining when that day came, the salmon had a chance and salmon fishermen had something to hope for. It also helped that in 1999 Canada and the United States concluded a new salmon treaty. The new arrangements contained many of the harmful features of the old treaty, but it was also significantly informed by advances in scientific understanding that had occurred since the first treaty was signed in the 1930s. And at least it was a treaty.

There was also the United Nations' 1992 Convention on Biodiversity. Signatories to the 1992 Convention declared themselves to be "conscious of the intrinsic value of biological diversity and of the ecological, genetic, social, economic, scientific, educational, cultural, recreational and aesthetic values of biological diversity and its components." This was a long way down the road that began with the Pacific fur seal treaty of 1911.

Managing fisheries for the simple purpose of achieving "maximum sustained yield" became a discredited practice by the 1990s, and throughout the North Pacific, management objectives were shifting to better reflect international concerns for preserving and restoring biological diversity. Mixed-stock fishing regimes, although partly re-entrenched in the Pacific salmon treaty that was renewed in 1999, were generally giving way to selective fisheries. This was a significant development, because so much of the diversity of North Pacific fish populations had been lost as a consequence of mixed-stock fisheries. In 1998, Canada's fisheries minister, David Anderson, declared that selective fishing practices would be the cornerstone of salmon management in British Columbia. South of the 49th parallel, fisheries managers were following the same course after the U.S. National Research Council advised the U.S. Congress that

American fisheries would have to move away from mixed-stock fishing and that long-term fisheries sustainability requires the protection of genetic diversity in fish populations.

In both Canada and the United States, decision makers were increasingly pressured to ensure that fisheries take an "ecosystem approach" to fisheries management, and salmon fisheries managers were being obliged not only to be mindful of the importance of maintaining salmon species throughout their range but also to be mindful of the need to protect subspecies and ecotypes, races, populations, and subpopulations of salmon.

But most important, a new restraint on science was presenting far-reaching consequences in the way we were all expected to conduct ourselves. "The precautionary principle," by the 1990s, was emerging as an effective standard by which governments were being expected to protect the North Pacific's marine resources while allowing the sustainable use of the ocean. First described in the context of marine pollution in the North Sea, the precautionary principle establishes, in law, that resource users, harvesters, and parties engaged in potentially harmful activities must bear the burden of proof with respect to conservation and habitat protection. In 1995, the precautionary principle was incorporated into the United Nations' Code of Conduct for Responsible Fisheries, developed by the UN's Food and Agriculture Organization. Throughout the late 1990s, the precautionary principle was being codified within a variety of international and domestic conventions, agreements, and statutes throughout the North Pacific.

This was another one of those paradigm shifts that was changing the course of the North Pacific's history, in the 1990s, in such confusing ways. The precautionary principle recognizes the limits of science in comprehending the dynamics of the North Pacific. It is a long-overdue acknowledgment that human beings simply don't know everything about what goes on out there. It is an admission that there are profound uncertainties in science, as a system of ways and means, and there will be uncertainty about the effects of human activities upon ecological systems.

The precautionary principle requires scientists to acknowledge uncertainty about the effects of natural resource extraction and prevents scientific uncertainty from being used as an excuse to allow industrial resource extraction to proceed. The UN's 1995 Code of Conduct for Responsible Fisheries states, in part, that "the absence of adequate scientific information should not be used as a reason for postponing or failing to take conservation and management measures." The code specifically admonishes its signatories to take into account uncertainties about the size and productivity of marine populations and also to take into account the impact of fisheries upon the socioeconomic conditions of coastal peoples.

In this way, the hubris of science, which so distorted the way humanity had come to see the North Pacific during the Industrial Age, was tamed. In this way, we are obliged to conform with a simple rule: Do what you will, but cause no harm. The precautionary principle recognizes that there are necessary mysteries in the North Pacific. There are mysteries about the place. There are also the mysteries of our own ways and means.

As the 20th century closed, technological utopianism, along with the temples to that religion that salmon hatcheries had become, was collapsing into ghost heaps. Throughout the range of the west coast's temperate rain forest, clear-cut logging had drawn widespread condemnation, in no small part because of the harm that conventional industrial forestry does to salmon habitat. Within salmon's terrestrial range, profound demographic and cultural changes had also altered the human landscape. It was from Vancouver, after all, that Greenpeace had sprung, and the century that began with whaling stations dotting the west coast of North America had ended with whale-watching businesses contributing far more to coastal economies than industrial whaling ever had.

And then at 6:55 A.M., Monday, May 17, 1999, a singular event was broadcast live from helicopters above the choppy waters at the mouth of Juan de Fuca Strait. On hundreds of thousands of television sets throughout British Columbia, Washington, and Oregon, voices with American television accents suggested we might want to avert our gaze or urge our children to leave the room. You'd think their president had just been shot.

After two years of false starts and failed attempts, a 10-meter (32-foot) cedar dugout canoe from the Makah village of Neah Bay had closed in on a gray whale, and a man at the bow had thrust a harpoon into the creature. The harpoon thrust was followed by a blast from a .50 calibre rifle, then another harpoon thrust, then another shot from the rifle. By 7:05 A.M., the whale was dead, and from Sequim to San Francisco, people in tie-dyed shirts wept for the cameras. Seattle editorial writers clucked their tongues and clacked away at their keyboards, and Portland radio phone-in shows lit up with every conceivable reason that the Makah were wrong to kill the whale: It was wrong because the harpoon was unnecessarily cruel, it was wrong because the rifle wasn't a traditional weapon, it was just wrong.

This event signaled just how completely the values of the Industrial Age had been overthrown during the late 20th century. But it had gone beyond a heightened public awareness of the need to conserve the marine resources of the North Pacific. The gray whales were no longer endangered. The Makah were entitled to do what they did by the solemn and legally enforceable promise of an 1855 treaty. What their whalers did that Monday morning was a thing for which they had been once held in awe by the tribes of the North Pacific. It was grotesque, courageous, tragic, defiant, bloody, and strangely beautiful. It was the Makahs' first whale in seventy years. It was an act carried out in defiance of a new orthodoxy, and as such it was an apostasy and a blasphemy. Whatever one might say in opposition to the Makah whale kill, a conservationist argument could not be raised against it.

Greenpeace, which was born in the blood of the world's whales and might be credited with saving several species of the North Pacific's whales from extinction, did not join the chorus of protest. There were no gaily painted Greenpeace protest ships lying in wait for Makah whalers in Juan de Fuca Strait. Greenpeace chose to stay outside the fray because the Makahs' plans amounted to nothing more than a sustainable, small-scale subsistence activity. When Greenpeace was born, there were about 12,000 gray whales making their annual migration from their calving grounds in Mexico to the krill-rich waters of the Bering Sea. By the morning of May 17, 1999, there were almost twice as many gray whales making that same migration. When Greenpeace was born, there were 11.4 square kilometers (4.4 square miles) of forest for every 1000 people on the planet. By May 17, 1999, there were 7.3 square kilometers (2.8 square miles) of forest for every 1000 people. To the dismay of so many of its traditional supporters, Greenpeace reckoned that there were a lot more important things to address than the distractions unfolding out in the chilly waters of Juan de Fuca Strait.

The Makah whale kill was not a conservation issue. For the protestors, as much as for the Makah whalers, the whale kill was about spirituality, sentiment, cosmology, and religion. There is absolutely nothing wrong with these things. They do not have to be justified to anyone. But that's what was going on.

Like whales, salmon, among the settler communities of North America's west coast, had become something far more than a mere contributor to gross domestic product calculations and corporate balance sheets. Salmon had become a cherished symbol of the west coast way of life, and protection of salmon habitat was becoming the litmus test by which most major land use decisions were judged, from urban development to logging plans to agricultural practices. Settler culture was changing, and it was something that had occurred over generations. It was difficult to explain to people from the other side of the Rocky Mountains.

Throughout the freshwater range of salmon, people and their governments were beginning to turn away from hatcheries and other technological "solutions" to the problem of sustainability and salmon. In Oregon, hatchery managers were being instructed to slaughter returning hatchery salmon rather than continue to allow hatchery fish to compete in the ocean with wild salmon. Meanwhile, those wild salmon, which swam at the vortex of aboriginal cultures down through the millennia, had come to occupy an iconic, almost sacramental place in the settler cultures of North America's west coast. Throughout the 1990s, public opinion polls in Oregon consistently showed overwhelming support for measures to protect wild salmon, and only 15 percent of Oregonians cited economic reasons for wanting salmon runs restored and maintained. In polls in Washington State, 75 percent of residents asserted that salmon had immeasurable value because they were a key aspect of the state's heritage and a key indicator of environmental health. In British

Columbia, meanwhile, more than 10,000 volunteers, all across the province, spent their weekends in the rain, clearing trash out of salmon creeks, monitoring water quality, and counting salmon fry. Salmon had become an "indicator species" in a much broader sense than the term is normally used by ecologists. All these things signaled that there was great hope for the future of salmon after all.

There were other reasons for hope. In the first few days of the first year of the new century, scientists at the Jet Propulsion Laboratory in Pasadena, California, announced that they had seen something happen in the North Pacific. Bill Patzert, a satellite oceanographer, said that whatever it was, it was bigger than El Niño. It was a rapid cooling of a massive stretch of the North Pacific, "a very strong signal," Patzert said, that a regime shift might be occurring. It meant that perhaps, just perhaps, a new chapter in the story of the North Pacific was beginning. It had all the signs of a chapter involving cold-water upwellings and lots of healing rain.

In the end, a lot of these things are really not about science. They never were. They are about faith, and they are about mysteries. That's the predicament.

Back home on Mayne Island, where I live, there is a certain crab fisherman by the name of Bob Strain. There are days when it's cold and pouring rain and there's nothing much to look forward to except sliding around the deck of the *Lorna Doone* pulling line after line of crab traps from a choppy sea while the boat heaves and shudders and you ache to your very bones by the time you're headed back to Horton Bay. And there are mornings when the whole world is sleeping, and the early-morning canopy of gray cloud dangles in the upper limbs of the arbutus and the cedar, and there is no sound, and nothing moves, except a single chattering kingfisher that plunges into the shallows now and then after a sandlance or a pipefish. A voice crackles on the marine radio, something about rippled seas and something about scattered rain somewhere, but nothing scatters from Campbell Point to Potato Point, and nothing ripples, and far out into the gulf, the sea is calm and fat and langorous.

There are the necessary mysteries. Horton Bay bites into Mayne Island's southeast side, behind Curlew Island, and Bob puts out in the

Lorna Doone to the places he sets his lines of traps, but to disclose where his traps are would be to violate a necessary rule of so many fisheries. You don't tell the world where your favorite fishing spots are. It's just not done.

There is also the mystery of place. It is true enough to say that Bob fishes in an area that Fisheries and Oceans knows as the southern section of the Gulf Islands quadrant on the crab-license charts known as Area H. I know the area as a place bordered by Curlew Island, which is infested with feral peacocks, and off the southern point of Curlew my son Eamonn caught his first rockfish. Older islanders might put the northern tip of Bob's fishing grounds at the spot where Harold Payne used to beach his little sailboat at Bennett Bay, in the 1890s, in the days when old Harold would sail up from Saturna Island, rain or shine, to collect the mail. Some of the older Tsartlip people, whose ancestors have known these waters from time out of mind, might identify the place marking the northern extent of Bob's crab traps as the site where the Tsartlips killed and buried a certain wicked man, hundreds of years ago, after the man had mistreated his brother's slaves by using their bodies as canoe skids.

There is the mystery of ways and means. Bob's boat is the *Lorna Doone*, a 37-foot lobster boat from Newcastle, New Brunswick, and nobody knows how it found its way to this coast. It's known to have been around the Gulf Islands since the 1950s, and it once belonged to the caretaker on Samuel Island. Bob bought it in 1984 to replace the *Andrea Leigh* (which was the 22-footer Bob owned when I first went out fishing with him, when he fished out of Boundary Bay on the mainland) which replaced a 21-foot Starcraft aluminum boat he'd bought up at Lasqueti Island in 1976, when his fishing days began with a $3500 loan. About the *Lorna Doone's* provenance, nothing more is known, but it can be said that the *Lorna Doone* is one of only about 220 crab-licensed boats coast-wide, and the crab fishery is puny compared with the herring fishery or the salmon fishery, and it is a reasonable and defensible fishery. It's a live-capture fishery. It's not only species-selective but selective by size and gender as well. It's managed by DFO scientists who are not so inflated by hubris that they cannot admit that there are mysteries about things, and there are mysteries about Dungeness crab, otherwise known as *Cancer magister*.

Bob insists, for instance, that there are "resident" crabs, which are gnarly and barnacle encrusted and don't appear to leave their own little bays, and there are "runs" of crabs, like salmon runs. Bob also observes that you can haul traps all day on the Plumper Sound side of Mayne Island and all you'll get is females, which, by regulation, have to go back in the water. But on the gulf side, the crabs are almost always males, which, if they are 165 millimeters (6½ inches) across the back, are keepers. There's one spot on the gulf side where the crabs have their own distinctive reddish color about their legs and pincers. Bob says there is a highway out there on the sea bottom, and if you're lucky enough to set a line of traps on top of it the traps will be full to bursting with big, beautiful Dungeness, but if you miss it by a couple of boat lengths your traps will come up empty. And the highway is always moving. So it's mysterious, but it is also quite maddening.

Anton Phillips, the federal fisheries biologist at the Pacific Biological Station who is expected to know something about these things, says this about Bob's observations: "The fishermen have their own individual religions. Us scientists have our own religion as well. We probably learn more from the fishermen than they learn from us. But that's the paradigm."

In Phillips's religion, the mysteries Bob observes can be accounted for in a number of ways. Every year, crabs shed their shells. But sometimes they skip a year, which would explain the barnacled residents. When crabs do molt, they get all limp and rubbery and gain a third in size during the few days that they're waiting for their new shells to harden. This is also when crab sex occurs. Once pregnant, the females spend most of the winter buried in the sand on the sea bottom, their little eyes poking up to keep a watch for any food that happens by, but come spring, the females release billions of larvae into the sea. The larvae become something called megalops, which are nasty-looking spiny creatures about the size of pencil erasers, and billions of megalops engage in a pattern of summer-long vertical migration: down on the ocean floor during the day, up at the surface at night. Around the Strait of Georgia they swirl, eventually settling down to become tiny crabs, which grow to become bigger crabs. Then they begin a pattern of counterclockwise marching, searching for food. This would account for Bob's crab highway. As for all the females in Plumper Sound, Phillips reckons the males really are down there, but because females are more ornery and aggressive, the males steer clear of them, and crab traps tend to come up with females. As for the preponderance of males on the gulf side, same deal. They're avoiding females. They're marching alone.

Bob and I considered these things one day in 1998, a fishing day when the water was calm and the rain fell gently and we returned to the dock at Horton Bay after pulling about 300 crabs from 95 traps, only 85 of which were keepers. This is not counting a significant volume of bladder wrack, sea lettuce, bull kelp fronds, a dozen or so starfish, and a 14-kilogram (30-pound) octopus, which is a mysterious creature altogether, and which Bob had admired for a few moments before allowing it to slither over the side, back into the deep.

Neither Bob's religion, nor Anton's, could explain why it is that in some places, like the Fraser River flats and Boundary Bay, all the crabs molt and have sex all at once, but in the Gulf Islands, crabs seem to be more leisurely about things, having sex whenever they feel like it. That is another mystery.

Bob was not sure of Anton's religion. Anton was not sure of Bob's. And that is what Anton calls the paradigm.

So it is about humility, and it is about faith, but it is also about deciding. In the epoch humanity has now entered, the decisions we make ultimately involve the very membrane of the planet itself, which is known to science as the ozone layer, a filament of a thing about as thin as the page upon which these words were printed. We are not just bit players in what goes on out there.

But we can decide what kind of world it will be, and the world is not coming to an end. As for faith, it's useless. But it is the only place where hope is.

Notes

CHAPTER 1: The Beginning of the World

PAGE 15 "There were no leafy . . . ," Wayne Suttles and Diamond Jenness, "The Katzie Book of Genesis," from "Katzie Ethnographic Notes and the Faith of a Coast Salish Indian," *Anthropology in B.C. Memoirs*, nos. 2 and 3 (Victoria: British Columbia Provincial Museum, 1955), p. 10.

PAGE 18 "the result of . . . ," Frederick H. West, "The Beringian Tradition and the Origin of American Indian Languages," *Proceedings, Circum-Pacific Prehistory Conference*, Seattle, August 1989, p. 6.

PAGE 19 Saint Lawrence Islanders' relationships with Russians, Carol Z. Jolles, "Late 19th and Early 20th Century Euro-American Contact and Its Effects on the Yup'ik Populations of Saint Lawrence Island: An Ethnohistorical Reconstruction," *Proceedings, Circum-Pacific Prehistory Conference*, Seattle, August 1989.

PAGE 19 Trade with Alaskans and Siberian Chukchis, Svetlana Fedorova, *The Russian Population in Alaska and California: Late 18th Century–1867*, trans. Richard A. Pierce and Alton S. Donelly (Kingston, Ont.: Limestone Press, 1973).

PAGES 19–20 Ecology of Beringia, Brian M. Fagan, *The Great Journey: The Peopling of Ancient America* (London: Thames and Hudson, 1987).

PAGE 21 Appearance of fully modern humans, Richard Leakey, *The Origin of Humankind* (New York: Harper Collins, 1994).

PAGES 22–24 Sinodonts and Sundodonts, Fagan, 1987.

PAGE 26 Aleut-Eskimo Sinodonts, Joseph H. Greenberg, Christy G. Turner, and Stephen L. Zegura, "The Settlement of the Americas: A Comparison of the Linguistic, Dental and Genetic Evidence," *Current Anthropology*, vol. 27, no. 5 (December 1986).

PAGE 27 "the whole speculative venture . . . ," Greenberg, Turner, and Zegura, 1986, p. 488.

PAGE 28 "but none have taken . . . ," Knut Fladmark, "Routes: Alternate Migration Corridors for Early Man in North America," *American Antiquity*, vol. 44, no. 1 (January 1979), p. 63.

PAGE 29 "Instead of despairing . . . ," Fladmark, 1979, p. 62.

PAGE 30 Account of Wai-Kai, Harry Assu and Joy Inglis, *Assu of Cape Mudge: Recollections of a Coastal Indian Chief* (Vancouver: University of British Columbia Press, 1989).

PAGE 31 Ecological upheaval around Seeley Lake, Terry Glavin, *A Death Feast in Dimlahamid* (Vancouver: New Star Books, 1990).

PAGE 34 Aleut migration, William S. Laughlin, *Aleuts: Survivors of the Bering Land Bridge* (New York: Holt, Rinehart and Winston, 1980).

PAGES 35–36 Burial sites on Hokkaido and at Port Moller, Atsuko Okada and Hiroaki Okada, "Port Moller: An ecological complex under Changing Climate," *Proceedings, Circum-Pacific Prehistory Conference*, Seattle, August 1989.

PAGE 37 Features of maritime societies, Hitoshi Watanabe, "The Northern Pacific Maritime Culture Zone: A Viewpoint of Hunter-Gatherer Mobility and Sedentism," *Proceedings, Circum-Pacific Prehistory Conference*, Seattle, August 1989.

PAGE 39 Study of shell middens, Clement W. Meighan, "Early Shell-mound Dwellers on the Pacific Coast of North America," *Proceedings, Circum-Pacific Prehistory Conference*, Seattle, August 1989.

PAGE 39 "Our perception of . . . ," Meighan, 1989.

PAGE 39 Evidence from bones, Richard L. Hill, "Bones Off Coast May Date Back 13,000 Years," *The Oregonian*, July 5, 1999.

PAGE 40 "Paradigmatic" academic blinders, Seonbok Yi, "Early Holocene Adaption in Korea: Current Status and Problems," *Proceedings, Circum-Pacific Prehistory Conference*, Seattle, August 1989.

PAGE 42 "At the bad rock . . . ," W. Kaye Lamb, ed., *The Letters and Journals of Simon Fraser, 1806–1808* (Toronto: Macmillan and Company, 1960).

CHAPTER 2: The Order of Things

PAGES 46–47 "wonderful proofs of . . . ," S. P. Krasheninnikov, *History of Kamtschatka and the Kurilski Islands, with the Countries Adjacent*, trans. James Grieve. (1754; reprint Chicago: Quadrangle Books, 1962).

PAGE 47 Michel Foucault, *Power/Knowledge: Selected Interviews and Other Writings, 1972–1977*, ed. Colin Gordon (New York: Pantheon Books, 1980).

PAGE 48 Renewed interest in Kamchatka, Fedorova, 1973.

PAGES 48–49 Walbaum's work, Cornelius Groot and Leo Margolis, *Pacific Salmon Life Histories* (Vancouver: University of British Columbia Press, 1991).

PAGES 55–56 Contribution of salmon, Mary F. Willson, Scott M. Gende, and Brian H. Marston, "Fishes and the Forest: Expanding Perspectives on Fish-Wildlife Interactions," *BioScience*, vol. 48, no. 6 (June 1998).

PAGE 56 Black-tailed gulls, Hiroshi Miztani and Eitaro Wada, "Nitrogen and Carbon Isotope Ratios in Seabird Rookeries and Their Ecological Significance," *Ecology*, vol. 69, no. 2 (1988).

PAGE 59 "one third of the . . . ," B. E. Riddell, "Spatial Organization of Pacific Salmon: What to Conserve?" in *Genetic Conservation of Salmonid Fisheries*, ed. G. Cloud and G. H. Thorgaard (New York: Plenum Press, 1993).

PAGE 63 Phosphorus in Karluk Lake, Willson, Gende, and Marston, 1998.

PAGE 68 "wonderful proofs . . . ," and "Nature, perhaps more . . . ," Jim Lichatowich, *Salmon Without Rivers: A History of the Pacific Salmon Crisis* (Washington, D.C.: Island Press, 1999).

PAGE 70 Ecological consequences of removing salmon, Ted Gresh, Jim Lichatowich, and Peter Schoonmaker, "Salmon Declines Create Nutrient Deficit in Northwest Streams," *Fisheries*, January 2000.

CHAPTER 3: From Sea Cows to Civilization

PAGE 77 Speculation about sea cow, Daryl P. Domning, "Steller's Sea Cow and the Origin of North Pacific Aboriginal Whaling," *Syesis*, vol. 5 (1972).

PAGE 78 Overharvesting of clam beds during the Jomon period, Hiroko Koike, "Exploitation Dynamics During the Jomon Period," *Proceedings, Circum-Pacific Prehistory Conference*, Seattle, August 1989.

PAGE 78 Overfishing in the Juan de Fuca Strait, Dale R. Croes and Steven Hackenberger, "Hoko River Archeological Complex: Modeling Prehistoric

Northwest Coast Economic Evolution," in *Prehistoric Economies of the Pacific Northwest Coast*, ed. Isaac B. L., Research in Economic Anthropology (Greenwich, Conn.: JAI Press, 1988).

PAGE 80 Fraser Canyon's pre-smallpox human population, Cole Harris, *The Resettlement of British Columbia: Essays on Colonialism and Geographical Change* (Vancouver: University of British Columbia Press, 1997).

PAGE 81 Pre-industrial harvests of salmon, G. W. Hewes, "Indian Fisheries Productivity in Pre-Contact Times in the Pacific Salmon Area," *Northwest Anthropological Research Notes*, vol. 7, no. 2 (1973).

PAGE 81 Precontact diet of aboriginal peoples, Brian Chisholm, "Reconstruction of Prehistoric Diet in British Columbia using Stable-carbon Isotope Analyses" (Ph.D. diss., Simon Fraser University, 1986).

PAGE 81 Study of thirty-eight skeletons, Brian S. Chisholm, D. Erle Nelson, and Henry P. Schwarcz, "Marine and Terrestrial Protein in Prehistoric Diets on the British Columbia Coast," *Current Anthropology*, vol. 24, no. 3 (June 1983).

PAGE 82 "well over 200,000," Cole Harris, 1997.

PAGE 83 Shalk's estimates of pre-industrial salmon harvests in the Columbia River basin, Joseph E. Taylor, *Making Salmon: An Environmental History of the Northwest Fisheries Crisis* (Seattle: University of Washington Press, 1999).

PAGE 83 Estimates of pre-industrial salmon harvests in the Fraser River basin, Terry Glavin, *Dead Reckoning: Confronting the Crisis in Pacific Fisheries* (Vancouver: David Suzuki Foundation/Greystone Books, 1996).

PAGE 84 Shellfish harvesting in the San Juan Islands, Bernhard J. Stern, *The Lummi Indians of Northwest Washington* (New York: Columbia University Press, 1934).

PAGE 84 Shellfish breeding on the Asian side of the North Pacific, D. L Brodianski and V. A. Rakov, "Aquaculture in Prehistory as a Branch of Ancient Economy on the Western Coast of the Pacific," *Proceedings, Circum-Pacific Prehistory Conference*, Seattle, August 1989.

PAGE 85 "banquet halls, theaters, and temples," Wayne Suttles and Kenneth Ames, "Pre-European History," in *The Rain Forests of Home*, ed. Peter K. Schoonmaker, Bettina Von Hagen, and Edward C. Wolf, (Washington, D.C.: Ecotrust/Interrain, Island Press, 1997).

PAGE 85 Ceramics in Asian maritime cultures, C. Melvin Aikens, "Jomon and Other Northeast Asian Hunter-Gatherers: Culture History, Environment, and Subsistence," *Proceedings, Circum-Pacific Prehistory Conference*, Seattle, August 1989.

PAGE 85 Overview of British Columbia's archeological sites, Roy Carlson, "The Native Fishery in British Columbia: The Archeological Evidence," unpublished paper (Department of Archeology, Simon Fraser University, 1992).

PAGE 86 "Beneath it the machines . . . ," W. Kaye Lamb, ed., *The Journals and Letters of Sir Alexander Mackenzie* (Toronto: MacMillan and Company, 1970).

PAGE 87 Katzie sale of potatoes and cranberries, Wayne Suttles, *Coast Salish Essays* (Seattle: University of Washington Press, 1987).

PAGE 88 "as many as 5,000 Indians," B. A. McKelvie, *Fort Langley: Outpost of Empire* (Vancouver: 1947).

PAGE 88 Cultivation of *Sagittaria*, Wayne Suttles and Diamond Jenness, 1955.

PAGE 89 "The women usually gather . . . ," Bernhard J. Stern, 1934.

PAGES 89–90 Camas production and "Among the Straits peoples . . . ," Wayne Suttles, "Economic Life of the Coast Salish of Haro and Rosario Straits" (Ph.D. diss., University of Washington, 1951).

PAGE 90 Tobacco smoking throughout the North Pacific, W. Bogoras, "The Chuckchee, Part I — Material Culture," *Memoirs of the American Museum of Natural History (Jesup Expedition)*, vol. XI (1904).

PAGES 90–91 Haida and Tlingit tobacco, Nancy J. Turner and Roy L. Taylor, "A Review of the Northwest Coast Tobacco Mystery," *Syesis*, vol. 5 (1972).

PAGES 91–92 Patricia Ann Berringer, "Northwest Coast Traditional Salmon Fisheries: Systems of Resource Utilization" (master's thesis, University of British Columbia, 1982).

PAGE 92 The Northwest Coast culture pattern, Knut Fladmark, "A Paleo-ecological Model for Northwest Coast Prehistory," paper 43, National Museum of Man Mercury Series (Ottawa: Archeological Survey of Canada, 1975).

PAGES 93–94 Japanese fisheries management, Evelyn Pinkerton and Martin Weinstein, "Fisheries That Work — Sustainability Through Community-Based Management" (Vancouver: David Suzuki Foundation, 1995).

CHAPTER 4: Spectral Flotillas and Lost Colonies

PAGE 96 Swaneset's voyage, Suttles and Jenness, 1955.

PAGE 98 Voyages of Hsu Fu, John Barber, "Oriental Enigma: Controversial New Evidence suggests Asian Sailors Explored the New World Centuries Before Europeans," *Equinox*, January/February 1990.

PAGES 98–99 Voyage of Huishen, Fang Zhongpu, "Did Chinese Buddhists

Reach America 1,000 Years Before Columbus?" *China Reconstructs*, August 1980.

PAGE 99 Controversy about Huishen, Michael Parks, "Historian Dismisses Argument that Chinese Monk Discovered America," *Los Angeles Times*, April 7, 1983.

PAGE 100 Inca as emigrants from China, Grant Keddie, "Early Chinese Exploration on the Pacific Coast?" *The Midden*, June 1980.

PAGE 103 Asian coins, Grant Keddie, "The Reliability of Dating Archeological and Ethnographic Materials with Associated Chinese Coins," *Datum*, vol. 3, no. 2 (1978).

PAGE 104 Wrecked Japanese ships, Charles Walcott Brooks, "Report of Japanese Vessels Wrecked in the North Pacific Ocean, From the Earliest Records to the Present Time," *Proceedings of the California Academy of Sciences*, no. 6 (1876).

PAGES 104–5 Japanese mariners held as slaves, Clifford M. Drury, "Early American Contacts with the Japanese," *Pacific Northwest Quarterly*, vol. 36, no. 4 (1945).

PAGE 105 George Quimby's estimates, George I. Quimby, "Japanese Wrecks, Iron Tools and Prehistoric Indians of the Northwest Coast," *Arctic Anthropology*, vol. 22, no. 2 (1985).

PAGE 106 Comparative analysis of Lake River ceramics, Alison T. Stenger, "Japanese-Influenced Ceramics in Pre-Contact Washington State: A View of the Wares and Their Possible Origin," *Proceedings, Circum-Pacific Prehistory Conference*, Seattle, August 1989.

PAGES 106–7 Possibility that Chinese and Japanese mariners ended up on west coast of North America, Nancy Yaw Davis, "The Zuni-Japanese Enigma," *Proceedings, Circum-Pacific Prehistory Conference*, Seattle, August 1989.

PAGES 108–9 Ethel G. Stewart's theories about Asiatic influence on North American aboriginal cultures, Ethel G. Stewart, *The Dene and Na-Dene Indian Migration, 1233 A.D: Escape from Genghis Khan to America*, (Columbus, Ga.: Institute for the Study of American Cultures, 1991).

PAGE 110 Charles Hill-Tout's theories about Asiatic origins of B.C. coastal peoples, Charles Hill-Tout, "Notes on the Cosmogony and History of the Squamish Indians of British Columbia," *Transactions of the Royal Society of Canada*, 1897.

PAGE 110 Studies of John Campbell, John Campbell, "The Origin of the Haidas of the Queen Charlotte Islands," *Transactions of the Royal Society of Canada*, 1897.

PAGE 111 Establishment of fur trade post at Okhotsk, Walter A. McDougall,

Let the Sea Make a Noise — A History of the North Pacific from Magellan to MacArthur (Toronto: HarperCollins, 1993).

PAGE 113 Russian expeditions, Fedorova, 1973.

PAGES 115–16 The second Kamchatka expedition, Corey Ford, *Where the Sea Breaks Its Back: The Epic Story of Early Naturalist Georg Steller and the Russian Exploration of Alaska* (Alaska Northwest Books, 1992).

PAGE 119 Voyage of Valerianos, John Kendrick, *The Men with Wooden Feet: The Spanish Exploration of the Pacific Northwest* (Toronto: NC Press, 1985).

PAGE 120 Voyages of Maldonado and de Fonte, John Kendrick, *Alejandro Malaspina: Portrait of a Visionary* (McGill/Queen's University Press, 1999).

PAGES 120–21 Voyages of Pérez and others, Donald C. Cutter, "Early Spanish-Indian Contacts in the Pacific Northeast, 1541–1795," *Proceedings, Circum-Pacific Prehistory Conference*, Seattle, August 1989.

PAGE 122 Cook's early life, Daniel Conner and Lorraine Miller, *Master Mariner: Captain James Cook and the Peoples of the Pacific* (Vancouver: Douglas and McIntyre, 1978).

PAGES 125–26 Voyage of Malasapina, John Kendrick, 1999.

PAGE 126 "Great was the joy . . . ," Donald C. Cutter, *Malaspina and Galiano: Spanish Voyages to the Northwest Coast, 1791 and 1792* (Vancouver: Douglas and McIntyre, 1991).

PAGE 127 "It is in . . . ," Conner and Miller, 1978.

PAGES 127–28 British and Spanish in Gulf of Georgia, John Kendrick, 1985.

PAGES 128–29 Voyage of Norman Kenny Luxton, Norman Kenny Luxton, *Luxton's Pacific Crossing* (Sidney, B.C.: Gray's Publishing, 1971).

CHAPTER 5: Muskets, Manchu Nobles, and Machines

PAGE 133 Quotes from journal of Archibald Menzies, G. P. V. Akrigg and Helen B. Akrigg, *British Columbia Chronicle, 1778–1846: Adventures by Sea and Land* (Vancouver: Discovery Press, 1975).

PAGE 135 "As things actually . . . ," Henry N. Michael, ed., *Lieutenant Zagoskin's Travels in Russian America, 1842–1844* (Toronto: Arctic Institute of North America/University of Toronto Press, 1967).

PAGE 135 Influence of Russian Orthodox Church, Sergei Kan, "Memory Eternal: Orthodox Christianity and the Tlingit Mortuary Complex," *Arctic Anthropology*, vol. 24, no. 1 (1987).

PAGES 135–36 Canonization of saints, Mark Stokoe and Leonid Kishkovsky, *Orthodox Christians in North America, 1794–1994* (Wayne, N.J.: Orthodox Christian Publications Centre, 1995).

PAGES 137–38 New Archangel, Fedorova, 1973.

PAGE 140 Russian gifts to Cook's expedition, Conner and Miller, 1978.

PAGE 141 Quotes from Cook, Conner and Miller, 1978.

PAGE 141 Sea otter trade, Robin Fisher, *Contact and Conflict: Indian-European Relations in British Columbia: 1774–1890* (Vancouver: University of British Columbia Press, 1977).

PAGE 142 Chinese shipwrights, Akrigg and Akrigg, 1975.

PAGES 143–44 Hawaiians on the Northwest Coast, Tom Koppel, *Kanaka: The Untold Story of Hawaiian Pioneers in British Columbia and the Pacific Northwest* (Vancouver: Whitecap Books, 1995).

PAGES 144–45 Whale hunting among aboriginal peoples, Margaret Lantis, "The Alaskan Whale Cult and Its Affinities," *American Anthropologist*, 1938.

PAGE 145 Whaling among the Salish peoples, Wayne Suttles, "Notes on Coast Salish Sea-Mammal Hunting," in *Anthropology in British Columbia*, no. 3, ed. Wilson Duff, (Victoria: British Columbia Provincial Museum, Department of Education, 1952).

PAGES 145–46 East India Company, Robert Lloyd Webb, *On the Northwest: Commercial Whaling in the Pacific Northwest, 1790–1967* (Vancouver: University of British Columbia Press, 1998).

PAGES 146–47 Right whales, Webb, 1988.

PAGES 147–48 Blue whale unit, Daniel Francis, *The Great Chase: A History of World Whaling* (Toronto: Pengun Books Canada, 1991).

PAGE 150 First whale-watching business, J. S. Matthews, ed., "Isla de Apodaca, 1791 (Bowen Island)," Vancouver City Archives, 1968.

PAGE 150 Pacific Whaling Company, Webb, 1988.

PAGE 151 Whaling in the Bering Sea, Francis, 1991.

PAGES 152–53 Asian whaling, Joseph Forester and Anne Forester, *British Columbia's Fishing History* (Saanichton, B.C.: Hancock House, 1975).

PAGE 153 Hapgood, Hume and Company, Terry Glavin, "The History of the Salmon Fisheries of North America's West Coast," *Proceedings, American Fisheries Society Annual General Meeting*, Hartford, Connecticut, 1998.

PAGES 153–54 The Jungles, Dianne Newell, ed., *The Development of the Pacific Salmon Canning Industry: A Grown Man's Game* (Montreal and Kingston, Ont.: McGill/Queen's University Press, 1989).

PAGES 154–55 Division of labor in coast's canneries, Alicja Muszynski, *Cheap Wage Labour: Race and Gender in the Fisheries of British Columbia* (Montreal and Kingston, Ont.: McGill/Queen's University Press, 1996).

PAGE 155 Japanese laborers, Muszynski, 1996.

PAGE 156 Racial tension, Muszynski, 1996.

PAGE 156 Chinook jargon, Charles Lillard and Terry Glavin, *A Voice Great Within Us* (Vancouver: Transmontanus Books/New Star, 1998).

PAGES 158–60 Sealing schooners, Peter Murray, *The Vagabond Fleet: A Chronicle of the North Pacific Sealing Schooner Trade* (Victoria: Sono Nis Press, 1998).

CHAPTER 6: Salmon Domains, Trophic Highways, and Bute Wax Episodes

PAGE 166 "In compensation for . . . ," Harold Sparck, "A New North Pacific International Order for Pelagic Fisheries," (master's thesis, University of Virginia, 1990).

PAGE 168 Soviet fishing fleet, Clarence Pautzke, "Russian Far East Fisheries Management," North Pacific Fishery Management Council Report to Congress, 1997.

PAGES 168–69 Depletion of animal populations, misc. stock status reports, Alaska Department of Fish and Game; Pacific Walrus (*Odobanus rosmarus divergens*), Marine Mammal Management document, U.S. Fish and Wildlife Service, Anchorage, Alaska, 1994; blue whale stock assessment, U.S. National Marine Mammal Laboratory, Southwest Fisheries Science Center, 1996.

PAGE 169 Sea otters, U.S. Fish and Widlife Service, "Sea Otter Conservation Plan," *Marine Mammals Management*, 1994.

PAGES 169–70 Walleye pollock, L. Fritz, "Stock Assessment Report for Groundfish Resources of the Gulf of Alaska," *Marine Fisheries Review*, 1996.

PAGE 170 Factory travelers, Ross Anderson, "Mammoth Factory Trawlers: To Be or Not to Be?" *Seattle Times*, March 25, 1998.

PAGE 171 Decline in Steller's sea lions, Andrew Trites and Peter Larkin, "Changes in the Abundance of Steller Sea Lions in Alaska from 1956 to 1992: How Many Were There?" Marine Mammal Research Unit paper (Vancouver: Fisheries Centre, University of British Columbia, 1996).

PAGE 172 Salmon from Canadian Rivers, T. L. Slaney, K. D. Hyatt, T. G. Northcote, and R. J. Fielden, "Status of Anadromous Salmon and Trout in British Columbia and the Yukon," *Fisheries*, October 1996.

PAGES 173–74 Canadian and American estimates, Terry Glavin, "Last Call: The Will to Save Pacific Salmon" (Vancouver: David Suzuki Foundation, 1998).

CHAPTER 7: The Necessary Mysteries of the North Pacific

PAGE 192 Important idea contrary to idea of steady state in nature, Frank N. Egerton, "Changing Concepts of the Balance of Nature," *The Quarterly Review of Biology*, vol. 48, no. 2 (June 1973).

PAGE 192 "The lack of success . . . ," Gary D. Sharp, "Fishery Catch Records, El Niño Southern Oscillation, and Longer-Term Climate Change as Inferred from Fish Remains in Marine Sediments," in *El Niño: Historical and Paleoclimatic Aspects of the Southern Oscillation* (Cambridge: Cambridge University Press, 1992).

PAGE 200 Study of regimes, R. J. Beamish and D. R. Bouillon, "Pacific Salmon Production Trends in Relation to Climate," *Canadian Journal of Fisheries and Aquatic Sciences*, vol. 50 (1993).

PAGE 200 More detail to regime shift picture, R. J. Beamish and D. R. Bouillon, "Marine Fish Production Trends Off the Pacific Coast of Canada and the United States," *Canadian Spec. Publ., Fisheries and Aquatic Sciences*, vol. 121 (1995).

PAGE 202 "There is good reason . . . ," Leonid B. Klyashtorin, "Cyclic Climate Changes and Pacific Salmon Stock Fluctuations: A Possibility for Long-term Forecasting," *Technical Report, Workshop on Climate Change and Salmon Production*, North Pacific Anadromous Fish Commission, Vancouver, 1998.

PAGE 203 Study of Santa Barbara Channel, T. R. Baumgartner, et al., *CalCOFI Rep.*, vol. 33 (1992), pp. 24–40.

PAGES 203–4 El Niño as independent of Pacific Decadal Oscillation, Robert Frances, Steven Hare, Anne Hollowed, and Warren Wooster, "Effects of Interdecadal Climate Variability on the Oceanic Systems of the N.E. Pacific," *Fisheries Oceanography*, vol. 7 (1998), p. 1.

PAGE 205 Anomalies, Gordon A. McFarlane, Jacquelynne R. King, and Richard J. Beamish, "Have There Been Recent Changes in Climate? Ask the Fish," in *Progress in Oceanography* (in press).

PAGE 208 Market distortions, Program Planning and Economics Branch, "Commercial Salmon Landings and Value, 1951–1997" (Vancouver: Department of Fisheries and Oceans, Pacific Region, 1998).

PAGE 211 UN Code of Conduct for Responsible Fisheries, United Nations Food and Agriculture Organization. "Precautionary Approach to Fisheries," *Technical Paper 350/1*, Rome, 1995; United Nations Convention on Biological Diversity, 1992.

Index